APPRECIATIVE INQUIRY

RETHINKING HUMAN ORGANIZATION TOWARD A POSITIVE THEORY OF CHANGE

Edited by

David L. Cooperrider
Professor of Organizational Behavior
Case Western Reserve University

Peter F. Sorensen, Jr.
Professor and Chairman of Management and Organizational Behavior
Benedictine University

Diana Whitney
President of Corporation for Positive Change

Therese F. Yaeger
Associate Director Ph.D. program of Organizational Development
Benedictine University

ISBN 87563-931-3

Published by

Stipes Publishing L.L.C.
Champaign, Illinois

CONTENTS

PART I

Rethinking Human Organization Toward a Positive Theory of Change   1

Chapter 1
A Positive Revolution in Change: Appreciative Inquiry   3
David L. Cooperrider and Diana Whitney

Chapter 2
Positive Image, Positive Action: The Affirmative Basis of Organizing   29
David Cooperrider

Chapter 3
Appreciative Inquiry in Organizational Life   55
David Cooperrider and Suresh Srivastva

Chapter 4
Five Theories of Change Embedded in Appreciative Inquiry   99
Gervase Bushe

PART II

Case Stories, Resources for Appreciative Inquiry Practice and
Empirical Testing 111

Chapter 5
Advances in Appreciative Inquiry as an Organization
Development Intervention 113
Gervase Bushe

Chapter 6
The "Child" as Agent of Inquiry 123
David L. Cooperrider

Chapter 7
Resources for Getting Appreciative Inquiry Started: An Example
OD Proposal 131
David L. Cooperrider

Chapter 8
An Appreciative Inquiry into the Factors of Culture Continuity During
Leadership Transitions: A Case Study of LeadShare, Canada 143
                    Mary Ann Rainey

Chapter 9
Survey Guided Appreciative Inquiry: A Case Study 155
                    Rita F. Williams

Chapter 10
Initiating Culture Change in Higher Education Through
Appreciative Inquiry.. 165
                    Robert L. Head and Michele M. Young

Chapter 11
Saving Tomorrow's Workforce 175
            Christopher Anne Easley, Therese Yaeger, and Peter Sorensen

Chapter 12
Appreciative Inquiry with Teams.................................. 183
                    Gervase R. Bushe

Chapter 13
A Field Experiment in Appreciative Inquiry 195
                    David A. Jones

Chapter 14
Appreciative Inquiry Meets the Logical Positivist.................... 207
            Peter F. Sorensen, Robert Head, Linda Sharkey, and Dale Spartz

PART III
New Horizons.. 215

Chapter 15
Is Appreciative Inquiry OD's Philosopher's Stone? 217
                    Thomas C. Head, Peter F. Sorensen, Jr.,
                    Joanne Preston, and Therese Yaeger

Chapter 16
Postmodern Principles and Practices for Large Scale Organization Change
and Global Cooperation 233
                    Diana Whitney

Chapter 17
Organizational Inquiry Model for Global Social Change Organizations ... 249
                    Jane Magruder Watkins and David Cooperrider

Chapter 18
From Deficit Discourse to Vocabularies of Hope: The Power of
Appreciation 265
                    James D. Ludema

PREFACE

This book is intended as a source book for our students, as a way of introducing them to and assisting them in their shared—our shared—mission for the creation of better, more fulfilling and more productive work places, places where the potential for OD and OD values are most fully realized.

Consistent with our intent to provide our students the opportunity to share in learning about appreciative inquiry, we have waived all royalties in an effort to provide the book at the lowest possible cost.

DEDICATION

To our families and students.

Introduction

Organization Development and Appreciative Inquiry: An Introduction to an Award-Winning Approach to OD

This book presents a series of articles on an approach to change known as Appreciative Inquiry, or AI for short. AI is an approach, which in its brief lifetime has made considerable impact on the field of Organization Development. It provides a critical new way of thinking about organizational change and improvement, yet at the same time is deeply rooted in the historical values of OD. Appreciative Inquiry draws on the best of "what is" and envisioning, and consequently creates what is at the heart of OD, which is perhaps best expressed by Marvin Weisbord as *the creation of productive workplaces with dignity, meaning, and community.* As the title of this introduction indicates it is very much an award-winning approach to OD. AI has been recognized by many of the OD professional associations, including an Award for Best Organizations Change Program from the American Society for Training and Development, and a Best Paper Award from the Academy of Management. It was part of the change effort that won the Outstanding OD Project of the Year Worldwide from the OD Institute, and was the topic of one of the articles selected and published as "The Best of the OD Journal in the 20th Century," and a special issue of the *OD Practitioner* published by the OD Network.

The book is clearly about a significant new approach to Organization Development. Throughout the book several major themes emerge:

1. Appreciative Inquiry is defined as a social construction based on a sociorationalist paradigm as opposed to the paradigm of logical positivism. Nevertheless it appears that AI is capable of drawing on the best of what exists from logical positivism and does not suffer, but in fact is strengthened by evaluation which draws from the logical positivist tradition.

2. Appreciative Inquiry contributes to the refinements and extension of established interventions at the core of OD such as action research, team building and survey feedback, and at the same time incorporates into the AI process

more recently developed approaches such as large group interventions and Search Conference methods.

3. Appreciative Inquiry addresses the large issues, which again reflects its rootedness in the fundamental values of OD. It deals with diversity, with global social change, and with conflict—conflict in the most meaningful way possible illustrated by the United Religions work and the drive, the hope and the vision of World Peace.

This book is divided into three sections. Part I, *Rethinking Human Organization toward a Positive Theory of Change*, is comprised of an introduction and overview of Appreciative Inquiry, followed by two classic articles in which AI was first articulated. The final chapter contains a review of the theoretical foundation of AI.

The second section describes various applications of AI and how it deals with the experiences, illustrations, applications and assessment of its impact as a way of changing groups and organizations are discussed.

In a sense the final section moves the reader and AI to a grander scale. Here questions are raised about the nature and possibility of AI's universal application, with illustrations of large-scale change and global applications. The book concludes, we feel, appropriately with a discussion of Appreciation and Hope, "that the very act of appreciation will itself contribute to transforming our organizations into places of genuine human hopefulness." (Ludema).

But rather than elaborate further we feel it best to let the contributors and their articles speak for themselves.

Awards and Recognition

Award	Recipient
Best Paper Award, International Management Association, 1999, entitled "Appreciative Inquiry as a Team Development Intervention for Newly Formed Heterogeneous Groups"	Robert Head
Best Organization Change Project Award from the American Society of Training and Development, 1997.	GTE
Best Paper Award, OD Institute 1998, entitled "Changing organizational culture through leadership development: A case in leadership transformation," *OD Journal*, Fall 1999.	Linda Sharkey
O.D. Institute's Outstanding OD Project Worldwide 1998 entitled "Changing Management Culture to Achieve Success", 1998.	Dale Spartz
Best Paper Award, OD Institute, entitled "A Field Experiment in Appreciative Inquiry," 1998.	David A. Jones
Finalist, Outstanding OD Project of the Award Worldwide, 1997.	Akinyinka O. Akinyele, Peter F. Sorensen, Jr., and Therese Yaeger
The Best of the *OD Journal* in the 20th Century "Advances in Appreciatve Inquiry as an Organization Development Intervention", Fall, 1995.	Gervase Bushe

Best Paper Award, Academy of Management, Organization Development and Change Division, "Using Generative Metaphor to Intervene in a System Divided by Turfism and Competition: Building Common Visions", 1988.	Frank Barrett and David Cooperrider
Catalyst Award for "Best Place to Work in the Country for Women 1997"	Avon – Mexico
"Award for Educational Achievement, 1998"	Scandinavian School System

About the Editors

David L. Cooperrider, Ph.D.
Case Western Reserve University

David L. Cooperrider is Chairman of the SIGMA Program for Human Cooperation and Global Action and Associate Professor of Organizational Behavior, at
Case Western Reserve University's Weatherhead School of Management.

David is past Chair at the National Academy of Management—the Division
of Organization Development—and he is a co-founder of The Taos Institute. He
has taught at Stanford University, Katholieke University in Belgium, Benedictine
University, Pepperdine University, and others. Currently he serves as the PI of a
multi-million dollar grant working with international organizations dealing with
global issues of human health, environment, peace, and sustainable economic development.

Dr. Cooperrider has served as researcher and consultant to a wide variety of
organizations including: Motorola, GTE, BP America, World Vision, Seattle Group
Health, Teledesic, Imagine Chicago, Technoserve, the Mountain Forum, and United
Way of America. Currently, as part of the above mentioned grant, David and his
colleagues have organizational learning projects active in 57 organizations working in over 100 countries in Africa, Asia, Europe, and North and South America.
Most of these projects are inspired by the Appreciative Inquiry methodologies for
which David is best known.

His ideas have been published in such journals as *Administrative Science Quarterly*, *Human Relations*, *Journal of Applied Behavioral Science*, *The OD Practitioner*, and in research series such as *Advances In Strategic Management*. More
popularly, his work has been covered by *The New York Times*, *Crain's Business*,
Cleveland's Plain Dealer, *San Francisco Chronicle* and others. He has been the
recipient of Innovation and Best Paper of the Year Awards at the Academy of
Management, and numerous clients have received awards for their work with Appreciative Inquiry—GTE, for example, has just been recognized as 1998 Best
Organization Change Program in the country by ASTD. David's most recent books
include *Organizational Courage and Executive Wisdom*; and *Appreciative Leadership and Management* (both with Suresh Srivastva); *International and Global
OD* (with Peter Sorensen); and *The Organization Dimensions of Global Change:
No Limits to Cooperation* (with Jane Dutton). David has just been named editor of
a new Sage Publication Book Series on the Human Dimensions of Global Change.

Peter F. Sorensen, Jr., Ph.D.
Benedictine University

Peter F. Sorensen, Jr., Ph.D., is Professor and Director of the Ph.D. program in Organization Development and the M.S. program in Management and Organizational Behavior at Benedictine University. He was instrumental in developing one of the first Masters Level programs in OD in 1967, and one of the first Ph.D. programs in OD in 1996.

He has authored more than 200 articles, papers and books, including several best paper selections. His work has appeared in the *Academy of Management Journal, Group and Organization Studies*, Leadership and *Organization Development Journal, Journal of Management Studies*, and *Organization and Administrative Sciences*, among others. In 1996, he was Guest Editor of a double issue of the *OD Practitioner* on Appreciative Inquiry. He is the invited Guest Editor for the first New Millennium issues for both the *OD Journal* and the *OD Practitioner*.

Sorensen's recent publications are *Perspectives on Organization Behavior and Global and International OD* with Cooperrider, Head, Mathys and Preston. He has worked with over 100 organizations including the U.S. Food and Drug Administration, U.S. Steel, DuPage County Health Department, Commonwealth Edison, and CNA.

He is a member of the Executive Committee of the Organization Development and Change Division of the Academy of Management, and serves on the Editorial Boards for the *OD Journal*, the *OD Practitioner*, and *Training Today*.

Peter was an invited, distinguished scholar to the first Academy of Management Conference on Global Change. In 1993, he received the "Outstanding OD Consultant of the Year Award" from the OD Institute. He holds a Ph.D. in Management from the Stuart School of Management, Illinois Institute of Technology.

Diana Whitney
President of Corporation for Positive Change

Diana Whitney, Ph.D., President of Corporation for Positive Change, is internationally recognized for her consulting, teaching and writing on innovative, large-scale processes for positive social and organizational change and has been instrumental in integrating appreciative inquiry in corporate change and leadership practices. Her work focuses on organization transformation, strategic culture change, communication and leadership development. Dr. Whitney applies social constructionist theory to mergers and acquisitions, organization development and strategic planning. She works collaboratively and creatively with executives, managers, and organization members, building teams and supporting them in the construction of the organization's future. She consults with corporate, nonprofit and government organizations including: Hunter Douglas, GTE, SmithKline Beecham, Johnson & Johnson, United Religions and Price

Waterhouse. Her recent publications and presentations include: "Partnership at Work," "The Appreciative Inquiry Summit: Overview and Applications," "Postmodern Principles and Practices for Large Scale Organization Change," and "Spirituality as a Global Organizing Potential." Diana is a cofounder of the Taos Institute, where appreciative inquiry is taught to consultants and leaders of change. She can be contacted through email at whitneydi@aol.com.

Therese Yaeger
Benedictine University

Therese Yaeger is Associate Director of the Organization Development Doctoral program at Benedictine University, where she also teaches Organization Development and Organizational Behavior courses to various audiences in graduate, undergraduate and corporate settings. She is also a Registered OD Consultant through the OD Institute.

She has more than eighteen years management experience, particularly in start-up operations and project management. Therese is an Editorial Associate of the *OD Journal*, and Chicago's ASTD's *Training Today*. She frequently presents at the Academy of Management, the OD Institute, and the International Association of Business Disciplines. She is 1999 Co-chair for the Organization Development Track of the Midwest Academy of Management Annual Conference.

Yaeger's research interests include international organization development, organizational change, and appreciative inquiry. Her most recent publications include "What Matters Most in Appreciative Inquiry: Review and Thematic Assessment" in an upcoming issue of *Human Systems*. She is recipient of various awards including Best OD Project of the Year from the OD Institute.

Yaeger is a member of the Academy of Management, the OD Network, and the OD Institute, and the American Society for Training and Development. She received both her BA in Literature and Communication and MS in Management and Organizational Behavior from Benedictine University, and continues her doctoral studies in the Benedictine Ph.D. Program.

PART I

Rethinking Human Organization Toward a Positive Theory of Change

Chapter 1

A POSITIVE REVOLUTION IN CHANGE: APPRECIATIVE INQUIRY

David L. Cooperrider
Case Western Reserve University
Diana Whitney
The Taos Institute

Introduction

Appreciative Inquiry (AI) begins an adventure. The urge and call to adventure has been sounded by many people and many organizations, and it will take many more to fully explore the vast vistas that are now appearing on the horizon. But even in the first steps, what is being sensed is an exciting direction in our language and theories of change—an invitation, as some have declared, to "a positive revolution".

The words just quoted are strong and, unfortunately, they are not ours. But the more we replay, for example, the high-wire moments of our several years of work at GTE, the more we find ourselves asking the very same kinds of questions the people of GTE asked their senior executives: "Are you really ready for the momentum that is being generated? This is igniting a grassroots movement . . . it is creating an organization in full voice, a center stage for the positive revolutionaries!"

Tom White, President of what was then called GTE Telops (making up 80% of GTE's 67,000 employees) responds, with no hesitation: "Yes, and what I see in this meeting are zealots, people with a mission and passion for creating the new GTE. Count me in, I'm your number one recruit, number one zealot." People cheer.

Enthusiasms continue, and they echo over subsequent months as a lot of hard work pays off. Fourteen months later—based on significant and measurable changes in stock prices, morale survey measures, quality/customer relations, union-management relations, etc.—GTE's whole system change initiative is given professional recognition by the American Society for Training and Development. It wins the 1997 ASTD award for best organization change program in the country. Appreciative inquiry is cited as the "backbone".

How Did They Do It?

This paper provides a broad update and overview of AI. The GTE story mentioned at the outset is, in many ways, just beginning but it is scarcely alone. In the ten years since the theory and vision for "Appreciative Inquiry Into Organizational Life" (Cooperrider and Srivastva, 1987; Cooperrider, 1986) was published, there have been literally hundreds of people involved in co-creating new practices for doing AI and in bringing its spirit and methodology into organizations all over the world. We believe the velocity and largely informal spread of the ideas suggest a growing sense of disenchantment with exhausted theories of change, especially those wedded to vocabularies of human deficit. This also suggests a corresponding urge to work with people, groups, and organizations in more constructive, positive, life-affirming, even spiritual ways.

In this paper we hope to serve as conduit to this impulse as we touch on exciting examples and concepts and provide references for future study. And while the outcomes and illustrations we have selected are often dramatic, we do want to emphasize, throughout, that AI is clearly only in its infancy. Questions are many, and we believe they will be a source of learning for many years.

Could it be, for example, that we as a field have reached "the end of problem solving" as a mode of inquiry capable of inspiring, mobilizing and sustaining significant human system change? What would happen to our change practices if we began all of our work with the positive presumption—that organizations, as centers of human relatedness, are "alive" with infinite constructive capacity? If so, how would we know? What do we mean by infinite capacity? What would happen to us, let's say, as leaders or catalysts of change if we approached the question of change only long after we have connected with people and organizations through systematic study of their already "perfect" form? How would we talk about "it"—this account of the ideal-in-the-real? Would we, in our work, have to go any further once we and others were connected to this positive core? How can we better inquire into organization existence in ways that are economically, humanly, and ecologically significant, that is, in ways that increasingly help people discover, dream, design and transform toward the greatest good?

What is Appreciative Inquiry?

Ap-pre'ci-ate, v., 1. valuing; the act of recognizing the best in people or the world around us; affirming past and present strengths, successes, and potentials; to perceive those things that give life (health, vitality, excellence) to living systems. 2.to increase in value, e.g., the economy has appreciated in value. Synonyms: VALUING, PRIZING, ESTEEMING, and HONORING.

In-quire' (kwir), v., 1. the act of exploration and discovery. 2. To ask questions; to be open to seeing new potentials and possibilities. Synonyms: DISCOVERY, SEARCH, and SYSTEMATIC EXPLORATION, STUDY.

AI has been described by observers in a myriad of ways: as a paradigm of conscious evolution geared for the realities of the new century (Hubbard, 1998); as a methodology that takes the idea of the social construction of reality to its positive extreme—especially with its emphasis on metaphor and narrative, relational ways of knowing, on language, and on its potential as a source of generative theory (Gergen, 1994); as the most important advance in action research in the past decade (Bushe, 1995); as offspring and "heir" to Maslow's vision of a positive social science (Chin, 1998; Curran, 1991); as a powerful second generation OD practice (French and Bell, 1995; Porras, 1991; Mirvis, 1988/89); as model of a much needed participatory science, a "new yoga of inquiry" (Harman, 1990); as a radically affirmative approach to change which completely lets go of problem-based management and in so doing vitally transforms strategic planning, survey methods, culture change, merger integration methods, approaches to TQM, measurement systems, sociotechnical systems, etc. (White, 1996); and lastly, as OD's philosopher's stone (Head and Sorensen, et al., 1996). Indeed it is difficult to sum up the whole of AI—as a philosophy of knowing, a normative stance, a methodology for managing change, and as an approach to leadership and human development. However, for purposes here, it might be most useful to begin with a practice-oriented definition of AI, one that is more descriptive than theoretical and one that provides a compass for the examples to follow:

Appreciative Inquiry is about the co-evolutionary search for the best in people, their organizations, and the relevant world around them. In its broadest focus, it involves systematic discovery of what gives "life" to a living system when it is most alive, most effective, and most constructively capable in economic, ecological, and human terms. AI involves, in a central way, the art and practice of asking questions that strengthen a system's capacity to apprehend, anticipate, and heighten positive potential. It centrally involves the mobilization of inquiry through the crafting of the "unconditional positive question," often involving hundreds or sometimes thousands of people. In AI, the arduous task of intervention gives way to the speed of imagination and innovation; instead of negation, criticism, and spiraling diagnosis, there is discovery, dream, and design. AI seeks, fundamentally, to build a constructive union between a whole people and the massive entirety of what people talk about as past and present capacities: achievements, assets, unexplored potentials, innovations, strengths, elevated thoughts, opportunities, benchmarks, high point moments, lived values, traditions, strategic competencies, stories, expressions of wisdom, insights into the deeper corporate spirit or soul, and visions of valued and possible futures. Taking all of these together as a gestalt, AI deliberately, in everything it does, seeks to work from accounts of this "positive change core"—and it assumes that every living system has many untapped and rich and inspiring accounts of the positive. Link the energy of this core directly to any change agenda and changes never thought possible are suddenly and democratically mobilized.

The positive core of organizational life, we submit, is one of the greatest and largely unrecognized resources in the field of change management today. As said earlier, we are clearly in our infancy when it comes to tools for working with it, talking about it, and designing our systems in synergistic alignment with it. But one thing is evident and clear as we reflect on the most important things we have learned with AI: human systems grow in the direction of what they persistently ask questions about and this propensity is strongest and most sustainable when the means and ends of inquiry are positively correlated. The single most prolific thing a group can do if its aims are to liberate the human spirit and consciously construct a better future is to make the positive change core the common and explicit property of all.

Let's Illustrate: The Appreciative Inquiry "4-D" Cycle

You have just received the following unsettling phone call:

My name is Rita Simmel. I am President of a New York consulting partnership. Our firm specializes in dealing with difficult conflict in organizations: labor-management issues, gender conflict, issues of diversity. We have been retained by a Fortune 500 corporation for the past several years. The contract is around sexual harassment, an issue that is deeper and more severe than virtually any corporation realizes. The issues are about power, the glass ceiling, and many things. As you know, millions of dollars are being expended on the issues. Our firm has specialized in this area for some years and now I'm beginning to ask myself the Hippocratic oath. Are we really helping? Here is the bottom line with our client. We have been working on the issues for two years, and by every measure—numbers of complaints, lawsuits, evaluations from sexual harassment training programs, word of mouth—the problem continues in its growth. Furthermore people are now voting with their feet. They are not coming to the workshops. Those that do seem to leave with doubts: our post-workshop interviews show people feel less able to communicate with those of the opposite gender, they report feeling more distance and less trust, and the glass ceiling remains. So here is my question. How would you take an appreciative inquiry approach to sexual harassment?

This was a tough one. We requested time to think about it, asking if we could talk again in a day or two. We can do the same for you right now (give you a bit of time) as we invite you to think about things you might seriously propose in the callback.

Before going further with the story let's pause and look at a typical flow for AI, a cycle that can be as rapid and informal as in a conversation with a friend or colleague, or as formal as an organization-wide analysis involving every stakeholder, including customers, suppliers, partners, and the like.

Figure 1.1 shows four key stages in AI: *Discovery*—mobilizing a whole system inquiry into the positive change core; *Dream*—creating a clear results-oriented vision in relation to discovered potential and in relation to questions of higher purpose, i.e., "What is the world calling us to become?"; *Design*—creating possibility propositions of the ideal organization, an organization design which

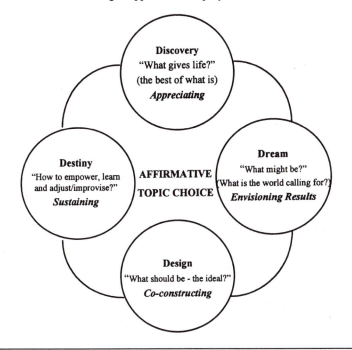

Figure 1.1. Appreciative Inquiry 4-D Cycle.

people feel is capable of magnifying or eclipsing the positive core and realizing the articulated new dream; and *Destiny*—strengthening the affirmative capability of the whole system enabling it to build hope and momentum around a deep purpose and creating processes for learning, adjustment, and improvisation, like a jazz group over time (Barrett, 1998).

At the core of the cycle, is Affirmative Topic Choice. It is the most important part of any AI. If, in fact, knowledge and organizational destiny are as intricately interwoven as we think, then isn't it possible that the seeds of change are implicit in the very first questions we ask? AI theory says yes and takes the idea quite seriously: It says that the way we know people, groups, and organizations is fateful. It further asserts the time is overdue to recognize that symbols and conversations, emerging from all our analytic modes, are among the world's paramount resources.

Topic Choice

Back to our phone call. If inquiry and change are a simultaneous moment, if the questions we ask set the stage for what we "find", and if what we "discover" (the data) creates the material out of which the future is conceived, conversed about, and constructed—then how shall we proceed with an appreciative approach to sexual harassment? Here is an excerpt from the response:

D.C.: Hello, Rita. Before we get into our proposal we have an important question. What is it that you want to learn about and achieve with this whole intervention, and by when?

Rita: We want to dramatically cut the incidence of sexual harassment. We want to solve this huge problem, or at least make a significant dent in it.

D.C.: O.K. Rita… But is that all?

Rita: You mean what do I really want to see? (Long pause . . . then she blurts out her response.) What we really want to see is the development of the new century organization—a model of high quality cross-gender relationships in the workplace!

DC: Great topic. What would happen if we put an invitation in the company newsletter, asking people to step forward in pairs to nominate themselves as candidates to study and share their stories of what it means to create and sustain high quality cross-gender relationships in the workplace? It might be interesting to do a large conference, and really put a magnifying lens to the stages of development, contextual factors, tough questions of adult attraction, breakthroughs in terms of power relations, and so on. What do you think?

To fastforward, a relatively small pilot project was created which surpassed everyone's expectations. Hundreds, not dozens, of pairs nominated themselves. That was surprise number one. Then other organizations got word of the pilot and a truly major effort, moving through the 4-D framework, was conceptualized by another consulting firm, Marge Schiller and Associates. The pioneering organization she worked with, which now can happily be named, was the Avon Corporation in Mexico. Again there were similar issues—including the glass ceiling at senior management levels—but again there was interest in framing the whole thing in terms of an inquiry.

To begin, a hundred people were trained in the basics of AI interviewing. They in turn went out into every part of the organization and over the next several weeks completed many more interviews, about 300 in all. At the end of each interview, the interviewers asked the person interviewed if they too could help do some interviewing. A waterfall was experienced. Stories poured in—stories of achievement, trust building, authentic joint leadership, practices of effective conflict management, ways of dealing with sex stereotypes, stages of development and methods of career advancement.

The second two Ds—articulating the new century dream and creating designs for an organization that maximally supported the development of high quality cross-gender relationships—came next. These were combined in a large group format much like a future search. Using stories from the interviews as a basis for imagining the future, expansive and practical propositions were created, for example, "Every task force or committee at Avon, whenever possible, is co-chaired by a cross-gender pairing." The significance of even this simple proposal proved to be big. Likewise, propositions in other areas of organization design were also carefully crafted. Soon, literally everything in the organization was opened to discussion: corporate structures, systems, work processes, communications, career opportunities, governance, compensation practices, leadership patterns, learning opportunities, customer connections, and more.

In the end, some 30 visionary propositions were created. Subsequent changes in system structures and behaviors were reported to be dramatic (Schiller, 1998). As it turns out, this story, like GTE's, gets even better. Avon Mexico was recently singled out, several years later, by the Catalyst organization. They received the 1997 Catalyst Award for best place in the country for women to work.

It is a classic example of the power of topic choice. Affirmative topics, always homegrown, can be on anything the people of an organization feel gives life to the system. As a rule of thumb most projects have between three and five topics. Words like empowerment, innovation, sense of ownership, commitment, integrity, ecological consciousness, and pride are often articulated as worthy of study. Topics can be on anything an organization feels to be strategically and humanly important. AI topics can be on technical processes, financial efficiencies, human issues, market opportunities, social responsibilities, or anything else. In each case of topic choice, the same premise is firmly posited: Human systems grow in the direction of their deepest and most frequent inquiries.

Discovery

The inquiry we are talking about is anything but wishful. If we were to underline one of the two words—appreciative or inquiry—our pen would immediately move to the latter. In "Vital Speeches of the Day" (1996), Tom White, President of what was then called GTE Telephone Operations, puts his interpretation of AI in executive language, months before GTE's change effort was recognized by ASTD:

Appreciative Inquiry can get you much better results than seeking out and solving problems. That's an interesting concept for me—and I imagine most of you—because telephone companies are among the best problem solvers in the world. We troubleshoot everything. We concentrate enormous resources on correcting problems that have relatively minor impact on our overall service and performance (and which)…when used continually and over a long period of time, this approach can lead to a negative culture. If you combine a negative culture with all the challenges we face today, it could be easy to convince ourselves that we have too many problems to overcome—to slip into a paralyzing sense of hopelessness. . . . Don't get me wrong. I'm not advocating mindless happy talk. Appreciative Inquiry is a complex science designed to make things better. We can't ignore problems—we just need to approach them from the other side.

What Tom White calls "the other side", we are describing as the positive change core. AI, most simply, is a tool for connecting to the transformational power of this core. Willis Harman (1990) talks about AI as a participatory science, a yoga of inquiry, where the term yoga comes from the Sanskrit root *yug* which means link or bond. In that sense, if we remember something or someone, it can be said that there is a form of yoga happening. AI helps make the memory link by concentrating systematic inquiry into all aspects of the appreciable world, into an organization's infinite and surplus capacity—past, present and future. By concentrating on the atom, human beings have unleashed its power. AI says we can do the same in every living system once we open this ever emergent positive core—every strength, innovation, achievement, resource, living value, imaginative story, benchmark, hope, positive tradition, passion, high point experience, internal genius, dream—to systematic inquiry.

The core task of the discovery phase is to discover and disclose positive capacity, at least until an organization's understanding of this "surplus" is exhausted (which has never happened in our experience). AI provides a practical way to ignite this "spirit of inquiry" on an organization-wide basis. Consider this example:

At LeadShare in Canada, AI was used to help this big eight accounting firm make the tough transition in the executive succession of a "legendary" managing partner. The managing partner seized the moment as an incredible leadership development opportunity for all 400 partners. Everyone was interviewed with AI. An extensive interview protocol was designed (ultimately taking about 2 hours per interview) focusing on affirmative topics like innovation, equality, partnership, speed to market, and valuing diversity (in Canada between francophone and anglophone). Not one outside consultant did the interviews. All were done internally, by 30 junior partners as part of a leadership development program. A powerful and instant intergenerational connection was made, and organizational history came alive in face-to-face stories. Instead of amnesia, or a problem-to-be-solved, people began to relate to their history in a whole new way. Like a good piece of poetry filled with endless interpretive meaning, people at Leadshare ascended into their history as a reservoir of positive possibility. At the next annual partners meeting, with over 400 people in the conference hall, the material was showcased and coupled to the future, as the strategic planning became one of the "best" the partners could ever remember (Rainey, 1996).

Perhaps it is obvious, but the process of doing the interviews is as important as the data collected. When managers ask us how many people should be interviewed or, who should do the interviews, we increasingly find ourselves saying "everyone." It is not uncommon in AI work to talk about doing thousands of interviews. A hospital in Seattle recently did three thousand interviews in preparation for an organization-wide Appreciative Inquiry Summit (Whitney and Cooperrider, 1998). People themselves, not consultants, generate the system-wide organization analysis using questions like this: "Obviously you have had ups and downs in your career here at XYZ. But for the moment I would like you to focus on a high point, a time in your work experience here where you felt most alive, most engaged, or most successful. Can you tell me the story? How did it unfold? What was it organizationally that made it stand out? What was it about you that made it a high point? What key insights do you have for all of us at XYZ?"

In Chicago, in one of the most exciting AI's we have seen, there is talk of over a million interviews. And guess whose interviews have produced the best data—the most inspiring, vision-generating stories? It is the children's. It is happening through inter-generational inquiry where the elders are valued and share hopes in settings with the young. One of our favorite papers is about the Imagine Chicago story and the leadership of Bliss Browne. It is titled "The Child as the Agent of Inquiry" (Cooperrider, 1996). It argues that the spirit of inquiry is something all of us in change work need to reclaim and aspire to: openness, availability, epistemological humility, the ability to admire, to be surprised, to be inspired, to inquire into our valued and possible worlds.

What distinguishes AI, especially in this phase of work, is that every carefully crafted question is positive. Knowing and changing are a simultaneous moment. The thrill of discovery becomes the thrill of creating. As people throughout a system connect in serious study into qualities, examples, and analysis of the positive core—each appreciating and everyone being appreciated—hope grows and community expands.

Dream

When an artist sits in front of a landscape the imagination is kindled not by searching for "what is wrong with this landscape," but by a special ability to be inspired by those things worth valuing. Appreciation, it appears, draws our eye toward life, stirs our feelings, sets in motion our curiosity, and provides inspiration to the envisioning mind. In his analysis of esthetics and the origins of creative images, Nietzsche once asked of the power of appreciation: "Does it not praise? Does it not glorify? Does it not select? Does it not bring [that which is appreciated] to prominence?" (Rader, 1973, p. 12) Then in the same passage he takes a next step, linking valuing (discovery) and imagination (dream). He elaborates: "Valuing is creating: hear it, ye creating ones! Valuation is itself the treasure and jewel of valued things."

During the dream phase, the interview stories and insights are put to constructive use. As people are brought together to listen carefully to the innovations and moments of organizational "life," sometimes in storytelling modes and sometimes in interpretive and analytic modes, a convergence zone is created where the future begins to be discerned in the form of visible patterns interwoven into the texture of the actual. The amplified interaction among innovators and innovations makes something important happen: very rapidly we start seeing outlines of the New World. Some organizations turn the data into a special commemorative report celebrating the successes and exceptional moments in the life of the organization (Liebler, 1997). Others have created a thematic analysis—careful to document rich stories and not succumb to "narrative thin" one line quotes (Ludema, 1996).

In all cases the data onto the positive change core serves as an essential resource for the visioning stages of the appreciative inquiry 4-D model.

Before their strategic planning session in 1997, Nutrimental Foods of Brazil closed down the plant for a full day to bring all 700 employees together for a day of Discovery into the factors and forces that have given life to the system when it had been most effective, most alive, and most successful as a producer of high quality health foods. With cheers and good wishes a "smaller" group of 150 stakeholders—employees from all levels, suppliers, distributors, community leaders, financiers, and customers—then went into a four day strategy session to articulate a new and bold corporate dream. The stories from the day before were used just as an artist uses a palette of colors—before painting a picture the artist assembles the red paints, blue, green, yellow and so on. With these "materials" in hand people were asked to dream: "What is the world calling us to become? What are those things about us that no matter how much we change, we want to continue into our new and different future? Let's assume that tonight while we were all asleep a miracle occurred where Nutrimental became exactly as we would like it to be—all of its best qualities are magnified, extended, multiplied the way we would like to see…in fact we wake up and it is now 2000 . . . as you come into Nutrimental today what do you see that is different, and how do you know?" After four days of appreciative analysis, planning, and articulation of three new strategic business directions, the organization launches into the future with focus, solidarity, and confidence. Six months later, record bottom line figures of millions of dollars are recorded—profits are up 300%. The co-CEOs, Rodrigo Loures and Arthur Lemme Netto, attribute the dramatic results to two things: bringing the whole system into the planning proces; and realizing that organizations are, in fact, "centers of human relatedness"(Loures and Lemme Netto, 1998) which thrive when there is an appreciative eye—when people see the best in one another, when they can dialogue their dreams and ultimate concerns in affirming ways, and when they are connected in full voice to create not just new worlds but better worlds.

Design

Once the strategic focus or dream is articulated (usually consisting of three things in our model—a vision of a better world, a powerful purpose, and a compelling statement of strategic intent) attention turns to the creation of the ideal organization, the social architecture or actual design of the system in relation to the world of which it is part. What we have found is that the sequencing is crucial, moving first through in-depth work on Dream before Design, followed with back and forth iterations. In Zimbabwe we recently worked with a partner organization of Save the Children. It was fascinating to observe how easy it was to re-design the organization in terms of structures and systems once broad agreement was reached on a powerful Dream. The articulation of the image of the future was simple: "Every person in Zimbabwe shall have access to clean water within five years." The critical design shift, demanded by the large dream, was to a new form of organization based on a network of alliances or partnerships, not bureaucracy's self-sufficient hierarchy.

One aspect that differentiates Appreciative Inquiry from other visioning or planning methodologies is that images of the future emerge out of grounded examples from an organization's positive past. Sometimes this "data" is complemented with benchmark studies of other organizations creating a "generative metaphor" for circumventing common resistances to change (Barrett and Cooperrider, 1990). In both cases, the good news stories are used to craft possibility propositions that bridge the best of "what is" with collective speculation or aspiration of "what might be". In the working of the material, people are invited to challenge the status quo as well as common assumptions underlying the design of the organization. People are encouraged to "wander beyond" the data with the essential question being: "What would our organization look like if it were designed in every way possible to maximize the qualities of the positive core and enable the accelerated realization of our dreams?"

When inspired by a great dream we have yet to find an organization that did not feel compelled to design something very new and very necessary. Here is an example of a possibility proposition, one of about twenty organization design visions that were created at DIA Corporation, a rapidly growing distributor of consumer products. Today this proposition is modus operandi at the corporation:

DIA has become a learning organization that fosters the cross fertilization of ideas, minimizes the building of empires, harnesses the synergy of group cooperation, and cultivates the pride of being a valued member of one outstanding corporation. DIA accelerates its learning through an annual strategic planning conference that involves all five hundred people in the firm as well as key partners and stakeholders. As a setting for "strategic learning," teams present their benchmarking studies of the best five other organizations, deemed leaders in their class. Other teams present an annual appreciative analysis of DIA, and together these databases of success stories (internal and external) help set the stage for DIA's strategic, future search planning.

Recently we have had the opportunity to team up with Dee Hock, one of the greatest visionary CEOs with whom we have ever worked. Dee was the founder of VISA, a breakthrough organization that has over 20,000 offices, and since 1970 has grown something like 10,000%; this year annual sales expected to pass $1 trillion. The whole Visa system, from Calcutta to Chicago, in over 200 countries is completely unmanageable from the perspective of using centralized, command-and-control design principles.

If General Motors once defined the shape of the old model, perhaps Dee's "chaordic organization"—combining chaos and order in ways which interweave (like nature's designs) infinite variety and self-organizing order—is a foreshadowing of an emerging prototype. What we have learned by working with Dee is how to move pragmatically and substantively from appreciative Discovery and

Dream to truly post-bureaucratic Design that distributes power and liberates human energy in a way we have never seen. Most recently we have collaborated on a re-constitution of the United Way of America as well as an initiative to design something akin to a United Nations among the world's great religions and spiritual traditions. (It is called United Religions.) In each case helping people agree on a set of design principles is crucial. That is "principles" as in, "We hold these truths to be self evident: that all people are created equal." Again, this is not a set of platitudes, but a manifesto, what people believe in and care about in their gut.

Destiny

William James said in 1902 that of all the creatures of earth, only human beings can change their pattern: "Man alone is the architect of his destiny."

In our early years of AI work, the fourth D was called Delivery. We emphasized planning for continuous learning, adjustment, and improvisation in the service of shared ideals. It was a time for action planning, developing implementation strategies, and dealing with conventional challenges of sustainability. But the word delivery simply did not go far enough. It did not convey the sense of liberation we were seeing—like the well documented hotel case, where the system tranformed itself from a one-star to four-star hotel by using AI and literally putting a moratorium on all the traditional problem solving efforts that it had going (Barrett and Cooperrider, 1990).

Executives like Jane Watkins (former Chair of the Board at NTL) and Jane Pratt (executive at the World Bank and now CEO of the Mountain Institute) argued that AI engenders a repatterning of our relationships, not only with each other, but also our relationship to reality itself. Reminiscent of Paulo Friere's concept of pedagogy of the oppressed—where people move in their relationship to reality from "submergence" to "reflexive awareness" to "co-participation"—these leaders insisted that AI's gift is at the paradigmatic level. AI is not so much about new knowledge but new knowing. Indeed people frequently talk, as they move through the pedagogy of life-giving Discovery, Dream, and Design, that something suddenly hits home: that interpretation matters—that the manner in which they/we read the world filters to the level of our imaginations, our relationships, and ultimately to the direction and meaning of our actions. We create the organizational worlds in which we live.

What we discovered, quite honestly, was that momentum for change and long-term sustainability increased the more we abandoned "delivery" ideas of action planning, monitoring progress, and building implementation strategies. What was done instead, in several of the most exciting cases, was to focus only on giving AI away to everyone, and then stepping back. The GTE story, still unfolding but already attracting national recognition, is suggestive. It is a story that says organizational change needs to look a lot more like an inspired movement than a neatly packaged or engineered product. Dan Young, the head of OD at GTE, and his colleagues Maureen Garrison and Jean Moore, call it "organizing for change from the grassroots to the frontline." Call it the path of positive protest, or a strategy for positive subversion—whatever it is called it is virtually unstoppable once "it" is up and running. Its structure is called the Positive Change Network (PCN). One especially dramatic moment gives the sense:

The headline article in GTE Together described what was spreading as a grassroots movement to build the new GTE. Initiated as a pilot training to see what would happen if the tools and theories of appreciative inquiry were made available to frontline employees, things started taking off. Suddenly, without permission having been granted, frontline employees are launching interview studies into positive topics like innovation, inspired leadership, revolutionary customer responsiveness, labor-management partnerships, and "fun". Fresh out of a training session on AI, one employee, for example, did 200 interviews into the positive core of a major call center. Who is going to say no to a complementary request like, "Would you help me out? . . . I'm really trying to find out more about the best innovations developing in your area and I see you as someone who could really give me new insight into creating settings where innovation can happen. . . . It is part of my leadership development. Do you have time for an interview? . . . would be glad to share my learnings with you later!" Soon the topics are finding their way into meetings, corridor conversations, and senior planning sessions—in other words the questions, enthusiastically received, are changing corporate attention, language, agendas, and learnings. Many start brainstorming applications for AI. Lists are endless. Have we ever done focus groups with the 100% satisfied customer? How about changing call center measures? What would happen if we replaced the entire deficit measures with equally powerful measures of the positive? How can we revitalize the TQM groups, demoralized by one fishbone analysis after another? What would happen if we augmented variance analysis with depth studies that help people to dream and define the very visions of quality standards? How about a star stories program to generate a narrative rich environment—where customers are asked to share stories of encounters with exceptional employees? How about a gathering with senior executives so we can celebrate our learnings with them, share with them how seeing the positive has changed our work and family lives, and even recruit them to join the PCN?

The pilot program now had a momentum all its own. The immediate response—an avalanche of requests for participation—confirmed that there were large numbers at GTE ready to be called to the task of positive change. To grow the network by the hundreds, even thousands, it was decided to do a ten region training session, all linked and downloaded by satellite conferencing. A successful pilot of three sites—Seattle, Indianapolis, and Dallas—confirmed the same kind of energy and response could happen through distance technologies. Quite suddenly the power of a 1000 person network caught people's attention. Just imagine the 1000 "students" of organization life coming together in a year at an AI Summit to share learning from 10,000 innovations discovered at GTE. Very rapidly, by connecting and consistently noticing breakthroughs, new patterns of organizing would become commonplace knowledge. Changes would happen not by organized confrontation, diagnosis, burning platforms, or piecemeal reform but through irresistibly vibrant and real visions. And when everyone's awareness grows at the same time—that basic change is taking place in this area and that area, it is easier to coalesce a new consensus that fundamental change is possible. PCN was becoming a lightning rod for energy and enthusiasm we all greatly underestimated. Then the unions raised questions. There were serious concerns, including the fact that they were not consulted in the early stages. We were told the initiative was over. There was to be a meeting of the unions and GTE at the Federal Mediation Offices in Washington, D.C. to put the whole thing to rest.

But at the meeting with the IBEW and the CWA, leaders from both groups said they saw something fresh and unique about AI. They agreed to bring 200 union leaders together for a two-day introduction. Their purpose: "to evaluate AI . . . to see if it should have any place in the future at GTE." A month later, the session took place. It looked as if it was going pretty well and then the moment of decision. Tables of eight were instructed to evaluate the ideas and cast a vote as a group: "Yes, we endorse moving forward with AI" or "No, we withhold endorsement." For thirty minutes the 30 groups deliberated. Dan Young calls the vote. Tensions were felt. "Table one, how do you vote?" The response was ready: "We vote 100% for moving forward with AI and feel this is an historic opportunity for the whole system." Then the next table: "We vote 100% with a caveat—that every person at GTE have the opportunity to get the AI training, and that all projects going forward be done in partnership, the unions and the company." On and on the vote goes. Thirty tables spoke. Thirty tables voted. Every single one voted to move forward. It was stunning. Eight months later AI was combined with the "conflictive partnership" model of John Calhoun Wells of the Federal Mediation Services at the kickoff session and announcement of a new era of partnership. The historic statement of Partnership states: "The company and the Unions realize that traditional adversarial labor-management relations must change in order to adapt to the new global telecommunications marketplace. It is difficult to move to cooperation in one quantum leap. However the company and the Unions have agreed to move in a new direction. This new direction emphasizes partnership."

AI accelerates the nonlinear interaction of organization breakthroughs, putting them together with historic, positive traditions and strengths to create a "convergence zone" facilitating the collective repatterning of human systems. At some point, apparently minor positive discoveries connect in accelerating manner and quantum change, a jump from one state to the next that cannot be achieved through incremental change alone, becomes possible. What is needed, as the Destiny Phase of AI suggests, are the network-like structures that liberate not only the daily search into qualities and elements of an organization's positive core but the establishment of a convergence zone for people to empower one another—to connect, cooperate, and co-create. Changes never thought possible are suddenly and democratically mobilized when people constructively appropriate the power of the positive core and simply... let go of accounts of the negative. But then the question is always voiced: "What do we do with the real problems?"

Basic Principles of Appreciative Inquiry

To address this question in anything other than Pollyannaish terms, we need to at least comment on the generative-theoretical work that has inspired and given strength too much of AI in practice. Here are five principles and scholarly streams we consider as central to AI's theory-base of change.

The Constructionist Principle: Simply stated—human knowledge and organizational destiny are interwoven. To be effective as executives, leaders, change agents, etc., we must be adept in the art of understanding, reading, and analyzing organizations as living, human constructions. Knowing (organizations) stands at the center of any and virtually every attempt at change. Thus, the way we know is fateful.

At first blush this statement appears simple and obvious enough. We are, as leaders and change agents, constantly involved in knowing/inquiring/reading the people and world around us—doing strategic planning analysis, environmental scans, needs analysis, assessments and audits, surveys, focus groups, performance appraisals, and so on. Certainly success hinges on such modes of knowing. And this is precisely where things get more interesting because throughout the academy a revolution is afoot, alive with tremendous ferment and implication, in regard to modernist views of knowledge. In particular, what is confronted is the Western conception of objective, individualistic, historic knowledge—"a conception that has insinuated itself into virtually all aspects of modern institutional life" (Gergen, 1985; p. 272). At stake are questions that pertain to the deepest dimensions of our being and humanity: how we know what we know, whose voices and interpretations matter, whether the world is governed by external laws independent of human choices and consciousness, and where is knowledge to be located (in the individual "mind", or out there "externally" in nature or impersonal structures)? At stake are issues that are profoundly fundamental, not just for the future of social science but for the trajectory of all our lives.

In our view, the finest work in this area, indeed a huge extension of the most radical ideas in Lewinian thought, can be found in Ken Gergen's Toward Transformation in Social Knowledge (1982) and Realities and Relationships: Soundings In Social Construction (1994). What Gergen does, in both of these, is synthesize the essential whole of the post modern ferment and crucially takes it beyond disenchantment with the old and offers alternative conceptions of knowledge, fresh discourses on human functioning, new vistas for human science, and exciting directions for approaching change. Constuctionism is an approach to human science and practice which replaces the individual with the relationship as the locus of knowledge, and thus is built around a keen appreciation of the power of language and discourse of all types (from words to metaphors to narrative forms, etc.) to create our sense of reality—our sense of the true, the good, the possible.

Philosophically it involves a decisive shift in western intellectual tradition from *cogito ergo sum*, to *communicamus ergo sum* and in practice constructionism replaces absolutist claims or the final word with the never ending collaborative quest to understand and construct options for better living. The purpose of inquiry, which is talked about as totally inseparable and intertwined with action, is the creation of "generative theory," not so much mappings or explanations of yesterday's world, but anticipatory articulations of tomorrow's possibilities. Constructionism, because of its emphasis on the communal basis of knowledge and its radical questioning of everything that is taken-for-granted as "objective" or seemingly immutable, invites us to find ways to increase the generative capacity of knowledge. However there are warnings: "Few are prepared," says Gergen (1985, p. 271) "for such a wrenching, conceptual dislocation. However, for the innovative, adventurous and resilient, the horizons are exciting indeed." This is precisely the call to which AI has responded. Principle number two takes it deeper.

The Principle of Simultaneity: Here it is recognized that inquiry and change are not truly separate moments, but are simultaneous. Inquiry is intervention. The seeds of change—that is, the things people think and talk about, the things people discover and learn, and the things that inform dialogue and inspire images of the future—are implicit in the very first questions we ask. The questions we ask set the stage for what we "find," and what we "discover" (the data) becomes the linguistic material, the stories, out of which the future is conceived, conversed about, and constructed.

One of the most impactful things a change agent or practitioner does is to articulate questions. Instinctively, intuitively and tacitly we all know that research of any kind can, in a flash, profoundly alter the way we see ourselves, view reality, and conduct our lives. Consider the economic poll, or the questions that led to the discovery of the atom bomb, or the surveys that, once leaked, created a riot at a unionized automobile plant in London. (See Cooperrider and Srivastva, 1987.) If we accept the proposition that patterns of social-organizational action are not fixed by nature in any direct biological or physical way, that human systems are made and imagined in relational settings by human beings (socially constructed), then attention turns to the source of our ideas, our discourses, our researches—that is, our questions. Alterations in linguistic practices—including the linguistic practice of crafting questions—hold profound implications for changes in social practice.

One great myth that continues to dampen the potential here is the understanding that first we do an analysis, and then we decide on change. Not so, says the constructionist view. Even the most innocent question evokes change—even if reactions are simply changes in awareness, dialogue, feelings of boredom, or even laughter. When we consider the possibilities in these terms, that inquiry and change are a simultaneous moment, we begin reflecting anew. It is not so much "Is my question leading to right or wrong answers?" but rather "What impact is my question having on our lives together...is it helping to generate conversations about the good, the better, the possible . . . is it strengthening our relationships?"

The Poetic Principle: A metaphor here is that human organizations are a lot more like an open book than, say, a machine. An organization's story is constantly being co-authored. Moreover, pasts, presents, or futures are endless sources of learning, inspiration, or interpretation—precisely like, for example, the endless interpretive possibilities in a good piece of poetry or a biblical text. The important implication is that we can study virtually any topic related to human experience in any human system or organization. We can inquire into the nature of alienation or joy, enthusiasm or low morale, efficiency or excess, in any human organization. There is not a single topic related to organizational life that we could not study in any organization.

What constuctionism does is remind us that it is not the "world out there" dictating or driving our topics of inquiry but again the topics are themselves social artifacts, products of social processes (cultural habits, typifying discourses, rhetoric, professional ways, power relations). It is in this vein that AI says: Let us make sure we are not just reproducing the same worlds over and over again because of the simple and boring repetition of our questions (not "one more" morale survey which everybody can predict the results ahead of time). AI also says, with a sense of excitement and potential, that there can be great gains made in a better linking of the means and ends of inquiry. Options begin to multiply. For example, informally, in many talks with great leaders in the NGO world (Save the Children, World Vision), we have begun to appreciate the profound joy that CEO's feel as "servant leaders"—and the role this positive affect potentially plays in creating healthy organizations. But then one questions: Is there a book on the Harvard Business book-list, or anywhere for that matter, titled Executive Joy? And even if there isn't, does this mean that joy has nothing to do with good leadership, or healthy human systems? Why aren't we including this topic in our change efforts? What might happen if we did?

What the poetic principle invites is re-consideration of aims and focus of any inquiry in the domain of change management. It is becoming clearer that our topics, like windsocks, continue to blow steadily onward in the direction of our conventional gaze. As we shall soon explore, seeing the world as a problem has become "very much a way of organizational life."

The Anticipatory Principle: The infinite human resource we have for generating constructive organizational change is our collective imagination and discourse about the future. One of the basic theorems of the anticipatory view of organizational life is that it is the image of the future, which in fact guides what might be called the current behavior of any organism or organization. Much like a movie projector on a screen, human systems are forever projecting ahead of themselves a horizon of expectation (in their talk in the haliways, in the metaphors and language they use) that brings the future powerfully into the present as a mobilizing agent. To inquire in ways that serve to refashion anticipatory reality—especially the artful creation of positive imagery on a collective basis—may be the most prolific thing any inquiry can do.

Our positive images of the future lead our positive actions—this is the increasingly energizing basis and presupposition of Appreciative Inquiry.

Whether we are talking about placebo studies in medicine (Ornstein and Sobel, 1987); reviews of a myriad of studies of the Pygmalion dynamic in the classroom

(Jussim, 1986); studies of the rise and fall of cultures (Boulding, 1966; Polak, 1973); research into the relationships between optimism and health (Seligman, 1990); studies of positive self-monitoring and ways for accelerating learning (Kirschenbaum, 1984); analysis of the importance of imbalance, positive inner dialogue to personal and relational well-being (Schwartz, 1986); research on positive mood states and effective decision making (Isen, 1983); studies from the domain of "conscious evolution" (Hubbard, 1998); or theories on how positive noticing of even "small wins" can reverberate throughout a system and change the world (Weick, 1984)—the conclusions are converging on something Aristotle said many years ago. "A vivid imagination," he said "compels the whole body to obey it." In the context of more popular writing, Dan Goleman (1987), in a well-written New York Times headline-article declares "Research Affirms the Power of Positive Thinking."

The Positive Principle: This last principle is not so abstract. It grows out of years of experience with appreciative inquiry. Put most simply, it has been our experience that building and sustaining momentum for change requires large amounts of positive affect and social bonding—things like hope, excitement, inspiration, caring, camaraderie, sense of urgent purpose, and sheer joy in creating something meaningful together. What we have found is that the more positive the question we ask in our work the more long lasting and successful the change effort. It does not help, we have found, to begin our inquiries from the standpoint of the world as a problem to be solved. We are more effective the longer we can retain the spirit of inquiry of the everlasting beginner. The major thing we do that makes the difference is to craft and seed, in better and more catalytic ways, the unconditional positive question.

Although the positive has not been paraded as a central concept in most approaches to organization analysis and change, it is clear we need no longer be shy about bringing this language more carefully and prominently into our work. And personally speaking, it is so much healthier. We love letting go of "fixing" the world. We love doing interviews, hundreds of them, into moments of organizational life. And we are, quite frankly, more effective the more we are able to learn, to admire, to be surprised, to be inspired alongside the people with whom we are working. Perhaps it is not just organizations—we too become what we study. So suggested, over and over again, is the life-promoting impact of inquiry into the good, the better, and the possible. A theory of affirmative basis of human action and organizing is emerging from many quarters—social contructionism, image theory, conscious evolution and the like. And the whole thing is beginning, we believe, to make a number of our change-management traditions look obsolete.

Appreciative Inquiry and Power in Organizations

We could have easily called this section "Eulogy for Problem Solving". In our view, the problem solving paradigm, while once perhaps quite effective, is simply out of sync with the realities of today's virtual worlds (Cooperrider, 1996). Problem solving approaches to change are painfully slow (always asking people to look backward to yesterday's causes); they rarely result in new vision (by definition we can describe something as a problem because we already, perhaps implicitly, assume an ideal, so we are not searching to expansive new knowledge of better ideals but searching how to close "gaps"); and in human terms problem approaches are notorious for generating defensiveness (it is not my problem but yours). But our real concern, from a social constructionist perspective, has to do with relations of power and control. It is the most speculative part of this chapter; and hopefully, it better illuminates the potentials advocated by AI. In particular is the more conscious linking of language, including the language of our own profession, to change. Words do create worlds—even in unintended ways.

There was an unforgettable moment in a conference in Chicago on AI for inner city change agents, mostly community mobilizers from the Saul Alinsky school of thought, Rules for Radicals. After two days a participant challenges: "This is naïve . . . Have you ever worked in the depths of the inner city, like the Cabrini Green public housing projects? You're asking me to go in and 'appreciate' it . . . Just yesterday I'm there and the impoverished children are playing soccer, not with a ball, no money for that, but with a dead rat. Tell me about appreciative inquiry in the housing projects!"

It was a powerful question. It was one that made us go deeper theoretically. At one level we were arguing typical approaches to problem diagnosis, including the Alinsky confrontation methods, would work, but at about half the speed of AI. But then as we explored the subject of the cultural consequences of deficit discourse we began seeing a disconcerting relationship between the society-wide escalation of deficit-based change methods and the erosion of people power. The analysis, from here, could proceed from virtually any professional discipline—the diagnostic vocabularies of social work, medicine, organization development, management, law, accounting, community development, editing—but let's begin with psychology and the social sciences (ample linkage will be made to our own field). Ken Gergen's (1994) work is at the forefront for anyone wanting something more than a suggestive summary.

Consider the following characterizations of the self: impulsive personality, narcissism, anti-social personality, reactive depressive, codependent, self-alienated, type-A, paranoid, stressed, repressed, authoritarian, midlife crisis. These are all terms commonly used by the mental-health professions and are now common among people in the culture itself. But importantly, these terms, and several thousand others (Gergen, 1994), have come into conventional usage only within the present century, many in only the last decade. But something else is noteworthy: the terminology's discredit, draws attention to problems, shortcomings, and incapacities. Interestingly, the trajectory of the "professional" development of vocabularies of human deficit is rising at geometric rates, correlated as might be expected with the sheer growth in numbers of the profession. In 1892 when the American Psychological Association was founded there were thirty-one members. By 1906 there were 181. The next thirty-one years witnessed an expansion of almost a hundredfold, to over 3,000. In the next twenty-two years the figure grew again by twenty times, over 63,000. Add to this similar growth figures in social work, psychiatry, community development, and organization development and one realizes that the spiraling production of languages of deficit have become quite a growth industry. By 1980 mental illness was the third most expensive category of health disorder in the United States at more than $20 billion annually. By 1983, the costs for mental illness, exclusive of alcoholism and drug abuse, were estimated to be almost $73 billion. We have no figures for the consulting industry, but we can guess. While intentions are good, argues Gergen, some of the unintended consequences may not be.

From a constructionist perspective one realizes that words do not so much innocently "mirror" a world out there as they become vehicles for coordinating our actions with one another. Words in any profession function a bit like tools of the trade. When I used to give my son Matt a hammer, inevitably everything in the house soon became a nail. What happens when the "scientifically" legitimated vocabularies of human deficit become the common and explicit tool kit of all? Gergen suggests not everything about it is healthy. Such deficit discourse, when chronically used, "generates a network of increasing entanglements for the culture at large. Such entanglements are not only self serving for the professions, they also add exponentially to the sense of human misery." (1994, p. 142)

In particular, deficit based change approaches have an unfortunate propensity to reinforce hierarchy, wherein "less than ideal" individuals, who learn to accept what sometimes becomes a lifelong label, are encouraged to enter "treatment programs" under expert supervision; to erode community, wherein the mental health professions appropriate the process of interpersonal realignment that might otherwise (in other eras) have happened in nonprofessional contexts like the family or community; to instill a sense of self-enfeeblement, wherein deficit terms essentialize the person and like a birthmark or fingerprint, the deficit is expected to inevitably manifest itself into many aspects of their lives (it is a "thing"); to stimulate endless vocabulary expansion wherein people increasingly construct their problems in the professional languages (diagnosing each other) and seek more help which in turn increased the numbers in the profession who are rewarded when they expand the vocabulary—"to explore a new disorder within the mental health sciences is not unlike discovering a new star in astronomy." (Gergen, p. 159) Gergen sums up: "As I am proposing, when the culture is furnished with a professionally rationalized language of mental deficit and people are increasingly understood according to this language, the population of 'patients' expands. This population, in turn, forces the profession to extend its vocabulary, and thus the array of mental deficit terms available for cultural use." (Gergen, p. 161) Is there no exit from such progressive infirmity?

After talking this over with the people in the inner city Chicago conference—and tracing the vocabularies of human deficit not only to the rise of the professions but also to the rise of bureaucracy, skeptical science, original sin theological accounts, the cynical media—the Alinsky-trained activist sat down with a gasp. He said: "In the name of entertainment, my people are being fed negative views of human violence—and they are surrounded by endless description of their negative 'needs' their 'problem lives'. Even in my methods, the same. And what do I see? I see people asleep in front of their TVs. Unable to move, like sleeping dogs. Yes, they have voice in the housing project assessments. But it is a certain kind of voice . . . it is visionless voice. They get to confirm the deficit analysis; all the reports are the same. 'Yes,' they say, 'the reports are true.' What is hitting me right now is how radical the AI message might be. Marx could have said it better: Perhaps the vocabularies of human deficit are the opiates of the masses. People have voice in the analyses—this involvement is what we fought for. But people are not mobilized by it anymore. No, they are asleep. Visionless voice is probably worse than no voice."

Elsewhere we have cautioned, in our own discipline, that it is not so much the problem solving methodologies per se that are of central concern, but the growing sense that we all, throughout the culture, have taken the tools a step further. It is not so much that organizations have problems, they are problems. (See Figure 1.2.) Somewhere a shift of this kind has taken place. Once accepted as fundamental truth about organizations, virtually everything in change-management becomes infused with a deficit consciousness. For example, as French and Bell (1995) define it, "Action-research is both an approach to problem solving—a model or paradigm, and a problem solving process—a series of activities and events" (p.88).

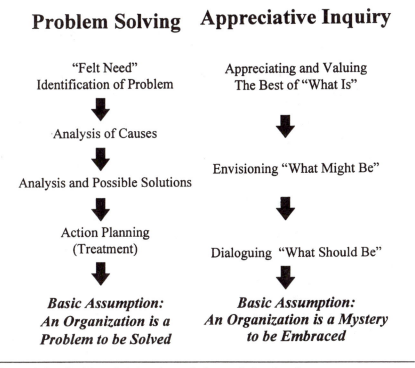

Problem Solving   Appreciative Inquiry

Problem Solving	Appreciative Inquiry
"Felt Need" Identification of Problem	Appreciating and Valuing The Best of "What Is"
↓	↓
Analysis of Causes	
↓	Envisioning "What Might Be"
Analysis and Possible Solutions	↓
↓	
Action Planning (Treatment)	Dialoguing "What Should Be"
↓	↓
Basic Assumption: *An Organization is a* *Problem to be Solved*	*Basic Assumption:* *An Organization is a Mystery* *to be Embraced*

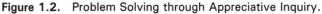

Figure 1.2. Problem Solving through Appreciative Inquiry.

Levinson, in the classic on Organizational Diagnosis (1972, p.37) likens it to therapy—"Like a therapeutic or teaching relationship it should be an alliance of both parties to discover and resolve these problems...looking for experiences which appear stressful to people. What kinds of occurrences disrupt or disorganize people?" Chris Argyris, in another classic, asserts: One condition that seems so basic as to be defined as axiomatic is the generation of valid information...Valid information is that which describes the factors, plus their interrelationships, that create the problem (1970, pp.16–17).

Tough questions remain about power and deficit discourse. And of course there are an array of new innovations in the field, many in this volume, that are signaling significant departures. So at this point all we want to do is make a call for reflection and caution, taking a lesson from the wisdom of anthropology — beware of the solid truths of one's own culture.

Conclusion

To be sure, Appreciative Inquiry (AI) begins an adventure. The urge for and call to adventure have been sounded by many people and many organizations, and it will take many more to fully explore the vast vistas that are now appearing on the horizon.

As said at the outset, we believe we are infants when it comes to our understanding of appreciative processes of knowing and social construction. Yet we are increasingly clear the world is ready to leap beyond methodologies of deficit based changes and enter a domain that is life-centric. Organizations, says AI theory, are centers of human relatedness, first and foremost. And relationships thrive where there is an appreciative eye—when people see the best in one another, when they share their dreams and ultimate concerns in affirming ways, and when they are connected in full voice to create not just new worlds, but better worlds. The velocity and largely informal spread of the appreciative learnings suggests, we believe, a growing sense of disenchantment with exhausted theories of change, especially those wedded to vocabularies of human deficit; and a corresponding urge to work with people, groups, and organizations in more constructive, positive, life-affirming, even spiritual ways. AI, we hope it is being said, is more than a simple 4-D cycle of discovery, dream, design, and destiny. What is being introduced is something deeper at the core.

Perhaps our inquiry must become the positive revolution we want to see in the world. Albert Einstein's words clearly compel: "There are only two ways to live your life. One is as though nothing is a miracle. The other is as though everything is a miracle."

Bibliography

Argyris, C. (1970). *Intervention Theory and Methods*. Reading, MA: Addison-Wesley.

Barrett, F. J. (1998). Creativity and Improvisation in Jazz and Organizations: Implications for Organizational Learning. *Organization Science*, 9 (5) 605–622.

Barrett, F. J., and Cooperrider, D. L. (1990). Generative Metaphor Intervention: A New Approach to Intergroup Conflict. *Journal of Applied Behavioral Science*, 26(2), 223–244.

Boulding, K. (1966). *The Image*. Ann Arbor: University of Michigan Press.

Bushe, G. R. (1995). Advances in Appreciative Inquiry as an Organization Development Intervention. *Organization Development Journal*, 13(3), 14–22.

Chin, A.L. (1998). Future Visions. *Journal of Organization and Change Management*, Spring.

Cooperrider, D. L. (1986). Appreciative Inquiry: Toward a methodology for understanding and enhancing organizational innovation. Unpublished Ph.D., Case Western Reserve University, Cleveland.

Cooperrider, D. L. (1996). The "Child" As Agent of Inquiry. *Organization Development Practitioner*, 28(1 and 2), 5–11.

Cooperrider, D. L. (1996). Resources for Getting Appreciative Inquiry Started: An Example OD Proposal. *Organization Development Practitioner*, 28(1 and2), 23–33.

Cooperrider, D. L., and Srivastva, S. (1987). Appreciative Inquiry in Organizational Life. *Research in Organizational Change and Development*, 1, 129–169.

Curran, M. (1991). Appreciative Inquiry: A Third Wave Approach to OD. *Vision/Action, December*, 12–14.

French, W., and Bell, C. (1994). *Organization Development: Behavioral Science Interventions for Organization Improvement. (5th ed.)*. Englewood Cliffs, NJ: Prentice Hall.

Gergen, K. (1982). *Toward Transformation in Social Knowledge*. New York: Springer-Verlag.

Gergen, K. (1985). The Social Constructionist Movement in Modern Psychology. *American Psychologist*, 40, 266–275.

Gergen, K. (1994). *Realities and Relationships: Soundings in Social Construction*. Cambridge, MA: Harvard University Press.

Goleman, D. (1987, Feb. 3). Research Affirms Power of Positive Thinking. New York Times, pp. 15–19.

Harman, W. W. (1990). Shifting Context for Executive Behavior: Signs of Change and Revaluation. In S. Srivastva, D. L. Cooperrider, and Associates (Eds.), Appreciative Management and Leadership: The Power of Positive Thought and Action in Organizations (1st ed., pp. 37–54). San Francisco, CA: Jossey-Bass Inc.

Head, T. and Sorensen, P., et.al. (1997) Is Appreciative Inquiry the Philosopher's Stone? An unpublished paper, Doctoral Program in Organizational Behavior. Naperville, IL. Benedictine University.

Hubbard, B. M. (1998). Conscious Evolution: Awakening the Power of Our Social Potential. Novato, CA: New World Library (See Chp. 11 on AI).

Isen, A., and Means, B. (1983). The Influence of Positive Affect on Decision Making Strategy. *Social Cognition*, 2, 18–31.

Jussim, C. (1986). Self-Fulfilling Prophecies: A Theoretical and Integrative Review. *Psychological Review*, 93(4), 429–445.

Kirschenbaum, D. (1984). Self-Regulation and Sport Psychology: Nurturing and Emerging Symbiosis. *Journal of Sport Psychology*, 8, 26–34.

Levinson, H. (1972). *Organizational Diagnosis*. Cambridge, MA: Harvard University Press.

Liebler, C. J. (1997 Summer). Getting Comfortable With Appreciative Inquiry: Questions and Answers. Global Social Innovations, *Journal of the GEM Initiative*, Case Western Reserve University, 1(2), 30–40.

Ludema, J. (1996). Narrative Inquiry. Unpublished Doctoral Dissertation, Case Western Reserve University, Cleveland, Ohio.

Mirvis, P. H. (1988/89). Organization Development: Part 1-An Evolutionary Perspective. In W. Pasmore and R. Woodman (Eds.), *Research in Organizational Change and Development (Vol. 2 and 3)*. Greenwich, CT: JAI Press, Inc.

Netto, L., and Netto, L. (1998). Journal of the Nutrimental Foods, 1(January), 2.

Ornstein, R., and Sobel, D. (1987). *The Healing Brain*. New York: Simon and Schuster.

Polak, F. (1973). *The Image of the Future*. New York: Elsevier.

Porras, J., I. (1991). Organization Development and Transformation. *Annual Review of Psychology*, 42, 51–78.

Rader, M. (1973). *A Modern Book of Esthetics: An Anthology*. New York: Holt.

Rainey, M. A. (1996). An Appreciative Inquiry Into the Factors of Culture Continuity During Leadership Transition. *Organization Development Practitioner*, 28(1 and 2), 34–41.

Schwartz, R. (1986). The Internal Dialogue: On the Assymmetry Between Positive and Negative Coping Thoughts. *Cognitive Therapy and Research*, 10, 591–605.

Seligman, M. (1990). *Learned Optimism*. New York: Pocket Books.

Weick, K. (1984). Small Wins: Redefining the Scale of Social Problems. *American Psychologist*, 39(1), 40–49.

White, T. W. (1996). Working In Interesting Times. Vital Speeches Of The Day, LXII(15), 472–474.

Whitney, D., and Cooperrider, D. (1998). The Appreciative Inquiry Summit: Overview and Applications. *Employment Relations Today*, Summer, 17–28.

Whitney, D., and Schau, C. (1998). Appreciative Inquiry: An Innovative Process for Organization Change. Employment Relations Today,(Spring)11–21.

Chapter 2

POSITIVE IMAGE, POSITIVE ACTION: THE AFFIRMATIVE BASIS OF ORGANIZING

David L. Cooperrider

Case Western Reserve University

> Be not afraid of life. Believe that life is worth living, and your belief will help you create the fact. —William James.

> We can easily forgive a child who is afraid of the dark.
> The real tragedy of life is when men are afraid of the light. —Plato.

Modern management thought was born proclaiming that organizations are the triumph of the human imagination. As made and imaged, organizations are products of human imagination. As made and imagined, organizations are products of human interaction and mind rather than some blind expression of an underlying natural order (McGregor, 1960; Berger and Luckmann, 1967; Pfeffer, 1981; Gergen, 1982; Srivastva and Associates, 1983; Schein, 1985; Unger, 1987). Deceptively simple yet so entirely radical in implication, this insight is still shattering many beliefs— one of which is the longstanding conviction that bureaucracy, oligarchy, and other forms of hierarchical domination are inevitable. Today we know that this simply is not true.

Recognizing the symbolic and socially constructed nature of the human universe, we now find new legitimacy for the mounting wave of sociocognitive and sociocultural research, all of which is converging around one essential and empowering thesis: that there is little about collective action or organization development that is preprogrammed, unilaterally determined, or stimulus bound in any direct physical or material way. Seemingly immutable ideas about people and organizations are being directly challenged and transformed on an unprecedented scale. Indeed, as we move into a postmodern global society we are breaking out of our parochial perspectives and are recognizing that organizations in all societies exist in a wide array of types and species and function within a dynamic spectrum of beliefs and lifestyles. And according to the social constructionist viewpoint, the possibilities are infinite.

S. Srivastva and D. L. Cooperrider and Associates (Eds.) *Executive Appreciation and Leadership: 91–125*. San Francisco: Jossey-Bass.

Interestingly, there is an important parallel to this whole area of thought that has grown out of the neurosciences and studies of cognition and mind–brain interaction. The "consciousness revolution" of the 1970s is well documented and represents, argues Nobel Laureate Roger Sperry (1988), more than a mere Zeitgeist phenomenon; it represents a profound conceptual shift to a different form of causal determinism. According to the mentalist paradigm, mind can no longer be considered the opposite of matter. Mental phenomena, this paradigm contends, must be recognized as being at the top of the brain's "causal control hierarchy" whereby, after millenniums of evolution, the mind has been given primacy over bioevolutionary (Darwinian) controls that determine what human systems are and can become. In direct contradiction to materialist and behaviorist doctrine, where everything is supposed to be governed from below upward through microdeterminist stimuli and physiochemical forces, the new mentalist view gives subjective mental phenomena a causal role in brain processing and thereby a new legitimacy in science as an autonomous explanatory construct. Future reality, in this view, is permeable, emergent, and open to the mind's causal influence; that is, reality is conditioned, reconstructed, and often profoundly created through our anticipatory images, values, plans, intentions, beliefs, and the like. Macrodeterminisim or the theory of downward causation is a scheme, asserts Sperry, that idealizes ideas and ideals over chemical interactions, nerve impulse traffic and DNA. It is a brain model in which conscious, mental, and psychic forces are recognized as the crowing achievement of some 500 million years or more of evolution.

The impetus for the present contribution grows from the exciting challenge that is implicitly if not explicitly posed by the social constructionist and mentalist paradigms: that to a far greater extent than is normally acknowledged, we human beings create our own realities through symbolic and mental processes and that because of this, consciousness evolution of the future is a human option. Taking this challenge—that of a future-creating mental activism—one step further, the thesis explored in this paper is that the artful creation of positive imagery on a collective basis may well be the most prolific activity that individuals and organizations can engage in if their aim is to help bring to fruition a positive and humanly significant future. Stated more boldly a *New York Times* headline recently apprised the public that "Research Affirms Power of Positive Thinking" (Goleman, 1987, p. 15). Implied in the popular news release and the scholarly research that we will soon sample is the intriguing suggestion that human systems are largely *heliotropic* in character, meaning that they exhibit an observable and largely automatic tendency to evolve in the direction of positive anticipatory images of the future. What I will argue is that just as plants of many varieties exhibit a tendency to grow in the direction of sunlight (symbolized by the Greek god Helios), there is an analogous process going on in all human systems.

As a whole this essay is intended to serve as an invitation to broadly consider a number of questions: What is the relationship between positive imagery and positive action? More specifically, what are the common processes, pathways, or global patterns whereby mental phenomena attract or even cause those actions that bring about movement toward an ideal? Where do positive images of some unknown and neutral future come from in the first place? Could it be that organizations are in fact affirmative systems, governed and maintained by positive projections about what the organization is, how it will function, and what it might become? If so, what are the implications for management? Is it true that the central executive task in a postbureaucratic society is to nourish the *appreciative* soil from which affirmative projections grow, branch off, evolve, and become collective projections?

To set the stage for our discourse, the first section will begin with a general introduction to the concept of imagery. The second will look specifically at the relationship between positive imagery and positive action by reviewing recent works from diverse areas of study—medicine, cognitive psychology, cultural sociology, and athletics. While I am careful not to suggest that the studies sampled make anything close to an exhaustive case, I do submit, nevertheless, that the convergence of insight, across disciples, represent an exciting step forward in our understandings of the intricate pathways that link mind and practice. Finally, in the third section, I will discuss how such knowledge from diverse quarters holds a thread of continuity that has broad relevance for understanding organizations. In particular, I will offer a set of eight propositions about the *affirmative basis of organizing*. These propositions are provided for discussion, elaboration, and active experimentation and converge around three basic conclusions: (1) Organizations are products of the affirmative mind; (2) when beset with repetitive difficulties or problems, organizations need less fixing, less problem solving, and more reaffirmation—or more precisely, more *appreciation*; (3) the primary executive vocation in a postbureaucratic era is to nourish the appreciative soil from which new and better guiding images grow on a collective and dynamic basis.

Imagery: An Introduction

Throughout the ages and from a diversity of perspectives, the image has been considered a powerful agent in the guidance and determination of action:

> A vivid imagination compels the whole body to obey it.
> —Aristotle (in Sheikh, 1984, p. 5).

> One of the basic theorems of the theory of image is that it is the image which in fact determines what might be called the current behavior of any organism or organization. The image acts as a field. The behavior consists in gravitating toward the most highly valued part of the world.
> —Kenneth Boulding (1966, p. 155).

> Mental anticipation now pulls the future into the present and reverses the direction of causality.
> —Erich Jantsch (1980, p. 14).

Man is a being who, being in the world, is ever ahead of himself, caught
up in bringing things alive with his projection. . . . Whatever comes to
light owes its presence to the fact that man has provided the overall imaginative sunlight for viewing.   —Edward Murray (1986, p. 64).

To the empowering principle that people can withhold legitimacy, and
thus change the world, we now add another. By deliberately changing
the internal image of reality, people can change the world.
                                                            —Willis Harman (1988, p. 1).

Imagination is more important than knowledge.
                                        —Albert Einstein (in Sheikh, 1984, p. 5).

It is clear that images are operative virtually everywhere: Soviet and U.S.
diplomats create strategies on the basis of images; Theory X managers construct
management structures that reflect the pictures they hold of subordinates; days or
minutes before a public speech we all feel the tension or anxiety that accompanies
our anticipatory viewing of the audience; we all hold self-images, images of our
race, profession, nation, and cultural belief systems; and we have images of our
own potential as well as the potential of others. Fundamentally, too, it can be
argued that every organization, product, or innovative service first started as a
wild but not idle dream and that *anticipatory realities* are what make collectivities
click. (This is why we still experience King, Jr's "I Have a Dream" and sometimes
find ourselves enlivened through the images associated with the mere mention of
such figures as John F. Kennedy, Gandhi, Winston Churchill, Buddha, or Christ.)

Given the central and pervasive role of the image in relation to action, it is not
surprising that research on the workings of the image has risen to be "one of the
hottest topics in cognitive science" (Block, 1981, p. 1). Theorists disagree over
definitions and argue whether images are direct encoding of perceptual experience (Pavid, 1971), are an artifact of the propositional structuring of reality
(Pylyshyn, 1973), represent the sensory system par excellence that undergirds and
constitutes virtually every area of cognitive processing, are primarily eidetic or
visual (Ashen, 1977), or represent constructive or reconstructive process (Kosslyn,
1980). But in spite of the largely technical differences, Richardson (1969, pp. 2–3)
seems to have provided adequate synthesis of a number of competing views in his
often-quoted definition of the image as quasi-sensory, stimulus-independent representative experience: "Mental imagery refers to (1) all those quasi-sensory or
quasi-perceptual experiences of which (2) we are self consciously aware and which
(3) exist for us in the absence of those stimulus conditions that are know to reproduce their sensory or perceptual counterparts, and which (4) may be expected to
have different consequences."

In subsequent work, Richardson (1983) retracts the fourth criterion; between
1969 and 1983 there was simply too much new evidence showing that self-initi-
ated imagery can and often does have consequences, many of them physiological,
that are indistinguishable from their genuine sensory counterparts. Merely an

anticipatory image, for example, of a hostile encounter can raise one's blood pressure as much as the encounter itself. Similarly, numerous new studies now show that consciously constructed images can lead directly to such things as blood glucose increases, increased gastric acid secretion, blister formation, and changes in skin temperature and pupillary size. In an example closer to home, Richardson (1983, p. 15) suggests that "it suffices to remind the reader of what every schoolboy (or girl) knows. Clear and unmistakable physiological consequences follow from absorption in a favorite sexual fantasy." Mind and body are indeed a unified interdependent system.

Perhaps most important, as the above begins to make clear, it is the time dimension of the future—what Harry Stack Sullivan (1947) referred to as "anticipatory reality"—that acts as a prepotent force in the dynamic of all images (for a decision theory counterpart to this view, see Mitchell, Rediker, and Beach, 1986; Polak, 1973). The recognition that every social action somehow involves anticipation of the future, in the sense that it involves a reflexive look-forward-to and backward-from, has been analyzed by Alfred Schultz (1967) and Karl Weick (1976). Similarly, in Heidegger's brilliant formulation it is our nature not only to be thrown into existence (*Geworfenheil*) but to always be ahead of ourselves in the world, to be engaged in the unfolding of projected realities; all action, according to Heidegger, has the nature of a project (Heidegger refers to this as *Entwurf*, the continuous projecting ahead of a design or a blueprint). Much like a movie projection on a screen, human systems are forever projecting ahead of themselves a horizon of expectation that brings the future powerfully into the present as a causal agent.

Recent Works on the Positive Image–Positive Action Relationship

What all this suggests, of course, is that the power of positive imagery is not just some popular illusion or wish but is arguably a key factor in every action. To illustrate the heliotropic propensity in human systems at several levels of functioning I will now turn to six areas of research as example—placebo, Pygmalion, positive emotion, internal dialogue, cultural vitality, and metacognitive competence.

Positive Imagery, Medicine, and the Placebo

The placebo response is a fascinating and complex process in which projected images, as reflected in positive belief in the efficacy of a remedy, ignite a healing response that can be every bit as powerful as conventional therapy. Though the placebo phenomenon has been controversial for some twenty years, most of the medical profession now accepts as genuine, the fact that anywhere from one-third to two-thirds of all patients will show marked physiological and emotional improvement in symptoms simply by believing they are given an effective treatment, even when that treatment is just a sugar pill or some other inert substance (Beecher, 1955; White, Tursky, and Schwartz, 1985).

Numerous carefully controlled studies indicate that the placebo can provide relief of symptoms in postoperative-wound pain, seasickness, headaches, angina, asthma, obesity, blood pressure, ulcers, and many other problems. In fact, researchers are now convinced that no system of the body is exempt from the placebo effect and that it is operative in virtually every healing encounter. Even more intriguing, the placebo is sometimes even more potent than typically expected drug effects: "Consider a series of experiments with a woman suffering from severe nausea and vomiting. Nothing the doctors gave her seemed to help. Objective measurement of her gastric contractions showed a disrupted pattern consistent with the severe nausea she reported. The doctors then offered her a 'new extremely powerful wonder drug' which would, they said, unquestionably cure her nausea. Within twenty minutes of taking this new drug, her nausea disappeared, and the same objective gastric tests now read normal. The drug which was given was not, of course, a new drug designed to relieve nausea. It was syrup of ipecac, which is generally used to induce vomiting, In this case, the placebo effect associated with the suggestion that the drug would relieve vomiting was powerful enough to counteract and direct an opposite pharmacological action of the drug itself" (Ornstein and Sobel, 1987, p. 79).

According to Norman Cousins, now a faculty member at the UCLA School of Medicine, and understanding of the way the placebo works may be one of the most significant developments in medicine in the twentieth century. Writing in *Human Options* (1981), Cousins suggests that beyond the central nervous system, the hormonal system, and the immune system, there are two other systems that have conventionally been overlooked but that need to be recognized as essential to the proper functioning of the human being: the healing and the belief system. Cousins (1983, p. 203) argues that the two work together: "The healing system is the way the body mobilizes all its resources to combat disease. The belief system is often the activator of the healing system."

Using himself as a living laboratory, Cousins (1983, p. 44) has movingly described how the management of his own anticipatory reality allowed him to overcome a life-threatening illness that specialists did not believe to be reversible and then, some years later, to again apply the same mental processes in his recovery from an acute heart attack: "What were the basic ideas involved in that recovery? The newspaper accounts had made it appear that I had laughed my way out of a serious illness. Careful readers of my book, however, knew that laughter was just a metaphor. . . . Hope, faith, love, will to live, cheerfulness, humor, creativity, playfulness, confidence, *great expectations*—all these, I believed, had therapeutic value."

In the end, argues Cousins, the greatest value of the placebo is that it tells us that indeed positive imagery can and often does awaken the body to its own self-healing powers. Research in many areas now confirms this view and shows that the placebo responses are neither mystical nor inconsequential and that ultimately mental and psychophysiological responses may be mediated through more than fifty different neuropeptide molecular messengers linking the endocrine, autonomic, and central nervous systems (White, Tursky, and Schwartz, 1985). While the complex mind-body pathways are far from being resolved, there is one area of clear agreement: Positive changes in anticipatory reality through suggestion and belief play a central role in all placebo responses. As Jaffe and Bresler (1980, pp.260–261) note, the placebo "Illustrates another important therapeutic use of imagery, namely, the use of positive future images to activate positive physical changes. Imagining a positive future outcome is an important technique for countering initial negative images, beliefs, and expectations a patient may have. In essence it transforms a negative placebo effect into a positive one. . . . The power of positive suggestion plants a seed which redirects the mind—and through the mind, the body—toward a positive goal."

Before moving on, there is one other perhaps surprising factor that adds significantly to the patient's placebo response—the expectancy or anticipatory reality of the physician. Placebo effects are strongest, it appears, when belief in the efficacy of the treatment is shared among a group (O'Regan, 1983). This then raises a whole new set of questions concerning not only the individual but the interpersonal nature of the positive image-positive action relationship.

Pygmalion and the Positive Construction of the Other

In effect, the positive image may well be the sine qua non of human development, as we now explore in the Pygmalion dynamic. As a special case of the self-fulfilling prophesy, Pygmalion reminds us that from the moment of birth we each exist within a complex and dynamic field of images and expectations, a vast share of which are projected onto us through an omnipresent environment of others.

In the classic Pygmalion study, teachers are led to believe on the basis of "credible" information that some of their students possess exceptionally high potential while others do not. In other words, the teachers are led, on the basis of some expert opinion, to hold a positive image (PI) or expectancy of some students and a negative image (NI) or expectancy of others. Unknown to the teachers, however, is the fact that the so-called high-potential students were selected at random; in objective terms, all student groupings were equivalent in potential and are merely dubbed as high, regular, or low potential. Then, as the experiment unfolds, differences quickly emerge, not on the basis of any innate intelligence factor or some other predisposition but solely on the basis of the manipulated expectancy of the teacher. Over time, subtle changes among students evolve into clear differences as the high-PI students begin to significantly overshadow all others in actual achievement. Over the last twenty years there have been literally hundreds of empirical studies conducted on this phenomenon, attesting both to its continuing theoretical and to its practical importance (Jussim, 1986; see Rosenthal and Rubin, 1978, for an analysis of over 300 studies).

One of the remarkable things about Pygmalion is that it shows us how essentially modifiable the human self is in relation to the mental projections of others. Indeed, not only do performance levels change, but so do more deeply rooted "stable" self-conceptions (Parsons and others, 1982). Furthermore, significant Pygmalion effects have been experimentally generated in as little time as fifteen minutes (King, 1971) and have the apparent capacity to transform the course of a lifetime (Cooper and Good, 1983). (I wonder how many researchers on this subject would volunteer their own children to be part of a negatively induced expectancy grouping?) Specific to the classroom, the correlation between teacher expectation and student achievement is higher than almost any predictive IQ or achievement measure, ranging in numerous studies from correlations of .5 all the way to an almost perfect (Brophy and Good, 1974; Crano and Mellon, 1978; Hymphreys and Stubbs, 1977). Likewise, in one of the earliest organizational examinations of this phenomenon, Eden and Shani (1982) reported that some 75percent of the variance in achievement among military trainees could be explained completely on the basis of induced positive expectation on the part of those in positions of authority.

Obviously the promise of Pygmalion as a source of human development depends more on the enactment of positive rather than negative interpersonal expectancy. But how does the positive dynamic work and why?

A summary of the three stages of the positive Pygmalion dynamic is presented in Figure 2.1. In the first phase of the model, positive images of the other are formed through any number of means—for example, stereotypes, reputation, hearsay, objective measures, early performances, and naive prediction processes. As interactions occur over time, positive images begin to take shape and consist not only of *prophesies* but also tend to become elaborated by one's sense of its other *possibilities* as well as one's sense of "what should be," or *normative valuations*. Taken together the prophesies, possibilities, and normative valuations combine to create a broad brushstroke picture of interpersonal expectancy that has its pervasive effect through two primary mediators—expectancy-consistent cognition and expectancy-consistent treatment.

Considerable evidence, for example, indicates that a positive image of another serves as a powerful cognitive tuning device that appears to trigger in the perceiver an increased capacity to (1) perceive the successes of another (Deaux and Ernswiller, 1974), (2) access from memory the positive rather than negative aspects of the other (Hastie and Kumar, 1979), and (3) perceive ambiguous situations for their positive rather than negative possibilities (Darley and Gross, 1983).

While often spoken about in pejorative ways as cognitive bias or distortion ("vital lies," to use Goleman's popular term), it is quite possible that this affirmative capacity to cognitively tune into the most positive aspects of another human being is in fact a remarkable human gift; it is not merely an aberration distorting some "given" reality but is a creative agent in the construction of reality. We see what our images make us capable of seeing. And affirmative cognition, as we will later highlight in our discussion of positive self-monitoring, is a unique and powerful competency that owes its existence to the dynamic workings of the positive image.

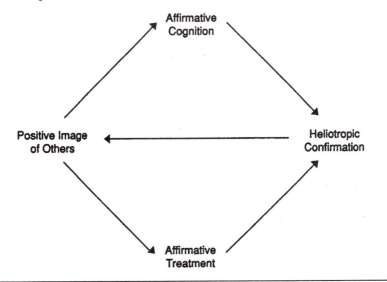

Figure 2.1. The Positive Pygmalion Dynamic (adapted from Jussim, 1986).

The key point is that all of our cognitive capacities—perception, memory, learning—are cued and shaped by the images projected through our expectancies. We see what our imaginative horizon allows us to see. And because "seeing is believing," our acts often take on a whole new tone and character depending on the strength, vitality, and force of a given image. The second consequence of the positive image of the other, therefore, is that it supports differential behavioral treatment in a number of systematic ways.

For example, it has been shown, both in the field and the laboratory, that teachers who hold extremely positive images of their students tend to provide those students with (1) increased emotional support in comparison to others (Rist, 1970; Rubovitz and Maeher, 1973); (2) clearer, more immediate, and more positive feedback around effect and performance (Weinstein, 1976; Cooper, 1979); and (3) better opportunities to perform and learn more challenging materials (Brophy and Good, 1974; Swann and Snyder, 1980).

Finally, in the third stage of the model, people begin to respond to the positive images that others have of them. When mediated by cognitive, affective, and motivational factors, according to Jussim (1986), heliotropic acts are initiated on the basis of increased effort, persistence, attention, participation, and cooperation, so that ultimately, high PIs often perform at levels superior to those projected with low-expectancy images. Research also shows that such effects tend to be long lasting, especially when the Pygmalion dynamic becomes institutionalized. High-PI students, for example, when assigned to the higher academic tracks, are virtually never moved to a lower track (the same is also true for negative-expectancy students, according to Brophy and Good's 1974 review of the "near permanence" of tracking).

The greatest value of the Pygmalion research is that it begins to provide empirical understanding of the relational pathways of the positive image-positive action dynamic and of the transactional basis of the human self. To understand the self as a symbolic social creation is to recognize—as George Herbert Mead, John Dewey, George Simmel, Lev Vygotsky, Martin Buber, and many others have argued—that human beings are essentially modifiable, are open to new development, and are products of the human imagination and mind. We are each made and imagined in the eyes of one another. There is an utter inseparability of the individual from the social context and history of the projective process. And positive interpersonal imagery, the research now shows, accomplishes its work very concretely. Like the placebo response discussed earlier, it appears that the positive image plants a seed that redirects the mind of the perceiver to think about and see the other with affirmative eyes.

Positive Affect and Learned Helpfulness

While often talked about in cognitive terms, one of the core features of imagery is that it integrates cognition and affect becomes a catalytic force through its sentiment-evoking quality. In many therapies, for example, it is well established that focusing on images often elicits strong emotional reactions; whereas verbal mental processes are linear, the image provides simultaneous representation, making it possible to vicariously experience that which is held in the imagination (Sheikh and Panagiotou, 1975).

So what about the relation between positive emotion—delight, compassion, joy, love, happiness, passion, and so on—and positive action? To what extent is it the affective side of the positive image that generates and sustains heliotropic movement so often seen in human systems? While still in the formative stages, early results on this issue are making clear that there is indeed a unique psychophysiology of positive emotion (as Norman Cousins has argued) and that individually as well as collectively, positive emotion may well be the pivotal factor determining the heliotropic potential of images of the future.

This line of research is partly predicated on knowledge growing out of studies of negative affectivity. In one of the most hotly pursued lines of research of the last decade, investigators are now convinced of the reciprocal connections between high negative affectivity and (1) experiences of life stress; (2) deficiency cognition; (3) the phenomenon of "learned helplessness"; (4) the development of depression; (5) the breakdown of social bonds; and (6) the triggering of possible physiological responses like the depletion of brain catecholamine, the release of corticosteroids, the suppression of immune functioning, and ultimately the development of disease (Watson and Clark, 1984; Seligman, 1975; Brewin, 1985; Peterson and Seligman, 1984; Beck, 1967; Schultz, 1984; Ley and Freeman, 1984). Table 2.1, for example, illustrates the linkage between negative affect and disease. In spite of diversity of subjects, methods, and measures, a salient pattern emerges: A host of diseases, especially various forms of cancer, are associated with chronic

TABLE 2.1. The Relationship Between Negative Affect and Disease: Conclusions from 28 Papers on Affect and Disease (adapted from Ley and Freeman, 1984, p. 57).

Disease	Affective State
Cancer	Depression
Cancer	Loss of hope
Leukemia	Depression, anxiety
Leukemia	Loss ofsignificant other
Neoplasm	Hopelessness, despair
Cancer	Self-directed aggression
Cancer	Depression
Cancer	Hopelessness
Cancer	Depression, hostility
Lung cancer	Rigidity, repression, hostility, despair
Cancer	Decreased depression
Cancer	Lethargy, depression
Cancer	Affective disorder
Cancer	Affective disorder
Cancer	Affective disorder
Cancer	Repression of anger
'Physical illness'	Depression
Pernicious anemia	Depression
Hay fever	Helplessness
Asthma	Helplessness
Tuberculosis	Poor coping with stress
Coronary heart disease	High and frustrated aspiration
Coronary bypass, mortality	Hopelessness, depression
Psychosomatic illness	Hostility, depression, frustration, anxiety, helplessness
Various illnesses	Helplessness, hopelessness

and persistent negative images, expressed and embodied in feelings of helplessness and hopelessness. As one physician from Yale concludes, "cancer is despair experienced at the cellular level" (Siegel, 1986).

Probably the one finding that emerges most conclusively on the other side of the ledger is that while negative affectivity is notably linked to the phenomenon of learned helplessness, positive affect is intimately connected with *social helpfulness*. Somehow positive affect draws us out of ourselves, pulls us away from self-oriented preoccupation, enlarges our focus on the potential good in the world, increases feelings of solidarity with others, and propels us to act in more altruistic and prosocial ways (see Brief and Motowildo, 1986, for a review of altruism and its implications for management).

According to the work of Alice Isen and her colleagues, mood, cognition, and action form an inseparable triad and tend to create feedback loops of amplifying intensity. Positive affect, the evidence indicates, generates superior recall or access to pleasant memories (Isen, Shalker, Clark, and Karp, 1978); helps create a heightened sense of optimism toward the future (Isen and Shalker, 1982); cues a person to think about positive things (Rosenhan, Salovey, and Hargis, 1981); and, as a result, predisposes people toward acts that would likely support continued positive affect, like the prosocial action of helping others (Cunningham, Stein-berg, and Grev, 1980; Isen and Levin, 1972; Isen, Shalker, Clark and Karp, 1978). In addition, positive affect has been associated with (1) increased capacity for creative problems solving (Isen, 1984); (2) more effective decision making and judgment (Isen and Means, 1983); (3) optimism and increased learning capac-ity—in particular, a sharpened capacity for perceiving and understanding mood-congruent or positive things (Bower, 1981; Clark and Isen, 1982).

In perhaps the most intriguing extension of this line of thought, Harvard's David McClelland has hypothesized a reinforcing set of dynamics between posi-tive imagery, positive affect, prosocial action, and improved immune functioning. McClelland has even gone so far as to argue that merely watching an altruistic act would be good for the observer. He may be right.

For example, in one of McClelland's experiments, students were shown a film of Mother Theresa, a Nobel Peace Prize recipient, attending to the sick and dying poor in Calcutta. During the film, measures were taken of the student's immune functioning as defined by increases in salivary immunogobulin A (IgA—a measure of defense against respiratory infection and viral disease). In all cases, it was found that IgA concentrations immediately increased during the film and for some observers remained elevated for a period of up to one hour afterward.

It should be emphasized that these findings are controversial and that we are clearly in our infancy when it comes to really understanding the role of positive emotion as it relates to individual and collective well-being. The most important fact, however, is that studies like these are even being done at all. They represent a vital shift in research attention across a whole series of disciplines and reflect a change in the mood and spirit of our times. For example, as Brendan O'Regan (1983, p. 3) observes in relation to the field of psychoneuroimmunology, "We will no longer be focused on only the reduction of symptoms or the removal of some-thing negative, and instead begin to understand health and well-being as the pres-ence of something positive. It [the focus on the psychophysiology of positive emotion] may well be the first step in the development of what might be called an affirmative science . . . a science for humankind."

The Off-Balance Internal Dialogue

One of the more fascinating refinements of the notion of positive imagery comes from Robert Schwart's development of a cognitive ethology: the study within human systems of the content, function, and structure of the internal dialogue. Here the image is conceptualized as self-talk. Traced back to Plato and Socrates, cognition is seen as discourse that the mind carries on with itself. As in James's stream of consciousness, it is argued that all human systems exhibit a continuing "cinematographic-show of visual imagery" (Ryle, 1949) or an ongoing "inner news-reel" (Becker, 1971) that is best understood in the notion of inner dialogue.

The inner dialogue of any system—individual, group, organization, society—can be understood, argues Schwartz (1986), by categorizing its contents at the

highest level of abstraction with respect to its functional role in achieving a specified aim. It is illustrated, for example, from a study of stressful medical procedure,
that people may have thoughts that either impede the aim of the clinical intervention ("the catheter might break and stick in my heart"—negative image) or conversely may facilitate the goals of the care ("this procedure may save my
life"—positive image). Hence, the inner dialogue functions as an inner dialectic
between positive and negative adaptive statements, and one's guiding imagery is
presumably an outcome of such an inner dialectic.

A whole series of recent studies have looked at this process, and results suggest a clear and definitive pattern of difference in the cognitive ecology of "functional" (healthy) versus "dysfunctional" (unhealthy) groups.

Table 2.2 presents data showing the ratios of positive to negative image statements for functional and dysfunctional groups across a series of seven independent
studies. In all cases, there is a definite *imbalance* in the direction of positive imagery
for those identified as more psychologically or socially functional. As can be seen,
the functional groups are characterized by approximately a 1.7 : 1 ratio of positive to
negative images. Mildly dysfunctional groups ("high" dysfunction was not studied)
demonstrate equal frequencies, a balanced 1 : 1 internal dialogue.

Obviously, the sheer quantification of cognition has certain weaknesses. For
one thing, it is clear that just one idea or image can transform the entire gestalt of
a thousand others. But the findings do have meaning, especially when linked to
other studies showing that images of hope or hopelessness can affect the body's
innate healing system, its immune functioning, and other neurochemical processes.
Especially disturbing are reports indicating that many of our children today are
growing up in family settings where as much as 90 percent of the home's internal
dialogue is negative, that is, what not to do, how bad things are, what was done
wrong, who is to blame (Fritz, 1984).

But it is not just our children. In his powerful *Critique of Cynical Reason*, Peter Sloterdijk (1987) observes that the whole of postmodern society is
living within an internal dialogue or cognitive environment of a universal,
diffuse cynicism. As a predominant mindset of the post-1960s era, Sloterdijk
takes the cynic not as an exception but rather as the average social character.
It is argued that at both the personal and institutional levels, throughout our
society there is a widespread disturbance of vitality, a bleakening of the life
feeling, a farewell to defeated idealisms, and a sense of paralyzing resentment. Sociologically, Sloterdijk contends, today's cynicism is bureaucratic
and it has become the predominant way of seeing things; psychologically, the
modernist character is said to be a borderline melancholic, one who is able to
keep the symptoms of depression under control and keep up appearances at
both home and work. Our internal dialogue, as a society, Sloterdijk laments,
has become more and more morose, and nowhere, he argues (1987, p. 12), is
this better exemplified than in the halls of academia: "The scenery of the
critical intelligensia is . . . populated by aggressive and depressive moralists,
problematists, 'problemholics,' and soft rigorists whose existential stimulus
is no."

TABLE 2.2. Ratios of Positive and Negative Thoughts for Functional and Dysfunctional Groups Across Seven Independent Studies (reported in Schwartz, 1986).

Focus of Study	Cognitive assessment	Functional M			Dysfunctional M		
		Positive	Negative	Ratio	Positive	Negative	Ratio
Assertiveness							
1. High vs. low assertive	Inventory/ASST[a]	57.0	33.0	1.7 : 1	48.0	51.0	1 : 1.1
2. High vs. low assertive	Inventory/ASST	59.0	35.0	1.7 : 1	48.0	51.0	1 : 1.1
3. High vs. low assertive	Inventory/ASST-R[b]	41.8	35.8	1.8 : 1	38.0	33.2	1.1 : 1
Social anxiety							
4. High vs. low socially anxious	Inventory/SISST[c]	54.9	33.0	1.7 : 1	42.7	47.3	1 : 1.1
Sample 2: Females and males combined							
5. High vs. low socially anxious	Production/thought listening[d]	1.6	1.2	1.3 : 1	1.5	2.0	1 : 1.3
Test anxiety							
6. High vs. low test-anxious	Production/talking aloud	67.3	32.0	2.1 : 1	45.0	61.3	1 : 1.4
Self-esteem							
7. High vs. low self-esteem	Production/though sampling	2.4	1.5	1.6 : 1	2.3	2.0	1.2 : 1
	Mean ratio		1.70 : 1		1 : 1.14		

[a]Assertiveness Self-Statement Test.
[b]ASST-Revised generalizes to a broader range of assertive situations.
[c]Social Interaction Self-Statement Test.
[d]Scores averaged across high and low anonymity conditions.

Whether one agrees with Sloterdijk or not, it is important to recognize that all human systems are conditioned by their internal dialogue. Our minds are bathed within any number of cognitive environments—family, school, church, play, and even the environments created by our research methods and problem-solving technologies—that provide cues to the ways we perceive, experience, and imagine reality.

So the question must therefore be asked, What kinds of cognitive environments maximize the "human possible"? What kinds of cognitive ecologies are we generating, and why? Can cognitive ecologies be developed, transformed, or enhanced? And what kinds of cognitive ecologies do we want?

The Positive Image as a Dynamic Force in Culture

As various scholars (for instance, Markley, 1976; Morgan, 1987) have noted, the underlying images held by a civilization or culture have an enormous influence on its fate. Ethical values such as "good" or "bad" have little force, except on an abstract level, but if those values emerge in the form of an image (for example, good = St. George, or bad = the Dragon), they suddenly become a power shaping the consciousness of masses of people (Broms and Gahmberg, 1983). Behind every culture there is a nucleus of images—the "Golden Age," "child of God," "Enlightenment," "Thousand-Year Reign of Christ," or "New Zion"—and this nucleus is able to produce countless variations around the same theme.

In his sweeping study of Western civilization, the Dutch sociologist Fred Polak (1973) argues essentially the same point concerning the heliotropic propensity of the positive image. For him (1973, p. 19), the positive image of the future is the single most important dynamic and explanatory variable for understanding cultural evolution: "Any student of the rise and fall of cultures cannot fail to be impressed by the role played in this historical succession of the future. *The rise and fall of images of the future precedes or accompanies the rise and fall of cultures.* As long as a society's image is positive and flourishing, the flower of culture is in full bloom. Once the image begins to decay and lose its vitality, however, the culture does not long survive."

For Polak, the primary question then is not how to explain the growth and decay of cultures, but how to explain the successful emergence or decay of positive images. Furthermore, he asks, how do the successive waves of optimism and pessimism or cynicism and trust regarding the images fit into the cultural framework and its accompanying dynamics? His conclusions, among others, include:

1. Positive images emerge in contexts of "influence-optimism" (belief in an open and influenceable future) and an atmosphere that values creative imagination mixed with philosophical questioning, a rich emotional life, and freedom of speech and fantasy.

2. The force that drives the image is only part cognitive or intellectual; a much greater part is emotional, esthetic, and spiritual.

3. The potential strength of a culture could actually be measured by the intensity, energy, and belief in its images of the future.

4. The image of the future not only acts as a barometer but actively promotes cognition and choice and in effect becomes self-fulfilling because it is self-propelling.

5. When a culture's utopian aspirations die out, the culture dies: "where there is no vision, the people perish" (Proverbs 29:18). Of special note here, anthropologists have shown that certain tribes have actually given up and allowed themselves to die when their images of the future have become too bleak. Ernest Becker (1971) notes the depopulation of Melanasia earlier in this century as well as the loss of interest by the Marquesan Islanders in having children. In the second case it appears that the islanders simply gave up when, in the face of inroads from white traders and missionaries, everything that gave them hope and a sense of value was eroded.

On this final point, Polak was intrigued with the following conclusion: Almost without exception, everything society has considered a social advance has been prefigured first in some utopian writing. For example Plato's *Politeia* opened the way, shows Polak, for a series of projections that then, via Thomas More's *Utopia*, had an impact on England's domestic and foreign policy. Similarly, Harrington's *Oceana* had immediate impact on France through the work of Abbé Sieyès, who used Harrington's model as a framework for his *Constitution de l'An VII* (about 1789). Later, these themes were "eagerly absorbed" by John Adams and Thomas Jefferson and emerged in a variety of American political institutions, not to mention the Declaration of Independence. While the word *utopia* has, in our society, often been a derogatory term, the historical analysis shows utopia to be, in Polak's words (1973, p. 138) "a powerhouse": "Scientific management, full employment, and social security were all once figments of a utopia-writer's imagination. So were parliamentary democracy, universal suffrage, planning, and the trade union movement. The tremendous concern for child-rearing and universal education, for eugenics, and for garden cities all emanated from the utopia. The utopia stood for the emancipation of women long before the existence of the feminist movement. All the concepts concerning labor, from the length of the work week to profit sharing (and sociotechnical systems design and QWL), are found in utopia. Thanks to the utopists, the twentieth century did not catch humanity totally unprepared."

Metacognition and Conscious Evolution of Positive Images

To the extent that the heliotropic hypothesis has some validity—that human systems have an observable tendency to macrodeterministically evolve in the direction of those "positive" images that are the brightest and boldest, most illuminating and promising—questions of volition and free agency come to the fore. Is it possible to create our own future-determining imagery? Is it possible to develop our metacognitive capacity and thereby choose between positive and negative ways of construing the world? If so, with what result? Is the quest for affirmative competence—the capacity to project and affirm an ideal image as if it is already so— a realistic aim or merely a romantic distraction? More important, is it possible to develop the affirmative competence of a large collectives, that is, of groups, organizations, or whole societies affirming a positive future together?

With the exception of the last question (there just has not been enough research here), most of the available evidence suggests quite clearly that affirmative competence can be learned, developed, and honed through experience, disciplined practice, and formal training.

Reviews on this topic, for example, are available in the areas of athletics and imagery, psychotherapy and imagery, imagery and healing, hypnosis and imagery, imagery and sexual functioning, and others related to overall metacognitive capacity (see Sheikh, 1983, for ten excellent reviews on these subjects).

In the case of athletics, as just one example, imagery techniques are fast becoming an important part of all successful training. In *Superlearning*, Ostrander (1979) discusses the mental methods used by Soviet and Eastern European athletes who have had such success in the Olympics in recent decades. Similarly, Jack Nicklaus's book *Golf My Way* (1974) offers a compendium of mental exercises to sharpen the affirmative function. For Nicklaus there is an important distinction to be made between a negative affirmation (for example, an image that says "don't hit it into the trees") and a positive affirmation (for instance, "I'm going to hit it right down the middle of the fairway"). Here again we find that the whole body, just like a whole culture, responds to what the mind imagines as possible. The important lesson, according to Nicklaus, is that affirmative competence can be acquired through discipline and practice and that such competence may be every bit as important to one's game as sheer physical capability.

Recent experimental evidence confirms this view and suggests something more: It is quite possible that the best athletes are as successful as they are because of a highly developed metacognitive capacity of differential self-monitoring. In brief, this involves being able to systematically observe and analyze successful performances (positive self-monitoring) or unsuccessful performances (negative self-monitoring) and to be able to choose between the two cognitive processes when desired. Paradoxically, while most in our culture seem to operate on the assumption that elimination of failures (negative self-monitoring) will improve performance, exactly the opposite appears to hold true, at least when it comes to learning new tasks. In one experiment, for example, Kirschenbaum (1984) compared a set of bowlers who received lessons on the components of effective bowling to those who did not receive the lessons (controls) and to groups who followed the lessons with several weeks of positive self-monitoring or negative self-monitoring (that is, they videotaped performances, edited out the positive or negative, and then selectively reviewed the corresponding tapes with the appropriate groups). As predicted, the positive self-monitors improved significantly more than all the others, and the unskilled bowlers (average of 125 pins) who practiced positive self-monitoring improved substantially (more than 100 percent) more than all other groups. Since then, these results have been replicated with other athletic activities such as golf, and evidence repeatedly indicates that positive self-monitoring significantly enhances learning on any task and is especially potent in the context of novel or poorly mastered tasks.

Some Implications for Management: Toward a Theory of the Affirmative Organization

> We are some time truly going to see our life as positive, not negative, as made up of continuous willing, not of constraints and prohibition.
> —Mary Parker Follett.

That was a judgment of one of the great management prophets of the early 1940s who, in moving out of step with her time, prefigured virtually every new development in organizational thought and practice. Today, her ideas do not seem quite as strange as they once must have been. As we have seen in our overview of the placebo effect, Pygmalion dynamic, positive emotion, imbalanced inner dialogue, and positive self-monitoring, as well as the role of utopian imagery in the rise and fall of cultures, scholars are recognizing that the power of positive imagery is not just some popular illusion or wish but an expression of the mind's capacity for shaping reality. A theory of affirmation is emerging from many quarters. Admittedly its findings are still limited; unifying frameworks are lacking, and generalization across levels of analysis and disciplines makes for unintelligible and often confusing logic. Nevertheless that knowledge–limited though it is—has important practical implications for organizations and management. In the rest of this discussion, I hope to push the current perspective onward by offering an exploratory set of propositions concerning what might be called the affirmative basis of organizing. When translated from the various disciplines into organizationally relevant terms, the emerging "theory of affirmation" looks something like this:

1. *Organizations as made and imagined are artifacts of the affirmative mind. As understanding of organizational life requires an understanding of the dynamic of the positive image as well as the process through which isolated images become interlocked images and of how nascent affirmations become guiding affirmations.* The starting point for a theory of affirmation is simply this: When it comes to understanding organizational existence from the perspective of human action, there is no better clue to a system's overall well-being than its guiding image of the future. In the last analysis, organizations exist because stakeholders who govern

and maintain them carry in their minds some sort of shared positive projection about what the organization is, how it will function, and what it might become. Although positive imagery (in the form of positive thinking, utopian visions, affirmation, and the like) has not been paraded as a central concept in organizational and management thought, it can be usefully argued that virtually every organizational act is based on some positive projection on the part of the individual or group. Organizational birth itself, to take just one example, is impossible in the absence of some affirmative projection. But positive or negative, enabling or limiting, conscious or unconscious — all action is conditioned by the fact that we live in an anticipatory world of images. These guiding images are not detailed objectives but are paintings created with a larger brush stroke. They encompass many aspects of organizational life that mission statements, corporate strategies, or plans alone do not reveal. Just as it has been observed that the rise and fall of images of the future precede or accompany the rise and fall of societies, it can be argued that as long as an organization's image is positive and flourishing, the flower of organizational life will be in full bloom.

2.   *No matter what its previous history is, virtually any pattern of organizational action is open to alteration and reconfiguration. Patterns of organizational action are not automatically fixed by nature in any blind microdeterminist way—whether biological, behavioral, technological, or environmental.* There is no such thing as an inevitable form of organization. There are no "iron laws." While affected by microdeterminist factors, existing regularities that are perceived are controlled by mentalist or "macro" factors exerting downward control. Just as in the Pygmalion dynamic reviewed earlier, organizations are genetically constituted socially in and through the images born in transaction among all participants. In this sense, existing regularities that are observed depend not on some dictate of nature but on the historically and contextually embedded continuities in what we might call (1) the prophetic image—expectancies and beliefs about the future; (2)the poetic image—imagined possibilities or alternatives of what might be; (3) the normative image—ideological or value-based images of what should be. When organizations continue to hold the same expectations and beliefs; when they continue to envision the same possibilities or alternatives; or when they continue to project the same conventional values, norms, or ideologies—it is under these macrodeterminist conditions that continuities in structures and practices will in fact be found.

3.   *To the extent that organizations' imaginative projections are the key to their current conduct, organizations are free to seek transformations in conventional practice by replacing conventional images with images of a new and better future.* To a far greater extent than is normally assumed, organizational evolution is isomorphic with the mental evolution of images. In many respects, it can usefully be argued that organizations are limited primarily or even only by (1) their affirmative capacities of mind, imagination, and reason, and (2) their collective or *coaffirmative capacity* for developing a commanding set of shared projections among a critical segment of stakeholders.

In regard to the latter point, it can be argued further that the guiding image of the future exists deep within the internal dialogue of the organization. The image is not, therefore, either a person-centered or a position-centered phenomenon; it is a situational and interactional tapestry that is a public "property" of the whole rather than of any single element or part. While such things as executive vision and charismatic leadership may be understood as parallels to what I am talking about, their emphasis on the "Great Man" leads them to seriously understate and miscast the complex cooperative aspect of an organization's guiding image of the future. When it comes to collective entities like groups, organizations, or even whole societies, we must emphatically argue that the guiding image of the future does not, even metaphorically, exist within some individual or collective mass of brain. It exists in a very observable and tangible way in the living dialogue that flows through every institution, expressing itself anew at every moment.

4.   *Organizations are heliotropic in character in the sense that organizational actions have an observable and largely automatic tendency to evolve in the direction of positive imagery. Positive imagery and hence heliotropic movement is endemic to organizational life, which means that organizations create their own realities to a far greater extent than is normally assumed.* As we have seen in the placebo, Pygmalion, and self-monitoring studies, the positive image carries out its heliotropic task by generating and provoking image-consistent affirmative cognition, image-consistent emotion, and self-validating action. Hence, it can be argued that positive images of the future generate in organizations (1) an affirmative cognitive ecology that strengthens peoples' readiness and capacity to recall the positive aspects of the past, to selectively see the positive in the present, and to envision new potentials in the future; (2) it catalyzes an affirmative emotional climate, for example, of heightened optimism, hope, care, joy, altruism, and passion; and (3) it provokes confident and energized action (see Weick, 1983, on this third point).

Another aspect of the heliotropic hypothesis is that it predicts the following: When presented with the option, organizations will move more rapidly and effectively in the direction of affirmative imagery (moving toward the light) than in the opposite direction of negative imagery (moving against the light or toward "overpowering darkness"). Existing in a dynamic field of images, it can be argued that organizations move along the path of least resistance (Fritz, 1984) toward those images that are judged to represent the organization's highest possibilities — those images that are the brightest, most purposeful, or most highly valued. Positive images whose prophetic, poetic, and normative aspects are congruent will show the greatest self-fulfilling potential.

5.   *Conscious evolution of positive imagery is a viable option for organized systems as large as global society or as small as the dyad or group. Also, the more an organization experiments with the conscious evolution of positive imagery the better it will become; there is an observable self-reinforcing, educative effect of affirmation. Affirmative competence is the key to the self-organizing system.* Through both formal and informal learning processes, organizations, like

individuals, can develop their metacognitive competence—the capacity to rise above the present and assess their own imaginative processes as they are operating. This enhances their ability to distinguish between the affirmative and negative ways of construing the world. The healthiest organizations will exhibit a 2 : 1 or better ratio of positive-to-negative imagery (as measured through inner dialogue), while less healthy systems will tend toward a 1 : 1 balanced ratio. Similarly, it can usefully be argued that positively biased organizational monitoring (with selective monitoring and feedback of the positive) will contribute more to heliotropic movement than either neutral (characterized by inattention) or negative organizational monitoring (with a focus on problems or deficiencies). This effect, we would expect based on studies in athletics, will be more pronounced in situations where the affirmative projection is of a novel or complex future and where the tasks or actions required to enact the images are not yet fully tested or mastered.

The more an organization experiments with the affirmative mode, the more its affirmative and heliotropic competence will grow. This is why, in many organizations that have experimented with it, people have come to believe that organizationwide affirmation of the positive future is the single most important act that a system can engage in if its real aim is to bring to fruitation a new and better future. An image that asserts that the future is worth living for will, as William James ([1895] 1956) argued, provoke those actions that help create the fact. While not every future can be created as locally envisioned, there is always a margin within which the future can be affected by positive affirmation. The size of this margin can never be known a priori. Put another way, an organization will rarely rise above the dominant images of its members and stakeholders; or as Willis Harman (1988, p. 1) hypothesizes, "perhaps the only limits to the human mind are those we believe in."

6.   *To understand organizations in affirmative terms is also to understand that the greatest obstacle in the way of group and organizational well-being is the positive image, the affirmative projection that guides the group or the organization.* Theorist Henry Wieman (1926, p. 286) gave a clear description of the seeming paradox involved here many years ago in his comparative analysis of *Religious Experience and Scientific Method*: "We are very sure that the greatest obstacle in the way of individual growth and social progress is the ideal [affirmative projection] which dominates the individual or group. The greatest instrument of achievement and improvement is the ideal, and therefore our constant failures, miseries, and wickedness are precisely due to the inadequacy of our highest ideals. Our ideals have in them all the error, all the impracticability, all the perversity and confusion that human beings that themselves erring, impractical, perverse and confused, can put into them. Our ideals are no doubt the best we have in the way of our constructions. But the best we have is pitifully inadequate. Our hope and full assurance . . . [are] that we can improve our ideals. If we could not be saved from our ideals, we would be lost indeed."

One of the ironies of affirmation is that it partially cripples itself in order to function. By definition, to affirm means to "hold firm." As we have seen, it is precisely the strength of affirmation, the degree of belief or faith invested, that allows the image to carry out its heliotropic task. So when our institutions are confronted with repetitive failure and amplifying cycles of distress; when time and energies are expended on such issues as compliance, discipline, obedience, motivation, and the like; or when almost every "new" surefire problem-solving technique does little but add a plethora of new problems—in every one of these cases the system is being given a clear signal of the inadequacy of its "firm" affirmative projections. To repeat, our positive images are no doubt the best we have, but the best is often not responsive to changing needs and opportunities. The real challenge, therefore, is to discover the processes through which a system's best affirmations can be left behind and better ones developed. For if we could not be saved from our best affirmative projections, "we would be lost indeed."

7.   *Organizations do not need to be fixed. They need constant reaffirmation. More precisely, organizations as heliotropic systems need to be appreciated. Every new affirmative projection of the future is a consequence of an appreciative understanding of the past or the present.* Up to this point we have examined the nature of the positive image-positive action relationship but have said nothing about the mental artistry by which guiding images—prophesies, possibilities, and normative values—are in fact generated. We seem to have become preoccupied with the question of "how to translate intention into reality and sustain it" (see for example Bennis and Nanus, 1985) and have ignored what is perhaps the more essential question.

An earlier set of writings (Cooperrider and Srivastva, 1987; Cooperrider, 1986) described a process of knowing that was preeminently suited to the task of providing both the data and mental inspiration through which human systems can fashion new affirmative projections on a dynamic and continuous basis. It was argued that appreciative inquiry is based on a "reverence for life" and is essentially biocentric in character: It is an inquiry process that tries to apprehend the factors that give life to a living system and seeks to articulate those possibilities that can lead to a better future. More than a method or technique, the appreciative mode of inquiry was described as a means of living with, being with, and directly participating in the life of a human system in a way that compels one to inquire into the deeper life-generating essentials and potentials of organizational existence.

As this concept relates specifically to leadership, an important clue to the meaning of executive appreciation is found in Isaiah Berlin's (1980, pp. 14–15) account of Winston Churchill's leadership during England's darkest hour:

> In 1940 he [Churchill] assumed an indomitable stoutness, an unsurrendering quality on the part of his people. . . . He idealized them with such intensity that in the end they approached his ideal and began to see themselves as he saw them: "the buoyant and inperturbable temper of Britain which I had the honour to express"—it was indeed, but he had the lion's

share in creating it. So hypnotic was the force of his words, so strong his faith, that by the sheer intensity of his eloquence he bound his spell upon them until it seemed to them that he was indeed speaking what was in their hearts and minds. Doubtless it was there; but largely dormant until he had awoken it within them.

After he had spoken to them in the summer of 1940 as no one else has ever before or since, they conceived a new idea of themselves. . . . They went forward into battle transformed by his words. . . . He created a heroic mood and turned the fortunes of the Battle of Britain not by catching the [life-diminishing] mood of his surroundings but by being impervious to it, as he had been to so many of the passing shades and tones of which the life around him had been composed.

Churchill's impact and the guiding images he helped create were the result of his towering ability to cognitively dissociate all seeming impossibilities, deficiencies, and imperfections from a given situation and to see in his people and country that which had fundamental value and strength. His optimism, even in Britain's darkest moment, came not from a Pollyanna-like sense that "everything is just fine" but from a conviction that was born from what he, like few others, could actually see in his country: "Doubtless it was there; but largely dormant until he had awoken it."

In almost every respect the cognitive and perceptual process employed by Churchill, like many great executives, was that of the artist. The appreciative eye we are beginning to understand apprehends "what is" rather than "what is not" and in this represents a rigorous cognitive ability to bracket out all seeming imperfections from that which has fundamental value. For as the poet Shelly suggests, appreciation "makes immortal all that is best and most beautiful in the world. . . . It exalts the beauty of that which is most beautiful. . . . It strips the veil of familiarity from the world, and lays bare and naked sleeping beauty, which is in the spirit of its forms" (in Cooperrider and Srivastva, 1987, p. 164).

But this is only part of the story: Appreciation not only draws our eye toward life, but stirs our feelings, excites our curiosity, and provides inspiration to the envisioning mind. In this sense, the ultimate generative power for the construction of new values and images is the apprehension of that which has value. Nietzsche once asked of appreciation, "Does it not praise? Does it not glorify? Does it not select? Does it not bring 'that which is appreciated' to prominence? In all this, does it not strengthen or weaken certain valuations?" (in Rader, 1973, p. 12).

No one has expressed this more effectively than the artist Vincent van Gogh, who, in a letter to his brother (in Rader, 1973, p. 10), spelled out what could actually be an entire leadership course on the relationship between appreciation and the emergence of new values:

I should like to paint a portrait of an artist friend, a man who dreams great dreams, who works as the nightingale sings, because it is in his nature. He'll be a fine man. I want to put into my picture of appreciation, the love

I have for him. So I paint him as he is, as faithfully as I can. But the picture is not finished yet. To finish it, I am now the arbitrary colorist. I exaggerate the fairness of the hair; I come even to use orange tones, chromes, and pale lemon-yellow. Behind the head, instead of painting the ordinary wall of the mean room, I paint infinity, a plain background of the richest, intensest blue that I can contrive—and by this simple combination of the bright head against the rich blue background, I get a mysterious effect, like a star in the depths of an azure sky.

Like Churchill, van Gogh began with a stance of appreciative cognition. He viewed his friend through a loving and caring lense and focused on those qualities that "excited his preference" and kindled his imagination. The key point is that van Gogh did not merely articulate admiration for his friend: He created new values and new ways of seeing the world through the very act of valuing. And again, as Nietzsche (in Rader, 1973, p. 12) has elaborated: "valuing is creating: hear it, ye creating ones! Valuation is itself the treasure and jewel of valuating things."

In contrast to the affirmative projection that seeks certainty and control over events, the appreciative eye actually seeks uncertainty as it is thrown into the elusive and emergent nature of organizational life itself. Appreciation is creative rather than conservative precisely because it allows itself to be energized and inspired by the voice of mystery. As an active process of valuing the factors that give rise to the life-enhancing organization, appreciation has room for the vital uncertainty, the indeterminancy that is the trademark of something alive. In this sense, too, it differs from affirmation in that it is not instrumental. It does not have the capability of shaping the world closer to preexisting wants because it tends, in the end, to transform those wants into something very different from that which was originally affirmed. Executive appreciation, then, represents the capacity to rediscover in organizations what Bruner refers to as the "immensity of the commonplace" or what James Joyce terms the "epiphanies of the ordinary" (see Bruner, 1986, p.198). Appreciation, as Churchill must have understood, is the mental strength that allows a leader to consciously peer into the life-giving present, only to find the future brilliantly interwoven into the texture of the actual.

8. *The executive vocation in a postbureaucratic society is to nourish the appreciation soil from which affirmative projections grow, branch off, evolve, and become collective projections. Creating the conditions for organizationwide appreciation is the single most important measure that can be taken to ensure the conscious evolution of a valued and positive future.* The "how" of appreciative inquiry is beyond the scope of this discussion. But a number of final thoughts can be offered on the organizational prerequisites of appreciation. These comments stem from the experiences with a number of systems that have actually experimented with appreciative inquiry on a collective and organizationwide basis.

First, it is clear that the appreciative process has been most spontaneous and genuine in relatively egalitarian systems—organizations committed to an ideology of inclusion, consent, and coevolution (Srivastva and Cooperrider, 1986). Put more strongly, experience suggests that the creative power of appreciation will never be realized in a world that continues to place arbitrary restrictions or constraints on speech and action. It is the realm of action, not mind, that is the preeminent basis of those creative images that have the power to guide us into a positive future.

Second, experience indicates that if pursued deeply enough, appreciative inquiry arrives at a dynamic interpersonal ideal. It arrives at knowledge that enlarges our sense of solidarity with other human beings and provides an ever-expanding universe of examples and images concerning the possibilities for a more egalitarian future.

We are infants when it comes to our understanding of appreciative processes of knowing and social construction. Yet we are beginning to see that the power of appreciation rests with its self-reinforcing and self-generative capacity. Through appreciation of organizational life, members of an organization learn to value not only the life-enhancing organization but also learn to affirm themselves. As new potentials for inquiry are revealed and experienced within the "student," new insights are made available and shared with others in the organization. As sharing occurs, the inquiry becomes a joint process of knowing—others are invited to explore and question their own ideals or affirmative projections. Through dialogue, new knowledge and new images of possibility are constantly being made available. And while such knowledge is always felt as an interruption in the status quo, it is valued and turned into a heliotropic project because it represents a joint creation of a world that corresponds to the jointly imagined projection of human and social possibility.

Chapter 3

APPRECIATIVE INQUIRY IN ORGANIZATIONAL LIFE

David L. Cooperrider and Suresh Srivastva
Case Western Reserve University

Abstract

This chapter presents a conceptual refiguration of action-research based on a "sociorationalist" view of science. The position that is developed can be summarized as follows: For action-research to reach its potential as a vehicle for social innovation it needs to begin advancing theoretical knowledge of consequence; that good theory may be one of the best means human beings have for affecting change in a postindustrial world; that the discipline's steadfast commitment to a problem solving view of the world acts as a primary constraint on its imagination and contribution to knowledge; that *appreciative inquiry* represents a viable complement to conventional forms of action-research; and finally, that through our assumptions and choice of method we largely create the world we later discover.

> We are sometime truly to see our life as positive, not negative, as made up of continuous willing, not of constraints and prohibition.
>
> —Mary Parker Follett.

> We are steadily forgetting how to dream; in historical terms, the mathematicist and technicist dimensions of Platonism have conquered the poetical, mythical, and rhetorical context of analysis. We are forgetting how to be reasonable in nonmathematical dialects.
>
> —Stanley Rosen.

W. A. Pasmore & R. W. Woodman (eds.), *Research in organizational change and development (Vol. I)*. Greenwich, CT: JAI Press, 1987.

Introduction

This chapter presents a conceptual reconfiguration of action research.[1] In it we shall argue for a multidimensional view of action-research which seeks to both generate theory and develop organizations. The chapter begins with the observation that action-research has become increasingly rationalized and enculturated to the point where it risks becoming little more than a crude empiricism imprisoned in a deficiency mode of thought. In its conventional *unidimensional* form action research has largely failed as an instrument for advancing social knowledge of consequence and has not, therefore, achieved its potential as a vehicle for human development and social-organizational transformation. While the literature consistently signals the worth of action-research as a managerial tool for problem solving ("first-order" incremental change), it is conspicuously quiet concerning reports of discontinuous change of the "second order" where organizational paradigms, norms, ideologies, or values are transformed in fundamental ways (Watzlawick, et al., 1974).

In the course of this chapter we shall touch broadly upon a number of interrelated concerns—scientific, metaphysical, normative, and pragmatic. Linking these streams is an underlying conviction that action-research has the potential to be to the postindustrial era what "scientific management" was to the industrial. Just as scientific management provided the philosophical and methodological legitimacy required to support the bureaucratic organizational form (Clegg and Dunkerly, 1980; Braverman, 1974), action-research may yet provide the intellectual rationale and reflexive methodology required to support the emergence of a more egalitarian "postbureaucratic" form of organization. Unlike scientific management however, which provided the means for a technorational science of administration, action-research holds unique and essential promise in the sociorational realm of human affairs. It has the potential to become the paradigmatic basis of a truly significant—a humanly significant—generative science of administration.

In the first part of the essay it is suggested that the primary barrier limiting the potential of action-research has been its romance with "action" at the expense of "theory." This tendency has led many in the discipline to seriously underestimate the power of theory as a means for social-organizational reconstruction. Drawing largely on the work of Kenneth Gergen (1978, 1982), we re-examine the character of theoretical knowledge and its role in social transformation, and then appeal for a redefinition of the scientific aims of action-research that will dynamically reunite theory and practice. The aim of science is not the detached discovery and

---

[1]While we draw most of our examples from the Organization Development (OD) school of action-research, the argument presented here should be relevant to other applications as well. As noted by Peters and Robinson (1984), the discipline of action-research has been prevalent in the literature of community action, education and educational system change, and organization change, as well as discussions of the social sciences in general.

verification of social laws allowing for prediction and control. Highlighted here instead, is an alternative understanding that defines social and behavioral science in terms of its "generative capacity," that is, its "capacity to challenge the guiding assumptions of the culture, to raise fundamental questions regarding contemporary social life, to foster reconsideration of that which is 'taken for granted' and thereby furnish new alternatives for social actions" (Gergen, 1978, p. 1346).

Assuming that generative theory is a legitimate product of scientific work and is, in fact, capable of provoking debate, stimulating normative dialogue, and furnishing conceptual alternatives needed for social transformation, then why has action-research till now so largely downplayed creative theorizing in its work with organizations? Here we will move to the heart of the chapter and argue that the generative incapacity of contemporary action-research derives from the discipline's unquestioned commitment to a secularized problem-oriented view of the world and thus to the subsequent loss of our capacity as researchers and participants to marvel, and in marveling to embrace, the miracle and mystery of social organization. If we acknowledge Abraham Maslow's (1968) admonition that true science begins and ends in wonder, then we immediately shed light on why action-research has failed to produce innovative theory capable of inspiring the imagination, commitment, and passionate dialogue required for the consensual re-ordering of social conduct.

Appreciative inquiry is presented here as a mode of action-research that meets the criteria of science as spelled out in generative-theoretical terms. Going beyond questions of epistemology, appreciative inquiry has as its basis a metaphysical concern: it posits that social existence as such is a miracle that can never be fully comprehended (Quinney, 1982; Marcel, 1963). Proceeding from this level of understanding we begin to explore the uniqueness of the appreciative mode. More than a method or technique, the appreciative mode of inquiry is a way of living with, being with, and directly participating in the varieties of social organization we are compelled to study. Serious consideration and reflection on the ultimate mystery of being engenders a reverence for life that draws the researcher to inquire beyond superficial appearances to deeper levels of the life generating essentials and potentials of social existence. That is, the action researcher is drawn to affirm, and thereby illuminate, the factors and forces involved in organizing that serve to nourish the human spirit. Thus, this chapter seeks to enrich our conception of administrative behavior by introducing a "second dimension" of action-research that goes beyond merely a secularized problem-solving frame.

The proposal that appreciative inquiry represents a distinctive complement to traditional action-research will be unfolded in the following way: First, the role of theory as an enabling agent of social transformation will be considered; such consideration can help to eliminate the artificial dualism separating theory from practice. Second, we will challenge the problem-oriented view of organizing inherent in traditional definitions of action-research, and describe an affirmative form of inquiry uniquely suited for discovering generative theory. Finally, these insights will be brought together in a general model of the conceptual underpinnings of appreciative inquiry.

Toward Generative Theory in Action-Research

The current decade has witnessed a confluence of thinking concerning the paradigmatic refiguration of social thought. As Geertz (1980) notes, there is now even a "blurring of genres" as many social scientists have abandoned—without apology—the misdirected quest to mimic the "more mature" physical sciences. Turning away from a Newtonian laws-and-instances-type explanation rooted in logical empiricist philosophy, many social theorists have instead opted for an interpretive form of inquiry that connects organized action to its contextually embedded set of meanings, "looking less for the sorts of things that connect planets and pendulums and more for the sorts that connect chrysanthemums and swords" (Geertz, 1980, p. 165).

In the administrative sciences, in particular, this recent development has been translated into observable movement away from mechanistic research designs intended objectively to establish universal causal linkages between variables, such as organizational size and level of centralization, or between technology, environment, and organizational structure. Indeed, prominent researchers in the field have publicly given up the logical positivist idea of "certainly through science" and are now embarking on approaches to research that grant preeminence to the historically situated and ever-changing "interpretive schemes" used by members of a given group to give life and meaning to their actions and decisions (Bartunek, 1984). Indicative of the shift away from the logical positivist frame, researchers are converging around what has been termed the "sociorationalist" metatheory of science (Gergen, 1982). Recognizing the symbolic nature of the human universe, we now find a flurry of innovative work supporting the thesis that there is little about human development or organizational behavior that is "preprogrammed" or stimulus-bound in any direct physical or biological way. In this sense, the social universe is open to indefinite revision, change, and self-propelled development. And, this recognition is crucial because to the extent to which social existence is situated in a symbolic realm, beyond deterministic forces, then to that extent the logical positivist foundation of social science is negated and its concept of knowledge rendered illusionary.

Nowhere is this better evidenced than in the variety of works concerned with such topics as organizational paradigms (Brown, 1978; McHugh, 1970); beliefs and master scripts (Sproull, 1981; Beyer, 1981); idea management and the executive mind (Srivastva, 1983; 1985); theories of action and presumptions of logic (Argyris and Schon, 1980; Weick, 1983); consciousness and awareness (Harrison, 1982; Lukes, 1974); and, of course, an array of work associated with the concept of organizational or corporate culture (Ouchi and Johnson, 1978; Schein, 1983; Van Maanen, 1982; Deal and Kennedy, 1982; Sathe, 1983; Hofstede, 1980). As Ellwood prophetically suggested almost half a century ago, "This is the cultural view of human society that is [or will be] revolutionizing the social sciences" (Ellwood, 1938, p. 561).

This developing consensus on the importance of the symbolic realm—on the power of ideas—by such independent sources embracing such diverse objectives reflects the reality of organized life in the modern world. However reluctantly, even the most traditional social thinkers are now recognizing the distinctiveness of the postindustrial world for what truly is—an unfolding drama of human interaction whose potential seems limited or enhanced primarily by our symbolic capacities for constructing meaningful agreements that allow for the committed enactment of collective life.

Never before in history have ideas, information, and beliefs—or theory—been so central in the formulation of reality itself. Social existence, of course, has always depended on some kind of idea system for its meaningful sustenance. The difference now, however, is that what was once background has become foreground. Today, the very fact that society continues to exist at all is experienced not so much mechanistically (an extension of machines) or even naturalistically (a by-product of fateful nature) but more and more humanistically as a social construction of interacting minds—"a game between persons" (Bell, 1973). And under these conditions—as a part of the change from an agrarian society to a goods-producing society at first and then to an information society—ideas and meaning systems take on a whole new life and character. Ideas are thrust center stage as the prime unit of relational exchange governing the creation or obliteration of social existence.

This line of argument applies no less potently to current conceptions of social science. To the extent that the primary product of science is systematically refined idea systems—or theory—science too must be recognized as a powerful agent in the enhancement or destruction of human life. And while this presents an unresolvable dilemma for a logical empiricist conception of science, it spells real opportunity (and responsibility) for a social science that wishes to be of creative significance to society. Put most simply, the theoretical contributions of science may be among the most powerful resources human beings have for contributing to change and development in the groups and organizations in which they live. This is precisely the meaning of Kurt Lewin's early view of action-science when he proposed: "There is nothing so practical as good theory" (1951, p. 169).

Ironically, the discipline of action-research continues to insist on a sharp separation of theory and practice, and to underrate the role of theory in social reconstruction. The irony is that it does so precisely at a time when the cultural view of organizing is reaching toward paradigmatic status. The sad and perhaps tragic commentary on action-research is that it is becoming increasingly inconsequential just as its opportunity to contribute is on the rise (Argyris, 1983).

Observers such as Rappaport (1970) and Bartunek (1983) have lamented the fact that action-researchers have come to subordinate research aims to action interests. Levinson (1972) has gone even further by branding the discipline "atheoretical." And, Friedlander and Brown (1974) have noted that the definition of action-research in classic texts give virtually no mention to theory-building as an integral and necessary component of the research/diagnostic process, or the process of organizational change. Whenever theory is mentioned, it is almost always referred to as a springboard for research or diagnosis, not the other way around. Bartunek (1983, pp. 3–4) concludes that "even the most recent papers that describe action-research strategies tend to focus primarily on the process of action-research and only secondarily on the specific theoretical contributions of the outcomes of such research" (e.g., Frohman, Sashkin, and Kavanaugh, 1976; Shani and Pasmore, 1982; Susman and Evered, 1978; see Pasmore and Friedlander, 1982, for an exception). For those of us trained in the field this conclusion is not surprising. Indeed, few educational programs in organizational behavior even consider theory-building as a formal part of their curriculum, and even fewer place a real premium on the development of the theoretical mind and imagination of their students.

According to Argyris (1983), this lack of useful theorizing is attributable to two major factors. On the one hand practice-oriented scholars have tended to become so client-centered that they fail to question their clients' own definition of a problem and thereby to build testable propositions and theories that are embedded in everyday life. Academics, on the other hand, who are trained to be more scientific in their bent, also undercut the development of useful theory by their very insistence on the criteria of "normal" science and research—detachment, rigor, unilateral control, and operational precision. In a word, creative theorizing has literally been assaulted on all fronts by practitioners and academic scientists alike. It must also be noted that implicit in this critique by Argyris (1983), and others (e.g., Friedlander and Brown, 1974), is an underlying assumption that action-research has built into it certain natural conflicts that are likely to lead either to "action" (consulting) or "research" (diagnosis or the development of organizational theory), but not to both.

The situation is summed up by Friedlander and Brown (1974) in their comprehensive review of the field:

> We believe that research will either play a far more crucial role in the advancement of this field, or become an increasingly irrevelant appendage to it. ... We have generally failed to produce a theory of change, which emerges from the change process itself. We need a way of enriching our understanding and action synergistically rather than at one or the other's expense—to become a science in which knowledge-getting and knowledge-giving are an integrated process, and one that is valuable to all parties involved (p. 319).

Friedlander and Brown concluded with a plea for a metatheoretical revision of science that will integrate theory and practice. But in another review over a decade later, Friedlander (1984) observed little progress coming from top scholars in the discipline. He then put words to a mounting frustration over what appears as a recurring problem:

> They pointed to the shortcomings of traditional research and called for emancipation from it, but they did not indicate a destination. There is as yet no new paradigm that integrates research and practice, or even optimizes useful

knowledge for organizations. . . . I'm impatient. Let's get on with it. Let's not talk it, write it, analyze it, conceptualize it, or research it. Instead let's actively engage and experiment with new designs for producing knowledge that is, in fact, used by organizations (p. 647).

This recurrent problem is the price we pay for continuing to talk about theory and practice in dualistic terms. In a later section in this chapter another hypothesis will be advanced on why there is this lack of creative theorizing, specifically as it relates to action-research. But first we need to look more closely at the claim that social theory and social practice are, indeed, part of a synthetic whole. We need to elaborate on the idea that scientific theory is a means for both understanding *and* improving social practice. We need to examine exactly what it means to merge the idea and the act, the symbolic and the sociobehavioral, into a powerful and integral unity.

The Sociorationalist Alternative

As the end of the twentieth century nears, thinkers in organizational behavior are beginning to see, without hesitation, why an administrative science based on a physical science model is simply not adequate as a means for understanding or contributing in relevant ways to the workings of complex, organized human systems (see, for example, Susman and Evered, 1978; Beyer and Trice, 1982). Kurt Lewin had understood this almost half a century earlier but his progressive vision of an action science fell short of offering a clear metatheoretical alternative to conventional conceptions of science (Peters and Robinson, 1984). Indeed, the epistemological ambiguity inherent in Lewin's writing has been cited as perhaps the critical shortcoming of all his work. And yet, in hindsight, it can be argued that the ambiguity was intentional and perhaps part of Lewin's social sensitivity and genius. As Gergen (1982) suggests, the metatheoretical ambiguity in Lewin's work might well have been a protective measure, an attempt to shield his fresh vision of an action science from the fully dominant logical positivist temper of his time. In any event, whether planned or not, Lewin walked a tightrope between two fundamentally opposed views of science and never did make clear how theory could be used as both an interpretive and a creative element. This achievement, as we might guess, would have to wait for a change in the intellectual ethos of social science.

That change, as we earlier indicated, is now taking place. Increasingly the literature signals a disenchantment with theories of science that grants priority to the external world in the generation of human knowledge. Instead there is growing movement toward granting preeminence to the cognitive processes of mind and the symbolic processes of social construction. In *Toward Transformation in Social Knowledge* (1982), Kenneth Gergen synthesizes the essential whole of this movement and takes it one crucial step beyond disenchantment to a bold, yet workable conception of science that firmly unites theory with practice—and thereby elevates the status of theoretical-scientific work. From a historical perspective there is no question that this is a major achievement; it brings to completion the work abruptly halted by Lewin's untimely death. But more than that, what Gergen offers, albeit indirectly, is a desperately needed clue to how we can revitalize an action-research discipline that has never reached its potential. While a complete statement of the emerging sociorationalist metatheory is beyond the scope of this chapter, it is important at least to outline the general logic of the perspective, including its basic assumptions.

At the heart of sociorationalism is the assumption of impermanence—the fundamental instability of social order. No matter what the durability to date, virtually any pattern of social action is open to infinite revision. Accepting for a moment the argument of the social constructionists that social reality, at any given point, is a product of broad social agreement (shared meanings), and further granting a linkage between the conceptual schemes of a culture and its other patterns of action, we must seriously consider the idea that alterations in conceptual practices, in ways of symbolizing the world, hold tremendous potential for guiding changes in the social order. To understand the importance of these assumptions and their meaning for social science, let us quote Gergen (1982) at length:

> Is not the range of cognitive heuristics that may be employed in solving problems of adaptation limited only by the human imagination?
>
> One must finally consider the possibility that human biology not only presents to the scientist an organism whose actions may vary in an infinity of ways, but it may ensure as well that novel patterns are continuously emerging ... variations in human activity may importantly be traced to the capacities of the organism for symbolic restructuring. As it is commonly said, one's actions appear to be vitally linked to the manner in which one understands or construes the world of experience. The stimulus world does not elicit behavior in an automatic, reflex-like fashion. Rather, the symbolic translation of one's experiences virtually transforms their implications and thereby alters the range of one's potential reactions. Interestingly, while formulations of this variety are widely shared within the scientific community, very little attention has been paid to their ramifications for a theory of science. As is clear, without such regularities the prediction of behavior is largely obviated ... to the extent that the individual is capable of transforming the meaning of stimulus conditions in an indeterminate number of ways, existing regularities must be considered historically contingent—dependent on the prevailing meaning systems of conceptual structure of the times. In effect, from this perspective the scientist's capacity to locate predictable patterns of interaction depends importantly on the extent to which the population is both homogeneous and stable in its conceptual constructions (pp. 16–17).

While this type of reasoning is consistent with the thinking of many social scientists, the ramifications are rarely taken to their logical conclusion: "Virtually unexamined by the field is the potential of science to shape the meaning systems of the society and thus the common activities of the culture" (Gergen, 1978, p.1349). Virtually unexamined is the important role that science can—and does—play in the scientific construction of social reality.

One implication of this line of thought is that to the extent the social science conceives its role in the logical positivist sense, with its goals being prediction and control, it not only serves the interests of the status quo (you can't have "good science" without stable replication and verification of hypotheses) but it also seriously underestimates the power and usefulness of its most important product, namely theory; it underestimates the constructive role science can have in the *development* of the groups and organizations that make up our cultural world. According to Gergen, realization of this fact furnishes the opportunity to refashion a social science of vital significance to society. To do this, we need a bold shift in attention whereby theoretical accounts are no longer judged in terms of their predictive capacity, but instead are judged in terms of their generative capacity— their ability to foster dialogue about that which is taken for granted and their capacity for generating fresh alternatives for social action. Instead of asking, "Does this theory correspond with the observable facts?" the emphasis for evaluating good theory becomes, "To what extent does this theory present provocative new possibilities for social action, and to what extent does it stimulate normative dialogue about how we can and should organize ourselves?" The complete logic for such a proposal may be summarized in the following ten points:

1. The social order at any given point is viewed as the product of broad social agreement, whether tacit or explicit.

2. Patterns of social-organizational action are not fixed by nature in any direct biological or physical way; the vast share of social conduct is potentially stimulus-free, capable of infinite conceptual variation.

3. From an observational point of view, all social action is open to multiple interpretations, no one of which is superior in any objective sense. The interpretations (for example, "whites are superior to blacks") favored in one historical setting may be replaced in the next.

4. Historically embedded conventions govern what is taken to be true or valid, and to a large extent govern what we, as scientists and lay persons, are able to see. All observation, therefore, is theory-laden and filtered through conventional belief systems and theoretical lenses.[2]

5. To the extent that action is predicated on ideas, beliefs, meanings, intentions, or theory, people are free to seek transformations in conventional conduct by changing conventional codes (idea systems).

---

[2]As physicist Jeremy Hayward (1984) has put it, "I'll see it when I believe it," or oppositely, "I won't see it because I don't believe it." The point is that all observation is filtered through belief systems which act as our personal theories of the world. Thus, what *counts* as "fact" depends largely on beliefs associated with theory and therefore, on the community of scientists espousing this belief system.

6. The most powerful vehicle communities have for transforming their conventions—their agreements on norms, values, policies, purposes, and ideologies—is through the act of dialogue made possible by language. Alterations in linguistic practices, therefore, hold profound implications for changes in social practice.

7. Social theory can be viewed as a highly refined language with a specialized grammar all its own. As a powerful linguistic tool created by trained linguistic experts (scientists), theory may enter the conceptual meaning system of culture and in doing so alter patterns of social action.

8. Whether intended or not, all theory is normative and has the potential to influence the social order—even if reactions to it are simply boredom, rebellion, laughter, or full acceptance.

9. Because of this, all social theory is morally relevant; it has the potential to affect the way people live their ordinary lives in relation to one another. This point is a critical one because there is no such thing as a detached/technical/scientific mode for judging the ultimate worth of value claims.

10. Valid knowledge or social theory is therefore a communal creation. Social knowledge is not "out there" in nature to be discovered through detached, value-free, observational methods (logical empiricism); nor can it be relegated to the subjective minds of isolated individuals (solipsism). Social knowledge resides in the interactive collectivity; it is created, maintained, and put to use by the human group. Dialogue, free from constraint or distortion, is necessary to determine the "nature of things" (sociorationalism).

In Table 3.1 the metatheory of sociorationalism is both summarized and contrasted to the commonly held assumptions of the logical empiricist view of science. Especially important to note is the transformed role of the scientist when social inquiry is viewed from the perspective of sociorationalism. Instead of attempting to present oneself as an impartial bystander or dispassionate spectator of the inevitable, the social scientist conceives of himself or herself as an active agent, an invested participant whose work might well become a powerful source of change in the way people see and enact their worlds. Driven by a desire to "break the hammerlock" of what appears as given in human nature, the scientist attempts to build theories that can expand the realm of what is conventionally understood as possible. In this sense the core impact of sociorationalist metatheory is that it invites, encourages, and requires that students of social life rigorously exercise their theoretical imagination in the service of their vision of the good. Instead of denial it is an invitation to fully accept and exercise those qualities of mind and action that make us uniquely human.

Now we turn to a question raised earlier: How does theory achieve its capacity to affect social practice, and what are some of the specific characteristics of generative theory?

TABLE 3.1. Comparison of Logical Empiricist and Socio-Rationalist Conceptions of Social Science

Dimension for Comparison	Logical Empiricism	Socio-Rationalism
1. Primary Function of Science	Enhance goals of understanding, prediction, and control by discerning general laws or principles governing the relationship among units of observable phenomena.	Enhance understanding in the sense of assigning meaning to something, thus creating its status through the use of concepts. Science is a means for expanding flexibility and choice in cultural evolution.
2. Theory of Knowledge and Mind	Exogenic—grants priority to the external world in the generation of human knowledge (i.e., the preeminence of objective fact). Mind is a mirror.	Endogenic—holds the processes of mind and symbolic interaction as preeminent source of human knowledge. Mind is both a mirror and a lamp.
3. Perspective on Time	Assumption of temporal irrelevance: searches for transhistorical principles.	Assumption of hstorically and contextually relevant meanings; existing regularities in social order are contingent on prevailing meaning systems.
4. Assuming Stability of Social Patterns	Social phenomena are sufficiently stable, enduring, reliable and replicable to allow for lawful principles.	Social order is fundamentally unstable. Social phenomena are guided by cognitive heuristics, limited only by the human imagination: the social order is a subject matter capable of infinite variation through the linkage ofideas and action.
5. Value Stance	Separation of fact and values. Possibility of objective knowledge through behavioral observation.	Social sciences are fundamentally nonobjective. Any behavioral event is open to virtually any interpretative explanation. All interpretation is filtered through prevailing values of a culture. "There is no description without prescription."

(continued)

TABLE 3.1. Comparison of Logical Empiricist and Socio-Rationalist Conceptions of Social Science *(continued)*

Dimension for Comparison	Logical Empiricism	Socio-Rationalism
6. Features of "Good" Theory	Discovery of transhistorically valid principles; a theory's correspondence with face.	Degree to which theory furnishes alternatives for social innovation and thereby opens vistas for action; expansion of "the realm of the possible."
7. Criteria for Confirmation or Verification (Life of a Theory)	Logical consistency and empirical prediction; subject to falsification.	Persuasive appeal, impace, and overall generative capacity; subject to community agreement; truth is a product of a community of truth makers.
8. Role of Scientist	Impartial bystander and dispassionate spectator of the inevitable; content to accept that which seems given.	Active agent and coparticipant who is primarily a source of linguistic activity (theoretical language) which serves as input into common meaning systems. Interested in "breaking the hammerlock" of what appears as given in human nature.
9. Chief Product of Research	Cumulation of objective knowledge through the production of empiracally disconfirmable hypothesis.	Continued improvement in theory building capacity; improvement in the capacity to create generative-theoretical language.
10. Emphasis in the Education of Future Social Science Professionals	Rigorous experimental methods and statistical analysis; a premium is placed on method (training in theory construction is a rarity).	Hermenuetic interpretation and catalytic theorizing; a premium is placed on the theoretical imagination. Sociorationalism invites the student toward intellectual expression in the service of his or her vision of the good.

The Power of Theory in Understanding Organizational Life

The sociorationalist vision of science is of such far-reaching importance that no student, organizational scientist, manager, educator, or action-researcher can afford to ignore it. Good theory, as we have suggested, is one of the most powerful means we have for helping social systems evolve, adapt, and creatively alter their patterns over time. Building further on this metatheoretical perspective we can talk about five ways by which theory achieves its exceptional potency:

1. Establishing a conceptual and contextual frame;
2. Providing presumptions of logic;
3. Transmitting a system of values;
4. Creating a group-building language;
5. Extending visions of possibility or constraint.

Establishing a Perceptual and Contextual Frame

To the extent that theory is the conceptual imposition of order upon an otherwise "booming, bustling, confusion that is the realm of experience" (Dubin, 1978), the theorist's first order of business is to specify what is there to be seen, to provide an "ontological education" (Gergen, 1982). The very act of theoretical articulation, therefore, highlights not only the parameters of the topic or subject matter, but becomes an active agent as a cueing device, a device that subtly focuses attention on particular phenomena or meanings while obscuring others. In the manner of a telescope or lens, a new theory allows one to see the world in a way perhaps never before imagined.

For example, when American eugenicists used the lens of biological determinism to attribute diseases of poverty to the inferior genetic construction of poor people, they literally could see no systematic remedy other than sterilization of the poor. In contrast, when Joseph Goldberg theorized that pellagra was not genetically determined but culturally caused (as a result of vitamin deficiency and the eating habits of the poor), he could discover a way to cure it (Gould, 1981). Similarly, theories about the "survival of the fittest" might well help executives locate "predators," "hostile environments," and a world where self interest reigns, where it is a case of "eat or be eaten." Likewise, theories of leadership have been known quickly to facilitate the discovery of Theory X and Theory Y interaction. Whatever the theory, it provides a potential means for members of a culture to navigate in an otherwise neutral, meaningless, or chaotic sea of people, interactions and events. By providing an "ontological education" with respect to what is there, a theory furnishes an important cultural input that affects people's cognitive set. In this sense "the world is not so constituted until the lens is employed. With each new distinction the groundwork is laid for alterations in existing patterns of conduct" (Gergen, 1982, p. 23).

As the reader may already surmise, an important moral issue begins to emerge here. Part of the reason that theory is, in fact, powerful is that it shapes perceptions, cognition's, and preferences often at a preconscious level, much like subliminal communications or even hypnosis. Haley (1973) talks about how Milton Erickson has made this a central feature of this psychotherapeutic work. But Lukes (1974) cautions that such thought control may be "the supreme and most insidious exercise of power," especially when it prevents people from challenging their role in the existing order of things and when it operates contrary to their real interests.

Providing Presumptions of Logic

Theories are also powerful to the extent to which they help shape common expectations of causality, sequence, and relational importance of phenomena within a theoretical equation. Consider, for example, the simple logic underlying almost every formal performance-appraisal system. Stripped to essentials, the theoretical underpinnings run something like this: "If you want to evaluate performance (P), then you must evaluate the individual employee (E); in other words, 'P = E'." Armed with this theory, many managers have entered the performance-appraisal meeting shaking with the thought of having to pass godlike judgment on some employee. Similarly, the employee arrives at the meeting with an arsenal of defenses, designed to protect his or her hard-won self-esteem. Little genuine communication occurs during the meeting and virtually no problem-solving takes place. The paperwork is mechanically completed, then filed away in the personnel office until the next year. So powerful is this subtle $P = E$ equation that any alternative goes virtually unnoticed, for example the Lewinian theory that behavior (performance) is a function of the person and the environment (in this case the organizational situation, the "OS" in which the employee works). Following this Lewinian line, the theory underlying performance appraisal would now have to be expanded to read $P = E \times OS$. That is, $P \neq E$. To adequately assess performance there must be an assessment of the individual *in relation* to the organizational setting in which he or she works and vice-versa. What would happen to the performance-appraisal process if this more complete theory were used as a basis for re-designing appraisal systems in organizations throughout the corporate world? Isn't it possible that such a theory could help shift the attribution process away from the person-blame to systems analysis?[3] By attributing causality, theories have the potential to create the very phenomena they propose to explain. Karl Weick, in a recent article examining managerial thought in the context of action, contends that thought and action are part and parcel of one another; thinking is best viewed as a kind of activity, and activity as the ground of thought. For him,

---

[3] A group of colleagues and we are engaged in a two-year study of a major industrial plant where introduction of this simple theory has led to changes in job design, work relations, training programs, motivational climate, and hierarchical ideology. For an introduction to this work see Pasmore, Cooperrider, Kaplan and Morris, 1983.

managerial theories gain their power by helping people overlook disorder and presume orderliness. Theory *energizes* action by providing a *presumption of logic* that enables people to act with certainty, attention, care, and control. Even where it is originally inadequate as a description of current reality, a forceful theory may provoke action that brings into the world a new reality that then confirms the original theory. Weick (1983) explains:

> Once the action is linked with an explanation, it becomes more forceful, and the situation is thereby transformed into something that supports the presumed underlying pattern. Presumptions [theories] enable actions to be tied to specific explanations that consolidate those actions into deterministic events. . . .
>
> The underlying explanation need *not* be objectively "correct." In a crude sense any old explanation will do. This is so because explanation serves mostly to organize and focus the action. The focused action then modifies the situation in ways that confirm the explanation, whatever it is.
>
> Thus, the adequacy of any explanation is determined by the intensity and structure it adds to potentially self-validating actions. More forcefulness leads to more validation and more perceived adequacy. Accuracy is subordinate to intensity. Since situations can support a variety of meanings, their actual content and meaning are dependent on the degree to which they are arranged in sensible, coherent configurations. More forcefulness imposes more coherence. Thus, those explanations that induce greater forcefulness become more valid, not because they are more accurate, but because they have a higher potential for self-validation. . . . the underlying explanations they unfold (for example, "This is war") have great potential to intensify whatever action is underway (1983, pp. 230–232).

Thus, theories are generative to the extent that they are forceful (e.g., Marx), logically coherent (e.g., Piaget), and bold in their assertions and consistency (e.g., Freud, Weber). By providing a basis for focused action, a logic for attributing causality, and a sequence specification that grounds expectations for action and reaction, a theory goes a long way toward forming the common expectations for the future. "And with the alteration of expectation, the stage is set for modification of action" (Gergen, 1982, p. 24).

Transmitting a System of Values

Beyond abstract logic, it is often the affective core of social theory that provides its true force and appeal, allowing it to direct perception and guide behavior. From the tradition of logical positivism, good "objective" theory is to be value-free, yet upon closer inspection we find that social theory is infused with values and domain assumptions throughout. As Gouldner (1970) so aptly put it, "Every social theory facilitates the pursuit of some, but not all, courses of action and thus, encourages us to change or accept the world as it is, to say yea or nay to it. In a way, every theory is a discrete obituary or celebration of some social system."

Nowhere is this better exemplified—negatively—than in the role scientific theory played in the arguments for slavery, colonialism, and belief in the genetic superiority of certain races. The scientific theory in this case was, again, the theory of biological determinism, the belief that social and economic differences between human beings and groups—differences in rank, status, political privilege, education privilege—arise from inherited natural endowments, and that existing social arrangements accurately reflect biological limits. So powerful was this theory during the 1800s that it led a number of America's highest-ranking scientific researchers unconsciously to miscalculate "objective" data in what has been brilliantly described by naturalist Steven Jay Gould (1981, p. 54) as a "patchwork of fudging and finagling in the clear interest of controlling a priori convictions". Before dismissing this harsh judgment as simple rhetoric, we need to look closely at how it was determined. One example will suffice.

When Samual Morton, a scientist with two medical degrees, died in 1851, the *New York Tribune* paid tribute saying, "Probably no scientific man in America enjoyed a higher reputation among scholars throughout the world than Dr. Morton" (in Gould, 1981, p. 51). Morton gained this reputation as a scientist who set out to rank racial groups by "objectively" measuring the size of the cranial cavity of the human skull, which he regarded as a measure of brain size. He had a beautiful collection of skulls from races throughout the world, probably the largest such collection in existence. His hypothesis was a simple one: The mental and moral worth of human races can be arrived at objectively by measuring physical characteristics of the brain; by filling skull cavities with mustard seed or lead shot, accurate measurement of brain size is possible. Morton published three major works, which were reprinted repeatedly as providing objective, "hard" data on the mental worth of races. Gould comments:

> Needless to say, they matched every good Yankee's prejudices—whites on top, Indians in the middle, and blacks on the bottom; and among whites, Teutons and Anglo-Saxons on top, Jews in the middle, and Hindus on the bottom. . . . Status and access to power in Morton's America faithfully reflected biological merit (p. 54).

Morton's work was undoubtedly influential. When he died, the South's leading medical journal proclaimed: "We of the South should consider him as our benefactor, for aiding most materially in giving the Negro his true position as an inferior race" (in Gould, 1981, p. 69). Indeed Morton did much more than only give "the Negro his true position," as the following remarks by Morton himself convey:

> Negroes were numerous in Egypt, but their social position in ancient time, was the same as it is now, that of servants and slaves. The benevolent mind may regret the inaptitude of the Indian civilization . . . [but

values must not yield to fact]. The structure of his mind appears to be different from that of the white man, or can the two harmonize in social relations except on the most limited scale. [Indians] are not only averse to restraints of education, but for the most part are incapable of a continued process of reasoning on abstract subjects (in Gould, 1981, p. 53).

The problem with these conclusions—as well as the numerical data, which supported them—was that they were based not on "fact" but purely and simply on cultural fiction, on Morton's belief in biological determinism. As Gould meticulously shows, all of Morton's data was wrong. Having reworked it completely, Gould concludes:

Morton's summaries are a patchwork of fudging and finagling in the clear interest of controlling a priori convictions. Yet—and this is the most intriguing aspect of the case—I find no evidence of conscious fraud; indeed, had Morton been a conscious fudger, he would not have published his data so openly.

Conscious fraud is probably rare in science. . . . The prevalence of unconscious finagling, on the other hand, suggests the general conclusion about the social context of science. . . . prior prejudice may be found anywhere, even in the basics of measuring bones and totaling sums (pp. 55–56).

Morton represents a telling example of the power of theory. Theory is not only a shaper of expectations and perceptions. Under the guise of "dispassionate inquiry" it can also be a peddler of values, typecasting arbitrary value as scientific "fact." Along with Gould, we believe that we would be better off to abandon the myth of "value-free" science and that theoretical work "must be understood as a social phenomenon, a gutsy, human enterprise, not the work of robots programmed to collect pure information" (Gould, 1981, p. 21). Even if Morton's data were correct, his work still could not be counted as value-free. His data and theories were not only shaped by the setting in which he worked; they were also used to support broad social policy. This is akin to making nature the source of cultural values, which of course it never can be ("What is" does not equal "what should be").

Creating a Group-Building Language

The sociorationalist perspective is more than a pessimistic epitaph for a strictly logical positivist philosophy. It is an invitation to inquiry that raises the status of theory from mere appendage of scientific method to an actual shaper of society. Once we acknowledge that a primary product of science—theory—is a key resource for the creation of groups, the stage is set for theory-building activity intended for the use and development of human society, for the creation of human options.

Students of human behavior have been aware of the group as the foundation of society since the earliest periods of classical thought. Aristotle, for example, discussed the importance of bands and families. But it was not until the middle of the present century that scientific interest in the subject exploded in a flurry of general inquiry and systematic interdisciplinary research (for a sample review of this literature see Hare, 1976). Among the conclusions of this recent work is the crucial insight that:

> The face-to-face group working on a problem is the meeting ground of individual personality and society. It is in the group that personality is modified and socialized and it is through the workings of groups that society is changed and adapted to its times (Thelen, 1954, p. vi).

Similarly, in the field of organization development, Srivastva, Obert, and Neilsen (1977) have shown that the historical development of the discipline has paralleled advances in group theory. And this, they contend, is no accident because:

> Emphasis on the small group is responsive to the realities of social change in large complex organizations. It is through group life that individuals learn, practice, develop, and modify their roles in the larger organization. To enter programmatically at the group level is both to confront and po- tentially co-opt an important natural source of change and development in these systems (p. 83).

It is well established that groups are formed around common ideas that are expressed in and through some kind of shared language which makes communi- cative interaction possible. What is less clear, though, is the exact role that science plays in shaping group life through the medium of language. However, the fact that science frequently does have an impact is rarely questioned. Andre Gorz (1973) offers an explosive example of this point.

In the early 1960s a British professor of sociology by the name of Goldthorpe was brought in from a nearby university to make a study of the Vauxhall automo- bile workers in Luton, England. At the time, management at the factory was wor- ried because workers in other organizations throughout the United Kingdom were showing great unrest over working conditions, pay, and management. Many strikes were being waged; most of them wildcat strikes called by the factory stewards, not by the unions themselves. Goldthorpe was called in to study the situation at Vauxhall, to find out for management if there was anything to worry about at their factory. At the time of the study there were at Vauxhall no strikes, no disruptions, and no challenges by workers. Management wanted to know why. What were the chances that acute conflict would break out in the "well-managed" and "advanced" big factory?

After two full years of research, the professor drew his conclusions. Manage- ment, he said, had little to worry about. According to the study, the workers were completely socialized into the system, they were satisfied with their wages and neither liked or disliked their work—in fact, they were indifferent to it, viewing it as boring but inevitable. Because their job was not intrinsically rewarding, most people did it just to be done with it—so they could go home and work on other more worthwhile projects and be with their family. Work was marginal and instrumental. It was a means to support other interests outside the factory, where "real life" began. Based then on his observations, Goldthorpe theorized that management had nothing to worry about: Workers were passively apathetic and well integrated into the system. They behaved according to middle-class patterns and showed no signs of strength as a group (no class-consciousness). Furthermore, most conflict with management belonged to the past.

The sociologist's report was still at the printer's when some employees got hold of a summary of his findings. They had the conclusions copied and distributed reports to hundreds of co-workers. Also at around this time, a report of Vauxhall's profits was being circulated, profits that were not shared with the employees. The next day something happened. It was reported by the *London Times* in detail:

> Wild rioting has broken out at the Vauxhall car factories in Luton. Thousands of workers streamed out of the shops and gathered in the factory yard. They besieged the management offices, calling for managers to come out, singing the 'Red Flag,' and shouting. 'String them up!' Groups attempted to storm the offices and battled police which had been called to protect them (quoted in Gorz, 1973).

The rioting lasted for two days. All of this happened, then, in an advanced factory where systematic research showed workers to be apathetic, weak as a group, and resigned to accept the system. What does it all mean? Had the researchers simply misread the data?

To the contrary. Goldthorpe knew his data well. He articulated the conclusions accurately, concisely, and with force. In fact, what happened was that the report gave the workers a *language* with which to begin talking to one another about their plight. It brought them into interaction and, as they discussed things, they discovered that Goldthorpe was right. They felt alike, apathetic but frustrated; and they were apathetic because they felt as individuals working in isolated jobs, that no one could do anything to change things. But the report gave them a way to discuss the situation. As they talked, things changed. People were no longer alone in their feelings, and they did not want things to continue as they were. As an emergent group, they now had a means to convert apathy into action, noninvolvement into involvement, and individual powerlessness into collective strength. "In other words," analyzes Gorz, "the very investigation of Mr. Goldthorpe about the lack of class-consciousness helped tear down the barriers of silence and isolation that rendered the workers apathetic" (p. 334).

The Vauxhall case is an important one for a number of reasons. At a general level it demonstrates that knowledge in the social sciences differs in quality and kind from knowledge generated in the physical sciences. For instance, our knowledge of the periodic chart does not change the elements, and our knowledge of the moon's orbit does not change its path. But our knowledge of a social system is different. It can be used by the system to change itself, thus invalidating or disconfirming the findings immediately or at some later time. Thus the human group differs from objects in an important way: Human beings have the capacity for symbolic interaction and, through language, they have the ability to collaborate in the investigation of their own world. Because of our human capacity for symbolic interaction, the introduction of new knowledge concerning aspects of our world carries with it the strong likelihood of changing that world itself.

Gergen (1982) refers to this as the "enlightenment effect" of scientific work, meaning that once the formulations of scientific work are made public, human beings may act autonomously either to disconfirm or to validate the propositions. According to logical positivist philosophy, potential enlightenment effects must be reduced or—ideally—eliminated through experimental controls. In social psychology, for example, deception plays a crucial role in doing research; enlightenment effects are viewed as contaminants to good scientific work. Yet there is an alternative way to look at the reactive nature of social research: it is precisely because of the enlightenment effect that theory can and does play an important role in the positive construction of society. In this sense, the enlightenment effect—which is made possible through language—is an essential ingredient making scientific work worthwhile, meaningful, and applicable. It constitutes an invitation to each and every theorist to actively participate in the creation of his or her world by generating compelling theories of what is good, and just, and desirable in social existence.

Extending Visions of Possibility

The position taken by the sociorationalist philosophy of science is that the conduct of inquiry cannot be separated from the everyday negotiation of reality. Social-organizational research is, therefore, a continuing moral concern, a concern of social reconstruction and direction. The choice of what to study, how to study it, and what to report each implies some degree of responsibility. Science, therefore, instead of being considered an endpoint, is viewed as one means of helping humanity create itself. Science in this sense exists for one singular overarching purpose. As Albion Small (1905) proposed almost a century ago, a generative science must aim at "the most thorough, intense, persistent, and systematic effort to make human life all that it is capable of becoming" (pp. 36–37).

Theories gain their generative capacity by extending visions that expand to the realm of the possible. As a general proposition it might be said that theories designed to empower organized social systems will tend to have a greater enlightenment effect than theories of human constraint. This proposition is grounded in a simple but important consideration which we should like to raise as it relates to the unity of theory and practice: Is it not possible that scientific theory gains its capacity to affect cultural practices in very much the same way that powerful leaders inspire people to new heights? Recent research on the functioning of the executive mind (Srivastva, 1983; 1985) raises a set of intriguing parallels between the possibilities of a generative science and the workings of the executive mind.

The essential parallel is seen in the primary role that ideas or ideals play in the mobilization of diverse groups in the common construction of a desired future. Three major themes from the research stand out in this regard:

1. **Vision:** The executive mind works largely from the present and extends itself out to the longer-term future. It is powerful to the extent that it is able to envision a desired future state which challenges perceptions of what is possible and what can be realized. The executive mind operates beyond the frontier of conventional practice without losing sight of either necessity or possibility.

2. **Passion:** The executive mind is simultaneously rational and intuitive, which allows it to tap into the sentiments, values, and dreams of the social collectivity. Executive vision becomes "common vision" to the extent that it ignites the imaginations, hopes, and passions of others-and it does so through the articulation of self-transcending ideals which lend meaning and significance to everyday life.

3. **Integrity:** The executive mind is the mental muscle that moves a system from the present state to a new and different future. As such, this muscle gains strength to the extent that it is founded upon an integrity able to withstand contrary pressures. There are three dimensions to executive integrity. The first, system integrity, refers to the fact that the executive mind perceives the world (the organization, group, or society) as a unified whole, not as a collection of individual parts. The second type of integrity is *moral integrity*. Common-vision leadership is largely an act of caring. It follows the "path of the heart," which is the source of moral and ethical standards. Finally, integrity of vision refers to consistency, coherence, and focus. Executive vision—to the extent to which it is compelling—is focused and unwavering, even in the midst of obstacles, critics, and conflicting alternatives.

Interestingly, these thematic dimensions of the executive mind have their counterparts in recent observations concerning the utilization of organizational research. According to Beyer and Trice (1982), the "affective bonding" that takes place during the research largely determines the attractiveness of its results and generates commitment to utilize their implications. For example, Henshel (1975) suggests that research containing predictions of an appealing future will be utilized and preferred over research that points to a negative or repelling future: "People will work for predicted states they approve of and against those they detest" (p.103). Similarly, Weiss and Bucavalas (1980) report that results which challenge the status quo are most attractive to high-level executives because they are the persons expected to make new things happen, at least on the level of policy. And, with respect to passion and integrity, Mitroff (1980) urges social scientists to become caring advocates of their ideas, not only to diffuse their theories but also to challenge others to prove them wrong and thus pursue those ideas which have integrity in action.

This section has explored a number of ways in which social theory becomes a powerful resource for change and development in social practice. The argument is simple. Theory is agential in character and has unbounded potential to affect patterns of social action—whether desired or not. As we have seen, theories are not mere explanations of an external world lying "out there" waiting to be objectively recorded. Theories, like powerful ideas, are formative. By establishing perceptual cues and frames, by providing presumptions of logic, by transmitting subtle values, by creating new language, and by extending compelling visions of possibility or constraint—in all these ways social theory becomes a powerful means whereby norms, beliefs, and cultural practices may be altered.

Reawakening the Spirit of Action-Research

The key point is this: Instinctively, intuitively, and tacitly we all know that important ideas can, in a flash, profoundly alter the way we see ourselves, view reality, and conduct our lives. Experience shows that a simple economic forecast, political poll, or technical discovery (like the atomic bomb) can forever change the course of human history. Thus one cannot help but be disturbed and puzzled by the discipline of action-research in its wide-ranging indifference to theory. Not only does it continue to underrate the role of theory as a means for organizational development (Friedlander and Brown, 1974; Bartunek, 1983; Argyris, 1983) but it appears also to have become locked within an assumptive base that systematically distorts our view of organizational reality and inadvertently helps reinforce and perfect the status quo (Brimm, 1972).

Why is there this lack of generative theorizing in action-research? And, more importantly, what can be done to rekindle the spirit, excitement and passion required of a science that wishes to be of vital significance to organizations? Earlier we talked about a philosophy of science congenial to the task. Sociorationalism, it was argued, represents an epistemological point of view conducive to catalytic theorizing. Ironically though, it can be argued that most action researchers *already do* subscribe to this or a similar view of science (Susman and Evered, 1978). Assuming this to be the case, it becomes an even greater puzzle why contemporary action-research continues to disregard theory-building as an integral and necessary component of the craft. In this section we shall broaden our discussion by taking a look at some of the metaphysical assumptions embedded in our conventional definitions of action-research—assumptions that can be shown to govern our thought and work in ways inimical to present interests.

Paradigm 1: Organizing As A Problem to be Solved

The intellectual and spiritual origins of action-research can be traced to Kurt Lewin, a social psychologist of German origin who coined the term *action-research* in 1944. The thrust of Lewin's work centered on the need to bridge the gap between science and the realm of practical affairs. Science, he said, should be used to inform and educate social practice, and subsequent action would then inform science: "We should consider action, research, and training as a triangle that should be kept together" (Lewin, 1948, p. 211). The twofold promise of an action science, according to Lewin, was to simultaneously contribute to the development of scientific knowledge (propositions of an if/then variety) and use such knowledge for bettering the human condition.

The immense influence of Lewin is a complete puzzle if we look only to his writings. The fact of the matter is that Lewin published only 2 papers—a mere 22pages—concerned directly with the idea of action-research (Peters and Robinson, 1984). Indeed, it has been argued that his enduring influence is attributable not to these writings but to the sheer force and presence of the man himself. According to biographer Alfred Marrow (1968), Lewin was a passionate and creative thinker, continuously knocking at the door of the unknown, studying "topics that had been believed to be psychologically unapproachable." Lewin's character was marked by a spirit of inquiry that burned incessantly and affected all who came in contact with him, especially his students. The intensity of his presence was fueled further by the belief that inquiry itself could be used to construct a more democratic and dignified future. At least this was his hope and dream, for Lewin had *not* forgotten his experience as a refugee from fascism in the late 1930s. Understanding this background, then, it is clear why he revolted so strongly against a detached ivory-tower view of science, a science that is immersed in trivial matters, tranquilized by its standardized methods, and limited in its field of inquiry. Thus, the picture we have of Lewin shows him to have been a committed social scientist pioneering uncharted territory for the purpose of creating new knowledge about groups and societies that might advance the democratic ideal (see, for example, Lewin, 1952). It was this spirit—a relentless curiosity coupled with a conviction of the need for knowledge-guided societal development—that marked Lewin's creative impact on both his students and the field.

Much of this spirit is now gone from action-research. What is left is a series of assumptions about the world which exhibits little, if any, resemblance to the process of inquiry as Lewin lived it. While many of the words are the same, they have been taken too literally and in their translation over the years have been bloated into a set of metaphysical principles—assumptions about the essence of social existence-that directly undermine the intellectual and speculative spirit. Put bluntly, under current norms, action-research has largely failed as an instrument for advancing social knowledge of consequence and now risks being (mis)understood as little more than a crude empiricism imprisoned in a deficiency mode of thought. A quick sketch of six sets of assumptions embedded in the conventional view of action-research will show exactly what we are talking about while also answering our question about the discipline's lack of contribution to generative theory:

Research equals problem-solving; to do good research is to solve "real problems." So ingrained is this assumption that it scarcely needs documentation. Virtually every definition found in leading texts and articles equates action research with problem solving—as if "real" problem solving is virtually the essence of the discipline. For example, as French and Bell (1978) define it, "Action-research is both *an approach to problem solving*—a model or paradigm, and *a problem-solving process*—a series of activities and events." (p. 88)[4] Or in terms of the Bradford, Gibb, and Benne (1964) definition, "It is an application of scientific methodology in *the clarification and solution of practical problems*" (p. 33). Similarly, Frohman, Sashkin, and Kavanaugh (1976) state: "Action research describes a particular process model whereby behavioral science knowledge is applied to help a client (usually a group or social system) *solve real problems and not incidentally learn the process involved in problem solving*" (p. 203). Echoing this theme, that research equals problem solving, researchers at the University of Michigan's Institute in Social Research state,

> Three factors need to be taken into account in an organization development [action-research] effort: The behaviors that are problematic, the conditions that create those behaviors, and the interventions or activities that will correct the conditions creating the problems. What is it that people are doing or not doing, that is a problem? Why are they doing or not doing these particular things? Which of a large number of possible interventions or activities would be most likely to solve the problems by focusing on why problems exist? (Hausser, Pecorella and Wissler, 1977, p. 2).

Here it is unmistakably clear that the primary focus of the action-research approach to organizational analysis is the ongoing array of concrete problems an organization faces. Of course, there are a number of differences in the discipline as to the overall definition and meaning of the emerging action-research paradigm. But this basic assumption—that research equals problem solving—is not one of them. In a recent review intended to discover elements of metatheoretical agreement within the discipline, Peters and Robinson (1984) discovered that out of 15 different dimensions of action-research studied, only 2 had unanimous support among leaders in the field. What were these two elements of agreement? Exactly as the definitions above suggest: Social science should be "action oriented" and "problem focused."

Inquiry, in action-research terms, is a matter of following the standardized rules of problem solving; knowledge is the result of good method. "In essence," write Blake and Mouton (1976), "it is a method of empirical data gathering that is

---

[4]Emphasis in this and the following definitions are ours, intended to underscore the points being made. Earlier we noted the importance of language as a subtle cueing device. Keeping this in mind, the reader is asked to pay special attention to the language of problem solving, and perhaps even count the sheer number of times the word problem is used in relation to definitions of action research.

comprised of a set of rather standardized steps: diagnosis, information gathering, feedback, and action planning" (pp. 101–102). By following this ritual list, they contend that virtually any organization can be studied in a manner that will lead to usable knowledge. As Chiles (1983) puts it, "The virtue of the model lies in the sequential process. . . . Any other sequence renders the model meaningless" (p.318). The basic idea behind the model is that "in management, events proceed as planned unless some force, not provided against by the plan, acts upon events to produce an outcome not contemplated in the plan" (Kepner and Tregoe, 1973, p. 3). Thus, a problem is a deviation from some standard, and without precise diagnosis (step one) any attempt to resolve the problem will likely fail as a result of not penetrating the surface symptoms to discover the true causes. Hence, like a liturgical refrain which is seldom questioned or thought about, Cohen, Fink et al. (1984) tell the new student that *knowledge is the offspring of processing information through a distinct series of problem-solving stages*:

> Action-research begins with an identified problem. Data are then gathered in a way that allows a diagnosis which can produce a tentative solution, which is then implemented with the assumption that it is likely to cause new or unforeseen problems that will, in turn, need to be evaluated, diagnosed, and so forth. *This action-research method assumes a constantly evolving interplay between solutions, results, and new solutions. . . . This model is a general one applicable to solving any kind of problem in an ongoing organization* (pp. 359–360).

Action-research is utilitarian or technical; that is, it should be initiated and designed to meet a need in an area specified by the organization, usually by "top management." The search is controlled by the "felt need" or object of inquiry; everything that is not related to this object should be dismissed as irrelevant. As we are beginning to see, action-research conventionally understood does not really refer to research per se but rather to a highly focused and defined *type* of research called problem solving. Taken almost directly from the medical model, the disease orientation guides the process of inquiry in a highly programmed way. According to Levinson (1972), diagnostic action-research, "like a therapeutic or teaching relationship should be an alliance of both parties to discover and resolve these problems. . . . [The researcher] *should look for experiences which appear stressful to people. What kinds of occurrences disrupt or disorganize people*" (p.37). Hence in a systematically limiting fashion, the general topic of research is largely prescribed—before inquiry even begins. As we would guess:

> Typical questions in [action-research] data gathering or "problem sensing" would include: *What problems* do you see in your group, including problems between people that are interfering with getting the job done the way you would like to see it done? And *what problems* do you see in the broader organization? Such open-ended questions provide latitude on the part of respondents and encourage a *reporting of problems* as the individual sees them (French, 1969, pp. 183–185).

In problem solving it is assumed that something is broken, fragmented, not whole, and that it needs to be fixed. Thus the function of problem solving is to integrate, stabilize, and help raise to its full potential the workings of the status quo. By definition, a problem implies that one already has knowledge of what "should be"; thus one's *re*search is guided by an instrumental purpose tied to what is already known. In this sense, problem solving tends to be inherently conservative; as a form of research it tends to produce and reproduce a universe of knowledge that remains sealed. As Staw (1984) points out in his review of the field, most organizational research is biased to serve managerial interests rather than exploring broader human and/or social purposes. But even more important, he argues, the field has not even served managerial interests well since research has taken a short-term problem focus rather than having formulated logic's of new forms of organization that do not exist. It is as if the discipline's *concept of social system development* means only clearing up distortions in current functioning (horizontal development) and does not include any conception of a stage-based movement toward an altogether new or transformed reality (vertical development or second-order change).

Action-research should not inquire into phenomena that transcend the competence of human reason. Questions that cannot be answered should not be asked and issues that cannot be acted upon should not be explored (i.e., action-research is not a branch of political philosophy, poetry, or theology). This proposition is a "smuggled-in" corollary to the preceding assumptions. It would appear that once one agrees with the ground rules of a pragmatic problem-solving science, the universe for inquiry is largely predetermined, defined, and delimited in scope. Specifically, what one agrees to a secularized view of a human universe that is predictable, controllable, and rational, one that is sequentially ordered into a series of causes and effects. As both a credit and a weakness, the problem-solving mode narrows our gaze in much the same manner that a blinder over one eye narrows the field of vision and distorts one's perception of depth. As a part of a long-term movement evidenced in social sciences, contemporary action-research embodies the trend toward metaphysical skepticism and denial (Quinney, 1982). That is, it operates out of a sacred void that cuts off virtually any inquiry into the vital forces of life. Indeed, the whole promise of modern science was that it would finally banish illusion, mystery, and uncertainty from the world. An inquiry process of immediate utility (problem solving), therefore, requires an anti-religious, secular spirit that will limit the realm of study to the sphere of the known. And because of the recognition that the formulation of a problem depends largely on one's views of what constitutes a solution, it is not surprising to find that *research on the utilization of research* shows a propensity for social scientists and organizations to agree on studying only those variables that can be manipulated (Beyer and Trice, 1982). As one might imagine, such a view has crippling implications for generative theorizing. For example, as typically practiced, action-research does little in the way of theorizing about or bringing beauty into organizational life. Does this mean that there is no beauty in organizing'? Does this mean that the realm of the esthetic has little or nothing to do with organizational dynamics'?

The tidy imagery of the problem-solving view is related to what Sigmund Koch (1981) has called, in his presidential address to the APA, the syndrome of "ameaningful thinking." One element of this syndrome is the perpetuation of the scientistic myth which uses the rhetoric of prediction and control to reassure people that their lives are not that complex, their situations not all that uncertain—and that their problems are indeed manageable through causal analysis. In the process, however, science tends to trivialize, and even evade, a whole class of issues that "transcend the competence of human reason" yet are clearly meaningful in the course of human experience. One way in which the field of inquiry is restricted, according to Koch, has to do with one's choice of methodology:

> There are times and circumstances in which able individuals, committed to inquiry, tend almost obsessively to frustrate the objectives of inquiry. It is as if uncertainty, mootness, ambiguity, cognitive infinitude were the most unbearable of the existential anguishes. . . . *Ameaningful* thought or inquiry regards knowledge as the result of "processing" rather than discovery. It presumes that knowledge is an almost automatic result of a gimmickry, an assembly line, a "metholology". . . . So strongly does it see knowledge under such aspects that it sometimes seems to suppose the object of inquiry to be an ungainly and annoying irrelevance (1981, p. 259).

To be sure, this is not to argue that all action-research is "ameaningful" or automatically tied to a standardized problem-solving method. Likewise, much of the success achieved by action-research until now may be attributed to its restricted focus on that which is "solvable. " However, it is important to recognize that the problem-solving method of organizational inquiry quite systematically paints a picture of organizational life in which a whole series of colors are considered untouchable. In this way the totality of being is obviously obscured, leading to a narrowed conception of human nature and cultural possibility.

Problems are "out there" to be studied and solved. The ideal product of action-research is a mirror-like reflection of the organization's problems and causes. As "objective third party " there is little role for passion and speculation. The action-researcher should be neither a passionate advocate nor an inspired dreamer (utopian thinker). One of the laudable and indeed significant values associated with action-research has been its insistence upon a collaborative form of inquiry. But unfortunately, from a generative-theory perspective, the term *collaboration* has become virtually synonymous with an idealized image of the researcher as a facilitator and mirror, rather than an active and fully engaged social participant. As facilitator of the problem-solving process, the action-researcher has three generally agreed-upon "primary intervention tasks": to help generate valid organizational data; to enable others to make free and informed choices on the basis of the data, and to help the organization generate internal commitment to their choices. Elaborating further, Argyris (1970) states:

> One condition that seems so basic as to be defined as axiomatic is the generation of *valid information. . . . Valid information is that which*

describes the factors, plus their interrelationships that create the problem (pp. 16–17).

Furthermore, it is also assumed that for data to be useful there must be a claim to neutrality. The data should represent an accurate reflection of the observed facts. As French and Bell (1978) describe it, it is important for the action-researcher to stress the objective, fact-finding features: "A key value inculcated in organizational members is a belief in the validity, desirability, and usefulness of the data" (p. 79). Then through feedback that "refers to activities and processes that 'reflect' or 'mirror' an objective picture of the real world" (p. 111), the action-researcher facilitates the process of prioritizing problems and helps others make choices for action. And because the overarching objective is to help the organization develop its own internal resources, the action-researcher should not play an active role or take an advocate stance that might in the long run foster an unhealthy dependency. As French and Bell (1978) again explain, an active role "tends to negate a collaborative, developmental approach to improving organizational processes" (p. 203).

As must be evident, every one of these injunctions associated with the problem-solving view of action-research serves directly to diminish the likelihood of imaginative, passionate, creative theory. To the extent that generative theory represents an inspired theoretical articulation of a new and different future, it appears that action-research would have nothing to do with it. According to French and Bell (1978) "Even the presenting of options can be overdone. If the [action-researcher's] ideas become the focal point for prolonged discussion and debate, the consultant has clearly shifted away from the facilitator role" (p. 206).

At issue here is something even more important. The fundamental attitude embodied in the problem-solving view is separationist. It views the world as something external to our consciousness of it, something "out there." As such it tends to identify problems not here but "over there": Problems are not ours, but yours; not a condition common to all, but a condition belonging to this person, their group, or that nation (witness the acid-rain issue). Thus, the action-researcher is content to facilitate *their problem solving* because he or she is not part of that world. To this extent, the problem-solving view dissects reality and parcels it out into fragmented groups, families, tribes, or countries. In both form and substance it denies the wholeness of a dynamic and interconnected social universe. And once the unity of the world is broken, passionless, mindless, mirror-like inquiry comes to make logical sense precisely because the inquirer has no ownership or stake in a world that is not his or hers to begin with.

Organizational life is problematic. Organizing is best understood as a historically situated sequence of problems, causes, and solutions among people, events, and things. Thus, the ultimate aim and product of action-research is the production of institutions that have a high capacity to perceive, formulate, and solve an endless stream of problems.

The way we conceive of the social world is of consequence to the kind of world we discover and even, through our reconstructions, helps to create it. Action-researchers, like scientists in other areas, approach their work from a framework based on taken-for-granted assumptions. To the extent that these assumptions are found useful, and are affirmed by colleagues, they remain unquestioned as a habitual springboard for one's work. In time the conventional view becomes so solidly embedded that it assumes the status of being "real," without alternative (Morgan, 1980; Mennhiem, 1936). As human beings we are constantly in symbolic interaction, attempting to develop conceptions that will allow us to make sense of and give meaning to experience through the use of language, ideas, signs, theories, and names. As many have recently shown, the use of metaphor is a basic mode under which symbolism works and exerts an influence on the development of language, science, and cognitive growth (Morgan, 1980; Ortony, 1979; Black, 1962; Keely, 1980). Metaphor works by asserting that A equals B or is very much like B. We use metaphors constantly to open our eyes and sensitize us to phenomenal realities that otherwise might go unnoticed. Pepper (1942) argues that all science proceeds from specifiable "world hypotheses" and behind every world hypothesis rests the boldest of "root metaphors."

Within what we are calling Paradigm I action-research, there lies a guiding metaphor which has a power impact on the theory-building activity of the discipline. When organizations are approached from the deficiency perspective of Paradigm I, all the properties and modes of organizing are scrutinized for their dysfunctional but potentially solvable problems. It is all too clear then that the root metaphor of the conventional view is that *organizing is a problem*. This image focuses the researcher's eye on a visible but narrow realm of reality that resides "out there" and is causally determined, deficient by some preexisting standard— on problems that are probably both understandable and solvable. Through analysis, diagnosis, treatment, and follow-up evaluation the sequential world of organizing can be kept on its steady and productive course. And because social existence is at its base a problem to be solved, real living equals problem solving, and living better is an adaptive learning process whereby we acquire new and more effective means for tackling tough problems. The good life, this image informs, depends on solving problems in such a way that problems of utility are identified and solutions of high quality are found and carried out with full commitment. As one leading theorist describes:

> For many scholars who study organizations and management, the central characteristic of organizations is that they are problem-solving systems whose success is measured by how efficiently they solve problems associated with accomplishing their primary mission and how effectively they respond to emergent problems. Kilmann's approach (1979, pp. 214–215) is representative of this perspective: "One might even define the essence of management as problem defining and problem solving, whether the problems are well-structured, ill-structured, technical, human, or environmental. . . . In this view, the core task of the executive is problem management. Although experience, personality, and specific technical expertise are important, the primary skill of the successful executive is the ability to manage the problem-solving process in such a way that

important problems are identified and solutions of high quality are found and carried out with the full commitment of organizational members (Kolb, 1983, pp. 109–110).

From here it is just a short conceptual jump to the idealized aim of Paradigm1 research:

Action-research tends to build into the client system an institutionalized pattern for continuously collecting data and examining the system's processes, as well as for the continuous review of *known* problem areas. *Problem solving becomes very much a way of organizational life* (Marguiles and Raia, 1972, p. 29).

I have tried in these few pages to highlight the almost obvious point that the deficiency/problem orientation is pervasive and holds a subtle but powerful grasp on the discipline's imagination and focus. It can be argued that the generative incapacity of contemporary action-research is securely linked with the discipline's guiding metaphor of social-organizational existence. As noted by many scholars, the theoretical output of the discipline is virtually nonexistent, and what theory there is, is largely problem-focused (theories of turnover, intergroup conflict, processes of dehumanization. See Staw, 1984 for an excellent review). Thus, our theories, like windsocks, continue to blow steadily onward in the direction of our conventional gaze. Seeing the world as a problem has become "very much a way of organizational life."

It is our feeling that the discipline has reached a level of fatigue arising from repetitious use of its standardized model. Fatigue, as Whitehead (1929) so aptly surmised, arises from an act of excluding the impulse toward novelty, which is the antithesis of the life of the mind and of speculative reason. To be sure, there can be great adventure in the process of inquiry. Yet not many action-researchers today return from their explorations refreshed and revitalized, like pioneers returning home, with news of lands unknown but most certainly there. Perhaps there is a different root metaphor from which to work.

Proposal for a Second Dimension

Our effort here is but one in a small yet growing attempt to generate new perspectives on the conduct of organizational research, perspectives that can yield the kind of knowledge necessary for both understanding and transforming complex social-organizational systems (Torbert, 1983; Van Maanen et al., 1982; Mitroff and Kilmann, 1978; Smirchich, 1983; Forester, 1983; Argyris, 1970; Friedlander, 1977). It is apparent that among the diverse views currently emerging there is frequently great tension. Often the differences become the battleground for fierce debate about theories of truth, the meaning of "facts," political agendas, and personal assertions of will. But, more fruitfully, what can be seen emerging is a heightened sensitivity to and interdisciplinary recognition of the fact that, based on "the structure of knowledge" (Kolb, 1984), there may be multiple ways of knowing, each of them valid in its own realm when judged according to its own set of essential assumptions and purposes. In this sense there are many different ways of studying the same phenomenon, and the insights generated by one approach are, at best, partial and incomplete. According to Jurgen Habermas (1971) different perspectives can be evaluated only in terms of their specified "human interests," which can broadly be differentiated into the realm of practical rationality and the realm of technical rationality. In more straightforward language Morgan (1983) states:

> The selection of method implies some view of the situation being stud-
> ied, for any decision on *how* to study a phenomenon carries with it cer-
> tain assumptions or explicit answers to the question, *"What is being stud-
> ied?"* Just as we select a tennis racquet rather than a golf club to play
> tennis because we have a prior conception as to what the game of tennis
> involves, so too, in relation to the process of social research, we select or
> favor particular kinds of methodology because we have implicit or ex-
> plicit conceptions as to what we are trying to do with our research (p. 19).

Thus, in adopting one mode over another the researcher directly influences what he or she will finally discover and accomplish.

It is the contention of this chapter that advances in generative theorizing will come about for action-research when the discipline decides to expand its universe of exploration, seeks to discover new questions, and rekindles a fresh perception of the extra ordinary in everyday organizational life. In this final section we now describe the assumptions and philosophy of an applied administrative science that seeks to embody these suggestions in a form of organization study we call appreciative inquiry. In distinction to conventional action-research, the knowledge-interest of appreciative inquiry lies not so much in problem solving as in social innovation. Appreciative inquiry refers to a research perspective that is uniquely intended for discovering, understanding, and fostering innovations in social-organizational arrangements and processes.[5] Its purpose is to contribute to the generative-theoretical aims of social science and to use such knowledge to promote egalitarian dialogue leading to social-system effectiveness and integrity. Whatever else it may be, social-system effectiveness is defined here quite specifically as a congruence between social-organizational values (the ever-changing non-native set of values, ideas, or interests that system members hold concerning the question, "How should we organize ourselves?") and everyday social-organizational practices (cf. Torbert, 1983). Thus, appreciative inquiry refers to

---

[5]Following Whyte (1982), a social innovation will be defined as: (1) a new element in organizational structure or interorganizational relations (2) innovative sets of procedures, reward systems, or interaction and activity and the relations of human beings to the natural and social environments (3) a new administrative policy in actual use; (4) new role or sets of roles; and (5) new belief systems of ideologies transforming basic modes of relating.

both a search for knowledge and a theory of intentional collective action which are designed to help evolve the normative vision and will of a group, organization, or society as a whole. It is an inquiry process that affirms our symbolic capacities of imagination and mind as well as our social capacity for conscious choice and cultural evolution. As a holistic form of inquiry, it asks a series of questions not found in either a logical-positivist conception of science or a strictly pragmatic, problem-solving mode of action-research. Yet as shown in Figure3.1, its aims are both scientific (in a sociorationalist sense) and pragmatic (in a social-innovation sense) as well as metaphysical and normative (in the sense of attempting ethically to affirm all that social existence really is and should become). As a way of talking about the framework as it is actually practiced, we shall first examine four guiding principles that have directed our work in the area to date:

PRINCIPLE 1: *Research into the social (innovation) potential of organizational, life should begin with appreciation.* This basic principle assumes that every social system "works" to some degree—that it is not in a complete state of entropy—and that a primary task of research is to discover, describe, and explain those social innovations, however small, which serve to give "life" to the system and activate members' competencies and energies as more fully functioning participants in the formation and transformation of organizational realities. That is, the appreciative approach takes its inspiration from the current state of "what is" and seeks a comprehensive understanding of the factors and forces of organizing (ideological, techno-structural, cultural) that serve to heighten the total potential of an organization in ideal-type human and social terms.

PRINCIPLE 2: *Research into the social potential of organizational life should be applicable.* To be significant in a human sense, an applied science of administration should lead to the generation of theoretical knowledge that can be used, applied, and thereby validated in action. Thus, an applicable inquiry process is neither utopian in the sense of generating knowledge about "no place" (Sargent, 1982) nor should it be confined to academic circles and presented in ways that have little relevance to the everyday language and symbolism of those for whom the findings might be applicable.

PRINCIPLE 3: *Research into the social potential of organizational life should be provocative.* Here it is considered axiomatic that an organization is, in fact, an open-ended indeterminate system capable of (1) becoming more than it is at any given moment, and (2) learning how to actively take part in guiding its own evolution. Hence, appreciative knowledge of what is (in terms of "peak" social innovations in organizing) is suggestive of what *might be* and such knowledge can be used to generate images of realistic developmental opportunities that can be experimented with on a wider scale. In this sense, appreciative inquiry can be both pragmatic and visionary. It becomes provocative to the extent that the abstracted findings of a study take on normative value for members of an organization, and this can happen only through their own critical deliberation and choice ("We feel

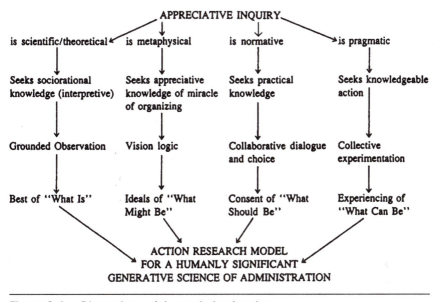

Figure 3.1. Dimensions of Appreciative Inquiry.

that this particular finding is [or not] important for us to envision as an ideal to be striving for in practice on a wider scale"). It is in this way then, that appreciative inquiry allows us to put intuitive, visionary logic on a firm empirical footing and to use systematic research to help the organization's members shape the social world according to their own imaginative and moral purposes.

PRINCIPLE 4: *Research into the social potential of organizational life should be collaborative.* This overarching principle points to the assumed existence of an inseparable relationship between the process of inquiry and its content. A collaborative relationship between the researcher and members of an organization is, therefore, deemed essential on the basis of both epistemological (Susman and Evered, 1978) and practical/ethical grounds (Habermas, 1971; Argyris, 1970). Simply put, a unilateral approach to the study of social innovation (bringing something new into the social world) is a direct negation of the phenomenon itself.

The spirit behind each of these four principles of appreciative inquiry is to be found in one of the most ancient archetypes or metaphorical symbols of hope and inspiration that humankind has ever known—the miracle and mystery of being. Throughout history, people have recognized the intimate relationship between being seized by the unfathomable and the process of appreciative knowing or thought (Marcel, 1963; Quinney, 1982; Jung, 1933; Maslow, 1968; Ghandi, 1958). According to Albert Schweitzer (1969), for example, it is recognition of the ultimate mystery that elevates our perception beyond the world of ordinary objects, igniting the life of the mind and a "reverence for life":

In all respects the universe remains mysterious to man. . . . As soon as man does not take his existence for granted, but beholds it as something unfathomably mysterious, thought begins. This phenomenon has been repeated time and time again in the history of the human race. Ethical affirmation of life is the intellectual act by which man ceases simply to live at random. . . . [Such] thought has a dual task to accomplish: to lead us out of a naive and into a profounder affirmation of life and the universe; and to help us progress from ethical impulses to a rational system of ethics (p. 33).

For those of us breastfed by an industrial giant that stripped the world of its wonder and awe, it feels, to put it bluntly, like an irrelevant, absurd, and even distracting interruption to pause, reflect deeply, and then humbly accept the depth of what we can never know—and to consider the ultimate reality of living for which there are no coordinates or certainties, only questions. Medicine cannot tell me, for example, what it means that my newborn son has life and motion and soul, anymore than the modern physicist can tell me what "nothingness" is, which, they say, makes up over 99 percent of the universe. In fact, if there is anything we have learned from a great physicist of our time is that the promise of certainty is a lie (Hiesenberg, 1958), and by living this lie as scientistic doctrine, we short-circuit the gift of complementarity—the capacity for dialectically opposed modes of knowing, which adds richness, depth, and beauty to our lives (Bohr, 1958). Drugged by the products of our industrial machine we lose sight of and connection with the invisible mystery at the heart of creation, an ultimate power beyond rational understanding.

In the same way that birth of a living, breathing, loving, thinking human being is an inexplicable mystery, so too it can be said in no uncertain terms that *organizing is a miracle* of cooperative human interaction, of which there can never be final explanation. In fact, to the extent that organizations are indeed born and re-created through dialogue, they truly are unknowable as long as such creative dialogue remains. At this point in time there simply are no organizational theories that can account for the life-giving essence of cooperative existence, especially if one delves deeply enough. But, somehow we forget all this. We become lulled by our simplistic diagnostic boxes. The dilemma faced by our discipline in terms of its creative contribution to knowledge is summed up perfectly in the title of a well known article by one of the major advocates of action-research. The title by Marv Wiesbord (1976), has proven prophetic: "Organizational diagnosis: six places to look for trouble, with or without a theory." Content to transfer our conceptual curiosity over to "experts" who finally must know, our creative instincts lie pitifully dormant. Instead of explorers we become mechanics.

This, according to Koch (1981), is the source of "ameaningful" thinking. As Kierkegaard (1954) suggests, it is the essence of a certain dull-minded routine called "philistinism:

Devoid of imagination, as the Philistine always is, he lives in a certain trivial province of experience as to how things go, what is possible. . . . Philistinism tranquilizes itself in the trivial (pp. 174–175).

As we know, a miracle is something that is beyond all possible verification, yet is experienced as real. As a symbol, the word *miracle* represents unification of the sacred and secular into a realm of totality that is at once terrifying and beautiful, inspiring and threatening. Quinney (1982) has suggested with respect to the rejuvenation of social theory, that such a unified viewpoint is altogether necessary, that it can have a powerful impact on the discipline precisely because in a world that is at once sacred and secular there is no place, knowledge, or phenomenon that is without mystery. The "miracle" then is pragmatic in its effect when sincerely apprehended by a mind that has chosen not to become "tranquilized in the trivial." In this sense, the metaphor "life is a miracle" is not so much an idea as it is—or can be—a central feature of experience enveloping (1) our perceptual consciousness; (2) our way of relation to others, the world, and our own research; and (3) our way of knowing. Each of these points can be highlighted by a diverse literature.

In terms of the first, scholars have suggested that the power of what we call the miracle lies in its capacity to advance one's perceptual capacity what Maslow (1968) has called a B-cognition or a growth-vs-deficiency orientation, or what Kolb (1984) has termed integrative consciousness. Kolb writes:

> The transcendental quality of integrative consciousness is precisely that, a "climbing out of". . . . This state of consciousness is not reserved for the monastery, but it is a necessary ingredient for creativity in any field. Albert Einstein once said, "The most beautiful and profound emotion one can feel is a sense of the mystical. . . . It is the dower of all true science" (p.158).

Second, as Gabriel Marcel (1963) explained in his William James lectures at Harvard on *The Mystery of Being*, the central conviction of life as a mystery creates for us a distinctly different relationship to the world than the conviction of life as a problem to be solved:

> A problem is something met which bars my passage. It is before me in its entirety. A mystery on the other hand is something I find *myself* caught up in, and whose essence is therefore not before me in its entirety. It is though in this province the distinction between "in me" and "before me" loses its meaning (p. 80).

Berman's (1981) recent analysis comes to a similar conclusion. The re-enchantment of the world gives rise to a "participatory consciousness" where there is a sense of personal stake, ownership, and partnership with the universe:

> The view of nature which predominated the West down to the eve of the Scientific Revolution was that of an enchanted world. Rocks, trees, rivers, and clouds were all seen as wondrous, alive, and human beings felt at home in this environment. The cosmos, in short, was a place of *belonging*. A member of this cosmos was not an alienated observer of it but a

direct participant in its drama. His personal destiny was bound up with its destiny, and this relationship gave meaning to his life.

Third, as so many artists and poets have shown, there is a relationship between what the Greeks called *thaumazein*—an experience which lies on the borderline between wonderment and admiration—and a type of intuitive apprehension or knowing that we call appreciative. For Keats, the purpose of his work was:

> to accept things as I saw them, to enjoy the beauty I perceived for its own sake, without regard to ultimate truth or falsity, and to make a description of it the end and purpose of my appreciations.

Similarly for Shelley:

> Poetry thus makes immortal all that is best and most beautiful in the world . . . it exalts the beauty of that which is most beautiful . . . it strips the veil of familiarity from the world, and lays bare the naked and sleeping beauty, which is in the spirit of its forms.

And in strikingly similar words, learning theorist David Kolb (1984) analyzes the structure of the knowing mind and reports:

> Finally, appreciation is a process of affirmation. Unlike criticism, which is based on skepticism and doubt (compare Polanyi, 1968, pp. 269ff.), appreciation is based on belief, trust, and conviction. And from this affirmative embrace flows a deeper fullness and richness of experience. This act of affirmation forms the foundation from which vital comprehension can develop. . . . Appreciative apprehension and critical comprehension are thus fundamentally different processes of knowing. Appreciation of immediate experience is an act of attention, valuing, and affirmation, whereas critical comprehension of symbols is based on objectivity (which involves a priori controls of attention, as in double-blind controlled experiments), dispassionate analysis, and skepticism (pp. 104–105).

We have cited these various thinkers in detail for several reasons: first, to underscore the fact that the powerful images of problem and miracle (in)form qualitatively distinct modes of inquiry which then shape our awareness, relations, and knowledge; and second, to highlight the conviction that the renewal of generative theory requires that we enter into the realm of the metaphysical. The chief characteristic of the modern mind has been the banishment of mystery from the world, and along with it an ethical affirmation of life that has served history as a leading source of values, hope, and normative bonding among people. In historical terms, we have steadily forgotten how to dream.

In contrast to a type of research that is lived without a sense of mystery, the appreciative mode awakens the desire to create and discover new social possibilities that can enrich our existence and give it meaning. In this sense, appreciative inquiry seeks an imaginative and fresh perception of organizations as "ordinary magic," as if seen for the first time—or perhaps the last time (Hayward, 1984). The appreciative mode, in exploration of ordinary magic, is an inquiry process that takes nothing for granted, searching to apprehend the basis of organizational life and working to articulate those possibilities giving witness to a better existence.

The metaphysical dimension of appreciative inquiry is important not so much as a way of finding answers but is important insofar as it heightens the living experience of awe and wonder which leads us to the wellspring of new questions—much like a wide-eyed explorer without final destination. Only by raising innovative questions will innovations in theory and practice be found. As far as action-research is concerned, this appears to have been the source of Lewin's original and catalytic genius. We too can re-awaken this spirit. Because the questions we ask largely determine what we find, we should place a premium on that which informs our curiosity and thought. The metaphysical question of what makes social existence possible will never go away. The generative-theoretical question of compelling new possibilities will never go away. The normative question of what kind of social-organizational order is best, most dignified, and just, will never go away, nor will the pragmatic question of how to move closer to the ideal.

In its pragmatic form appreciative inquiry represents a data-based theory building methodology for evolving and putting into practice the collective will of a group or organization. It has one and only one aim—to provide a generative theoretical springboard for normative dialogue that is conducive to self-directed experimentation in social innovation. It must be noted, however, that the conceptual world which appreciative inquiry creates remains—despite its empirical content—an illusion. This is important to recognize because it is precisely because of its visionary content, placed in juxtaposition to grounded examples of the extraordinary, that appreciative inquiry opens the status quo to possible transformations in collective action. It appreciates the best of "what is" to ignite intuition of the possible and then firmly unites the two logically, caringly, and passionately into a theoretical hypothesis of an envisioned future. By raising ever new questions of an appreciative, applicable, and provocative nature, the researcher collaborates in the scientific construction of his or her world.[6]

Conclusion

What we have tried to do with this chapter is present conceptual refiguration of action-research; to present a proposal arguing for an enriched multidimensional

---

[6]For an example of the type of theory generated through appreciative inquiry, see "The Emergence of the Egalitarian Organization" (Srivastva and Cooperrider, 1986).

view of action-research which seeks to be both theoretically generative and progressive in a broad human sense. In short, the argument is a simple one stating that there is a need to re-awaken the imaginative spirit of action-research and that to do this we need a fundamentally different perspective toward our organizational world, one that admits to its uncertainties, ambiguities, mysteries, and unexplicable, miraculous nature. But now we must admit, with a certain sense of limited capabiiity and failure, that the viewpoint articulated here is simply not possible to define and is very difficult to speak of in technological, step-by-step terms. From the perspective of rational thought, the miraculous is impossible. From that of problem solving it is nonsense. And from that of empirical science, it is categorically denied (Reeves, 1984). Just as we cannot prove the proposition that organizing is a problem to be solved, so, too, we cannot prove in any rational, analytical, or empirical way that organizing is a miracle to be embraced. Each stance represents a commitment—a core conviction so to speak—which is given to each of us as a choice. We do, however, think that through discipline and training the appreciative eye can be developed to see the ordinary magic, beauty, and real possibility in organizational life; but we are not sure we can so easily transform our central convictions.

In sum, the position we have been developing here is that for action-research to reach its potential as a vehicle for social innovation, it needs to begin advancing theoretical knowledge of consequence—that good theory may be one of the most powerful means human beings have for producing change in a post-industrial world; that the discipline's steadfast commitment to a problem-solving view of the world is a primary restraint on its imagination, passion, and positive contribution; that appreciative inquiry represents a viable complement to conventional forms of action- research, one uniquely suited for social innovation instead of problem solving; and that through our assumptions and choice of method we largely create the world we later discover.

References

Argyris, C. (1973). Action science and intervention. *The Journal of Applied Behavioral Science,* 19, 115–140.

Argyris, C. (1970). *Intervention theory and methods.* Reading, MA: Addison-Wesley.

Argyris, C. and Schon, D. (1978). *Organizational learning: A theory of action perspective.* Reading. MA: Addison-Wesley.

Bartunek, J. (1983). How organization development can develop organizational theory. *Group and Organizational Studies.* 8, 303–318.

Bartunek, J. (1984). Changing interpretive schemes and organizational restructuring: The example of a religious order. *Administrative Science Quarterly,* 27, 355–372.

Bell, D. (1973). *The coming of the Post-Industrial society*. New York: Basic Books.

Beyer, J. (1981). Ideologies, values and decision making in organizations. In P. C. Nystrom and W. H. Starbuck (Eds.), *Handbook of organizational design, Vol.2*. Oxford University Press.

Beyer, J. and Trice, H. (1982). Utilization process: Conceptual framework and synthesis of findings. *Administrative Science Quarterly*, 22, 591–622.

Blake. R. and Mouton. J. (1976). *Consultation*. Reading, MA: Addison Wesley.

Bohr, N. (1958). *Atomic theory and human knowledge*. New York: John Wiley.

Bradford, L. P., Gibb, J. R., and Benne, K. (1964). *T-group theory and laboratory method*. New York: John Wiley.

Braverman, H. (1974). *Labor and monopoly capital*. New York: Monthly Review Press.

Brimm, M. (1972). When is change not a change? *Journal of Applied Behavioral Science*, 1, 102–107.

Brown, R. H. (1978). *Leadership*. New York: Harper and Row.

Chiles, C. (1983). Comments on "design guidelines for social problem solving interventions." *Journal of Applied Behavioral Science* 19, 189–191.

Clegg, S. and Dunkerley. D. (1980). *Organization, class, and control*. Boston: Routledge and Kegan Paul.

Cohen, A. R., Fink, S. L., Gadon, H., and Willits, R. D. (1984). *Effective behavior in organizations*. Homewood, IL: Irwin.

Cooperrider, D. (I 986). *Appreciative Inquiry: Toward a methodology for understanding and enhancing organizational innovation*. Unpublished Ph.D. dissertation, Case Western Reserve University, Cleveland, OH.

Deal, T. E. and Kennedy, A. A. (1982). *Corporate cultures*. Reading, Mass.: Addison-Wesley.

Dubin, R. (1978). *Theory Building*. New York: The Free Press.

Ellwood, C. (1938). *A history of social philosophy*. New York: Prentice-Hall.

Forester, John (1983). Critical theory and organizational analysis. In G. Morgan (Ed.). *Beyond methods* Beverly Hills, CA: Sage Publications.

French, W. L. (1969). Organization development objectives, assumptions, and strategies. *Management Review*, 12(2), 23–34.

French, W. L. and Bell, C. H. (1978). *Organization development*. New Jersey: Prentice-Hall.

Friedlander, F. (1984). Producing useful knowledge for organizations. *Administrative Science Quarterly*, 29, 646–648.

Friedlander, F. (1977). Alternative methods of inquiry. Presented at APA Convention. San Francisco, Ca.

Friedlander, F. and Brown, L. D. (1974). Organization development, *Annual Review of Psychology*, 25, 313–341.

Frohman, M., Sashkin, M., and Kavanaugh, M. (1976). Action-research as applied to organization development. *Organization and Administrative Sciences*, 1, 129–161.

Geertz, C. (1980). Blurred genres: The refiguration of social thought. *American Scholar*, 49, 165–179.

Gergen, K. (1982). *Toward transformation in social knowledge.* New York: Springer-Verlag.

Gergen, K. (1978). Toward generative theory. *Journal of Personality and Social Psychology*, 36, 1344–1360.

Ghandi, M. (1958). *All men are brothers.* New York: Columbia University Press.

Gorz, A. (1973). Workers' control is more than just that. In Hunnius, Garson. and Case (Eds.), *Workers control.* New York: Vintage Books.

Gould, S. J. (1981). *The mismeasure of man.* New York: Norton and Company.

Gouldner, A. (1970). *The coming crisis of Western sociology.* New York: Basic Books.

Habermas, J. (1971). *Knowledge and human interests.* Boston: Beacon Press.

Haley, J. *Uncommon therapy.* New York: W. W. Norton, 1973.

Hare, P. H. (1976). *Handbook of small group research.* New York: The Free Press.

Harrison, R. (1982). *Leadership and strategy for a new age: Lessons from "conscious evolution."* Menlo Park, CA: Values and Lifestyles Program.

Hausser, D., Pecorelia, P., and Wissler, A. (1977). *Survey-guided development 11.* LaJolla, Calif.: University Associates.

Hayward, J. (1984). *Perceiving ordinary magic.* Gouldner: New Science Library.

Hiesenberg, W. (I 958). *Physics and philosophy: The revolution in modern science.* London: Allen and Urwig.

Henshel, R. (1975). Effects of disciplinary prestige on predictive accuracy. *Futures*, 7, 92–106.

Hofstede, G. (1980). *Culture's consequences.* Beverly Hills, CA: Sage.

Jung, C. (1933). *Modern man in search of a soul.* New York: Harcourt, Brace and Company.

Keeley, M. (1980). Organizational analogy: Comparison of orgasmic and social contract models, *Administrative Science Quarterly*, 25, 337–362.

Kepner, C. and Trego, B. (1973). *Executive problem analysis and decision making.* Princeton, NJ.

Kierkegaard, S. (1954). *The sickness unto death.* New York: Anchor Books. Translated by Walter Lowrie.

Kilmann, R. (1979). Problem management: A behavioral science approach. In G. Zaltman (Ed.). *Management principles for non-profit agencies and organizations.* New York: American Management Association.

Koch, S. (1981). The nature and limits of psychological knowledge. *American Psychologist, 36,* 257–269.

Kolb, D. A. (1984). *Experiential learning.* Englewood Cliffs, NJ: Prentice-Hall.

Kolb, D. A. (1983). Problem management: Learning from experience. In S. Srivastva (Ed.), *The executive mind.* San Francisco: Jossey-Bass.

Levinson, H. (1972) The clinical psychologist as organizational diagnostician. *Professional Psychology, 10,* 485–502.

Levinson, H. (1972). *Organizational diagnosis.* Cambridge, MA: Harvard University Press.

Lewin, K. (1948). Action research and minority problems. In G. W. Lewin (Ed.), *Resolving social conflicts.* New York: Harper and Row.

Lewin, K. (1951). *Field theory in social science.* New York: Harper and Row.

Lukes, S. (1974). *Power: A radical view.* London: Macmillan.

Mannheim, K. (1936). *Ideology and utopia.* New York: Harcourt, Brace and World.

Marcel, G. (1963). *The existential background of human dignity.* Cambridge: Harvard University Press.

Margulies, N. and Raia, A. P. (1972). *Organization development: Values, process and technology.* New York: McGraw Hill.

Marrow, A. (1968). *The practical theorist.* New York: Basic Books.

Maslow, A. (1968). *Toward a psychology of being.* New York: Van Nostrand Reinhold Co.

McHugh, P. (1970). On the failure of positivism. In J. Douglas (Ed.), *Understanding everyday life.* Chicago: Aldine.

Mitroff, I. (1980). Reality as a scientific strategy: Revising our concepts of science. *Academy of Management Review, 5,* 513–515.

Mitroff, I. and Kilmann, R. (1978). *Methodological approaches to social sciences.* San Francisco: Jossey-Bass.

Morgan, G. (1983). *Beyond method.* Beverly Hills: Sage Publications.

Morgan, G. (1980). Paradigms, metaphors, and puzzle solving in organization theory. *Administrative Science Quarterly, 24,* 605–622.

Ortony, A. (Ed.) (1979). *Metaphor and thought.* Cambridge: Cambridge University Press.

Ouchi, W. G. and Johnson, J. B. (1978). Types of organizational control and their relationship to emotional well-being. *Administrative Science Quarterly, 23,* 293–317.

Pasmore, W., Cooperrider, D., Kaplan, M. and Morris, B. (1983). Introducing managers to performance development. In *The ecology of work,*. Proceedings of the Sixth NTL Ecology of Work Conference, Cleveland, Ohio.

Pasmore, W. and Friedlander, F. (1982). An action-research program for increasing employee involvement in problem solving. *Administrative Science Quarterly*, 27, 343–362.

Pepper, S. C. (1942). *World hypothesis*. Berkeley, CA: University of California Press.

Peters, M. and Robinson, V. (1984). The origins and status of action research. *Journal of Applied Behavioral Science*, 20, 113–124.

Quinney, R. (1982). *Social existence: Metaphysics, Marxism, and the social sciences*. Beverly Hills, CA: Sage Publications.

Rappaport, R. W. (1970). Three dilemmas of action-research. *Human Relations*, 23, 499–513.

Reeves, G. (1984). The idea of mystery in the philosophy of Gabriel Marcel. In J. Schlipp, and L. Hahn, (Eds.), *The philosophy of Gabriel Marcel*. LaSalle, IL: Open Court.

Sargent, L. T. (1982). Authority and utopia: Utopianisms in political thought. *Polity*, 4, 565–584.

Sathe, V. J. (1983). Implications of corporate culture. *Organizational Dynamics*, Autumn, 5–23.

Schein, E. (1983). The role of the founder in creating organizational culture. *Organizational Dynamics*, Summer, 12–28.

Schweitzer, A. (1969). *The teaching of reverence for life*. New York: Holt, Rinehart and Winston.

Small, A. (1905). *General sociology: An exposition of the main development in sociological theory from Spencer to Ratzenhofer*. Chicago: University of Chicago Press.

Smirchich, L. (1983). Studying organizations as cultures. In G. Morgan (Ed.), *Beyond method*. Beverly Hills, CA: Sage Publications.

Sproull, L. S. (1981). Beliefs in organizations. In P. C. Nystrom and W. H. Starbuck (Eds.), *Handbook of organizational design, Vol. 2*. New York: Oxford University Press.

Srivastva, S. (1985). *Executive power*. San Francisco: Jossey-Bass Publishers.

Srivastva, S. (1983). *The executive mind*. San Francisco: Jossey-Bass Publishers.

Srivastva, S. and Cooperrider, D. (1986). The emergence of the egalitarian organization. *Human Relations*, London: Tavistock.

Srivastva, S., Obert, S. and Neilsen, E. (1977). Organizational analysis through group process: A theoretical perspective for organization development. In C. Cooper (Ed.) *Organization development in the U.K. and U.S.A.* New York: The Macmillan Press.

Staw, B. (1984). Organizational behavior: A review and reformulation of the field's outcome variables. *Annual Review of Psychology*, 35, 626–666.

Susman, G. and Evered, R. (1978). An assessment of the scientific merits of action-research. *Administrative Science Quarterly*, 23, 582–603.

Thelen, H. (1954). *Dynamics of groups at work*. Chicago University of Chicago Press.

Torbert, W. (1983). Initiating collaborative inquiry. In G. Morgan (Ed.). *Beyond method*. Beverly Hills, CA: Sage Publications.

Van Maanen, J., Dabbs, J. M., and Faulkner, R. R. (I 982). *Varieties of qualitative research*. Beverly Hills, Calif.: Sage Publications.

Watzlawick, P., Weakland, J., and Fish, R. (1974). *Change: Principles of problem formation and problem resolution*. New York: Horton.

Weick, K. E. (1983). Managerial thought in the context of action. In S. Srivastva (Ed.), *The executive mind*. San Francisco: Jossey-Bass.

Wiesbord, M. (1976). Organization diagnosis: Six places to look for trouble with or without a theory. *Group and Organization Studies*, 1, 430–447.

Weiss, C. H. and Bucuvalas, M. (1980). The challenge of social research to decision making. In C. H. Weiss (Ed.), *Using social research in public policy making*. Lexington, MA: Lexington Books.

Whitehead, A. N. (1929). *The function of reason*. Boston: Beacon Press.

Whyte, W. F. (1982). Social inventions for solving human problems. *American Sociological Review*, 47, 1–13.

Chapter 4

FIVE THEORIES OF CHANGE EMBEDDED IN APPRECIATIVE INQUIRY

Gervase R. Bushe Ph.D.
Simon Fraser University

In this paper I will describe five different ways of thinking about how an appreciative inquiry can create change in social systems. Appreciative inquiry is a form of action research that attempts to create new theories/ideas/images that aid in the developmental change of a system (Cooperrider and Srivastva, 1987). The key data collection innovation of appreciative inquiry is the collection of people's stories of something at it's best. If we are interested in team development, we collect stories of people's best team experiences. If we are interested in the development of an organization we ask about their peak experience in that organization. If enhanced leadership is our goal, we collect stories of leadership at its best. These stories are collectively discussed in order to create new, generative ideas or images that aid in developmental change of the collectivity discussing them.

I am concerned that as appreciative inquiry becomes "fashionable" two undesirable things are happening. One is that any inquiry that focuses on the "positive" in some way gets called appreciative inquiry (AI). I have already come across a consulting firm that asked people to rate how good the organization was on a number of items on a 5-point scale and called this appreciative inquiry. The result will be that the unique power of this idea gets corrupted and lost and appreciative inquiry becomes just another discarded innovation on the junk heap of "failed" management effectiveness strategies, like QWL, TQM, BPR, etc. Anyone involved in any of these processes knows they all contained excellent ideas and useful techniques but "failed" because of consultants calling whatever they did by the currently fashionable acronym who sold these to managers who didn't know the difference.

A second concern is that some practitioners, especially graduate students, can develop a zealous attention to "appreciation" without any theoretical rhyme or

Appeared in R. Engdahl (ed.) *Proceedings of the 18th World Organization Development Congress.* Wilmington, NC: Cameron School of Business, UNCW, pp. 1.01–1.09.

reason to their practice. Promoting appreciation where there has been little can, of itself, generate a wave of energy and enthusiasm but that will go away just as quickly as the next challenge or tragedy to a social system rears its head.

In this paper I want to appreciate appreciative inquiry as, itself, a generative metaphor that has led me to new ideas and images of how to change social systems. I do this also to caution against the indiscriminant application of appreciative inquiry, calling for a disciplined and reasoned approach to its use. I believe that AI can be very helpful in the right time and the right place. We need, however, to develop a model of where and when that is. Some people seem to believe that use of appreciative inquiry is more an ideological than practical question, and that its use will always have a positive effect. I strongly question that. From a purely practical standpoint I think researchers and consultants will find that systems full of deeply held and unexpressed resentments will not tolerate an appreciative inquiry until there has been some expression and forgiving of those resentments. From a theoretical perspective there is the question of what happens to negative images and affect if they are "repressed" from collective discussion by a zealous focus on the "positive". Experience from psychoanalysis, sociology and medicine suggest repression usually results in some nasty side effects.

Secondly, we need to embrace different ways of inquiring appreciatively but to do so, we need theory that tells us what ways will work—how and why. In this paper, I offer a way to begin thinking about both questions, especially the latter. I will first review two key theories of change contained in the writings of Cooperrider: the social construction of reality and the "heliotropic hypothesis". Then I will present three ideas that I have stumbled across in my use of AI: the organization's "inner dialogue", resolving paradoxical dilemmas, and appreciative process. Each directs us to different ways of thinking about and implementing an appreciative inquiry when our purpose is developmental change.

Socially Constructing Reality

Those familiar with AI know that the dominant theoretical rational for AI is post modernist European philosophy (for an excellent summary related to this theory of change see Barrett, Thomas and Hocevar, 1995). From this point of view there is nothing inherently real or true about any social form. All social organization is an arbitrary, social construction. Our ability to create new and better organizations is limited only by our imagination and collective will. Furthermore, language and words are the basic building blocks of social reality. Rather than seeing language as a passive purveyor of meaning between people, post modernists see language as an active agent in the creation of meaning. As we talk to each other, we are constructing the world we see and think about, and as we change how we talk we are changing that world. From this perspective, theory, especially theory that is encoded in popular words or images, is a powerful force in shaping social organization because we "see what we believe". Creating new and better theories/ideas/ images is, therefore, a powerful way of changing organizations. Appreciative inquiry seeks these new images in and among people's best intentions and noblest aspirations, attempting a collective envisioning of what the group could be at its very best.

From the practical standpoint the problem is how do we get people to dream alternative futures together, to envision new patterns of social organization that are better than what they currently have or may ever have individually experienced? My own experience as an OD consultant is that it is very difficult to get a group of people who work together to talk about things they might hope for but have never seen. This is especially true in business organizations which tend to have a culture that values "hard headedness" and devalues "fanciful thinking". It is scary to verbalize those basic human desires for community, love, fealty, making a contribution in an organization where that is not the norm. To talk about "how things could be" when no one has ever actually seen them that way is to open oneself up to ridicule and embarrassment. Indeed, if there is a lot of repressed yearning in the system, anyone who names what is yearned for is sure to be ridiculed and shamed as a defense against experiencing that yearning. About the best one can expect is that people will talk about things they have experienced elsewhere, or read about, since they can defend themselves against ridicule by pointing to places where those noble aspirations and intentions are being lived.

I have found that an appreciative inquiry, where people listen to each other's stories about micro moments in organizational life where the best in us is touched, can create a unique climate for collective dreaming where the forces of ridicule and repression are momentarily suspended. There is something about telling one's story of "peak" organizational experiences, and listening to others, that can make a group ready to be open about deeply held desires and yearnings. I am sure that there are other factors, beside the AI technique, that are necessary to make this happen (e.g., quality of leadership) but the technique is astounding in the speed with which it can create such a climate in the right place at the right time. Into this climate, then, a different kind of conversation can take place and from that, a different social reality can evolve.

One more point about the social construction of reality. From this point of view means create ends and this is especially true about our means of inquiry. How we go about studying something will impact what we "see" and in some cases, will even create what we then "discover". At the core of appreciative inquiry is "inquiring with the heart". What that means is difficult to describe on paper, a lot easier to teach in practice. For myself it means that before I ask a question or make a statement I locate my consciousness in my heart region and notice how my thoughts and questions are shaped and let those be what I say. In my personal and professional life this has had a consistent, profound, healing effect on my interactions with others. I think it was Jung who said that inquiry with the head only can never heal as the head is concerned with analysis which only serves to cut things up and examine them in parts. The heart, however, is concerned with bringing things together and wholeness and it is from here that inquiry can be healing. Can analytical forms of action research, which cut up an organization or group for analysis, attending to all the "problems" and "deficiencies" (based on the theory of the researcher/consultant) ever hope to really heal a system; to make old wounds go away and add health and vitality to the relationships in that system? I no longer think so. Can appreciative inquiry? If it is carried out with an open heart, I think it can.

More could be said about the social construction of reality theory of change embedded in AI but let me turn to implications of this theory for OD practice. First, it means that the way the inquiry is carried out is very important. Techniques which help to open the hearts of those engaged in the inquiry should aid it. For example, Cooperrider (1996) has talked about the heightened quality of interview data that come from having children interview adults and I think some of this impact can be explained by the heart opening potential of that. Secondly, this means that the key to creating change in the organization is creating new theories/ideas/images that enter the everyday language of system members. Therefore, both the process of creative ideation and the process of importation of that creativity into popular usage are critical for change. Once we collect the stories, then what? From this perspective the hard work of change begins. I do not think nearly enough about these two processes has been written about.

The Heliotropic Hypothesis

In an intriguing paper Cooperrider (1990) presented his "heliotropic hypothesis" which is that social systems evolve toward the most positive images they hold of themselves. These images are not necessarily conscious in that they may not be discussible by the members of that social system, but nevertheless he argues that such images exist and the more they "affirm" the group the more firmly they hold the group to a pattern of being prescribed by the theory/idea/image the group has of itself at its very best. When these images are out of step with the requirements the social system faces the group will experience itself as dysfunctional and rational attempts to fix itself will not work until the underlying "affirmative image" of the group is changed. Appreciative inquiry, therefore, attempts to create a new and better affirmative image for the social system, one better aligned with the organization's critical contingencies.

Surprisingly, there have been no published attempts to assess the validity of this hypothesis and I will not attempt to argue for or against it here. But it is an important theory of change embedded in AI and as such, has important implications for OD practice. From this point of view the quality of the output of the AI, the affirming image, is all important for its change potential.

How this affirming image is constructed needs to be thought about carefully. Does it have to be a managed process or can we trust that the process of AI will itself unfreeze the system so that a better affirmative image will naturally form? If managed, who needs to be involved in generating the image? How do we know when we have a good enough new image? How can we know which images will "stick" while others fall quickly into disuse? These are the sorts of questions that the AI practitioner, operating under this theory of change, ought to have answers to.

The Organization's Inner Dialogue

Now we turn to 3 theories of change that have been evoked for me by AI. The first I call changing the organization's inner dialogue and it comes from the observation that if you think of organizations using the metaphor of human consciousness, with many different voices saying things within one's mind, there are layers of awareness in the organization, just as there are in the human mind, of what is being said. In the human mind we have the most conscious layer, which tends to be a rational layer, of things we are aware we are saying to ourselves. The organizational analog for this are the things that are said between people in "official" meetings of the organization—things that are said out loud so that everyone present can hear. These are events like committee meetings, departmental meetings, workshops and offsite retreats, strategic planning sessions and the like. This I call the conscious, rational part of the organizational mind. What is said here is "discussible" by all employees who are in attendance and in that sense the organization as an entity is consciously aware of it.

Between and around events, however, are things people talk about in smaller groups or in confidential conversations. Often these entail interpretations and judgements about the events that these people would not verbalize in an "official forum of organizational business", like a meeting. As such, the organization as an entity is only partially aware and to the extent that these perceptions, interpretations and judgements are not discussible in any official forum of organizational business, they are out of awareness. They are like the "inner dialogue" of the human mind that operates at a subconscious level. In individuals these are the day dreams that we quickly forget or may not even notice that we are having, the patterns of thinking and judgement that operate just out of awareness but powerfully effect our conscious, "rational" thoughts. Psychologist call these scripts or schemas and some therapies, like neuro-linguistic programming and rational-emotive therapy, operate mainly at this level of consciousness.

I want to suggest 3 things that can form the basis of using AI as a change strategy:

1. Organizations have an inner dialogue made up of the things people say to each other in small confidential groups that are undiscussible in official forums of organizational business.

2. This inner dialogue is a powerful stabilizing force in social systems that accounts for the failure to follow through on rationally arrived at decisions. It is here where people's real thoughts and feelings about what is discussed in official forums are revealed and communicated.

3. This inner dialogue is mainly carried through the stories people tell themselves and each other to justify their interpretation of events and decisions.The change theory is: If you change the stories you change the inner dialogue. Nothing the "rational mind" decides it wants will actually happen if the "inner dialogue" is resistant to it.

When people talk in the hallways and over coffee it is often stories of past events that they use to justify the interpretations and judgements of current events. These stories get passed on and embellished with time and their historical veracity is irrelevant to the impact they have on how people make sense of organizational events. From this point of view AI can change an organization if it changes the stories that circulate in the organization's inner dialogue. Let me give an example.

One organization I work with has a strong and deep (but changing) inner dialogue about the lack of "real leadership" in the organization. Of course this is not discussed in official forums. Just the opposite. Those in authority are praised and accolades given for their leadership prowess. But in the inner dialogue, just the opposite happens. Authorities are described as gutless wonders who have no integrity, blow with whatever wind is strongest and can only be relied on to act politically in their best interest. Little wonder then, that almost none of the "soft" organizational strategies agreed upon during a major strategic planning exercise had been implemented three years later. In an appreciative inquiry into leadership, people in this organization interviewed their executives about the greatest acts of leadership they had seen in the organization as well as what they would considered their own peak leadership experiences.

The interviewees were stunned by the stories their leaders told – almost always stories about great personal integrity and courage where someone took the "right" stand even though it was politically unpopular or highly risky. Stories about events from the past that involved these leaders were radically changed as new appreciations about the motives and meanings behind their actions evolved. As these stories changed, greatly different interpretations of the current actions of leaders began to emerge in the parts of the organization that had been involved in the appreciative inquiry. Leaders were now being supported by the inner dialogue where in the past they were resisted, and some really different organizational strategies were implemented in the "soft" side of the business.

From this theoretical point of view, the key to OD practice is the stories and the way in which these are communicated to others in the organization. Those most impacted by the new stories are those who get to hear them, first hand, from those who tell them. Finding ways to help make that happen are clearly important. The use of interview protocols where people simply capture a few key images or "quoatable quotes" does not make sense from the inner dialogue view of change. Rather, what is required are richly woven short stories, written in the first person. The interviewer's job is not to simply transcribe what the interviewee said, like a journalist, but to use the craft of the literary writer to make a document full of vignettes that will invite and delight those who read them. As well, it is critical that the data not be anonymous, as in typical action research feedback reports, but directly attributed to whomever the story came from. Following on from the logic of the inner dialogue view, it might even be better to skip the writing all together and help people really hear each other's stories. Some possibilities are using edited videotapes of people telling their stories and bringing large numbers of people together where individuals take turns at a microphone telling their stories. From the inner dialogue view of change, what is critical to creating change is not the generation of new images/theories but the telling and retelling of stories that create new and more efficacious meanings that support organizational evolution.

Resolving Paradoxical Dilemmas

Another way in which I have seen AI lead to developmental change is in offering images that resolve paradoxical dilemmas for groups (Bushe 1998). All groups, especially those in organizations, face paradoxical requirements where they are asked to simultaneously do mutually incompatible things. In one study I was able, in about 2 hours, to help project managers in an MIS organization list 28 paradoxical requirements they experience in their organizational life. These are things like organizational injunctions to "staff up projects to ensure the best people are doing the work" and "staff up projects to ensure developmental opportunities for staff"; "always meet deadlines" and "never give customers defective work"; and so on. For the most part managers find ways to work around such paradoxical dilemmas and they get the work done in spite of them. But as Smith and Berg (1987) point out, groups can become stuck in a paradox where the nature of the paradoxical dilemma facing the group is unconscious or undiscussible. In such a case, a group will look and feel "stuck", constantly repeating failing patterns, finding itself with the same issues over and over that never seem to get resolved, all the while losing energy and motivation to continue operating as a group.

An AI with a team can evoke stories and images that aid the team in moving through the paradox it is stuck in. Let me give an example. An "empowered work team" of analysts was stuck over what Smith and Berg (1987) call the paradox of authority. The issue was that people were not willing to authorize others to act on the group's behalf but at the same time some wanted authority to act on the group's behalf in dealing with others in and outside the organization. The group had not discussed the problem this way. Rather, a sense was developing that "this empowered work team stuff just doesn't work" as the group became paralyzed by the inability of members to take action without having to convene a meeting of the group to get sanction. This was experienced by all as very frustrating.

As a team building intervention each member described to the whole team the best team he or she had ever been a member of (Bushe and Coetzer, 1995). One member told the story of working on a charity fund-raising drive with people who had been loaned, full time for 3 months, from their respective companies. Each person had pursued independent, creative initiatives in raising funds while at the same time fully supporting the initiatives of others. There was a program of activities to be done that had built up over the years and was fully documented for them. Over and above that, individuals pursued the group's core mission however they thought best.

The team reacted a little differently to this story than it had to others. Members were quieter and more withdrawn. It then dawned on me that this story offered a way out of the authority paradox (which, at the time, was one of a number of alternative explanations I had for their stuckness). I asked how the group was able to let others have free reign without fearing someone, due to inexperience or eagerness, would get them into a bind? He said "we decided we had no way of knowing if we could trust each other so we figured we had more to lose by not trusting than by trusting". At this another member piped in "so trust costs less".

The image of "trust costs less" blended this groups bottom-line business identity with the essential element for the resolution of the paradox. Because it was such a novel combination of those words, it opened up new gateways to emotional issues in this group. They were able to explore what the price of distrust was. Some were angry about how much other's distrust had cost them. People were able to admit that they hadn't felt trusted, hadn't been trusting others and that they believed trust would cost less. From there it was easy to decide on the "core program" and general objectives for individual initiatives.

It is probably true that all sizes of social systems can become stuck in an undiscussible paradoxical dilemma. One way out, and perhaps the only way out, is the development of new images that jostle conventional thinking and offer new ways of acting. Take for example the impact the image "sustainable development" had on what, to that point, seemed the intractable opposition of the business community and environmentalists. From this point of view, then, the change potential of AI is in it's capacity to offer such images. The implications for OD practice lead to very different implementation scenarios. For instance, we would want to have some kind of diagnosis, or set of hypothesis, about the kinds of paradoxical dilemmas facing the system before we begin the inquiry so that we can be sensitive to possible ways out presented in the stories. We would be most concerned with 'word smithing", the creation of an image that captures people's energy and offers the solution to the dilemma they are caught in. The conduct of an AI from this perspective requires a much greater consultant, manager, or researcher-driven focus than one from any of the other change perspectives where there is a greater emphasis on fostering openness to what emerges from the collective inquiry.

Appreciative Process

While the first four theories I have described relate to AI as an action research process, "appreciative process" (Bushe and Pitman, 1991) is more a change agent technique. I mention it here because the theory of appreciation and its impact on organizations is clearly an important justification for appreciative inquiry (Cooperrider, 1991; Barrett, 1995) and because it has had the greatest personal impact on my consulting practice.

Appreciative process theorizes that you can create change by paying attention to what you want more of rather than paying attention to problems. Cooperrider's (1991) review of the research on sports psychology, the Pygmalion effect and brain functioning supported the ancient wisdom that you get more of whatever you pay attention to. As a change technique, appreciative process involves tracking and fanning. Tracking is a state of mind where one is constantly looking for what one wants more of. It begins with the assumption that whatever one wants more of already exists, even if in small amounts. Fanning is any action that amplifies, encourages, and helps you to get more of whatever you are looking for.

Recently I had a group of Executive-MBA students use appreciative process to create a change in any social system they chose. We were all blown away by the results. For example, one manager's "problem person" became his star employee when he looked for examples of her being a star. Another manager's conflicted and competitive team became a cohesive, cooperative unit when he looked for examples of cohesion and cooperation. Those using it with spouses or children felt that major positive transformations had occurred in their families.

It would be a mistake to say these are only examples of behavioral modification—of reinforcing desired behaviors. While there is some of this, the most critical part of appreciative process required for it to work is a change in the consciousness of the change agent. It begins with an act of belief, often in the face of accumulated evidence to the contrary. It requires a real change of "attitude" for those of us used to being "critical" or providing "corrective feedback". It seems much easier for many of us to know what is missing, what we don't want, what is lacking in others and ourselves All too often the main themes of discussions in organizations are what isn't working, what is wrong, what goals or standards are not being met. What is the impact of that on us? As my EMBA students found out, it seems to be more difficult and take more effort to notice what isn't missing and get clear about what we really want more of.

While working with a manager who can be bossy, sarcastic, demeaning and nasty, I worked on "seeing" the part of him that is compassionate, wise and wants to be a good leader. The result was that I not only observed much more compassionate and wise behavior, but the part of him that wants to be that way recognized me as an ally and we developed a deep, trusting relationship. I am sure that would never have happened if I had mainly paid attention to the behavior I didn't like. As I was to find out, he was well aware, usually after the fact, of his own meanness.

He still acts "poorly", but not as often and as people who work for him come to see him as I do, with not nearly as harmful an impact.

From this point of view, then, appreciative inquiry creates change by focusing attention on where things are working and amplifying them through fanning. Utilizing such a theory, the collection of stories and creation of generative images is not nearly so important, perhaps not even necessary. Instead, what is necessary is a change in the problem oriented, deficiency focused consciousness of those intervening into the system to an appreciative one that believes that there is an abundance of good people, processes, intentions and interactions, just waiting to be seen and fanned.

Summary

In this paper I have reviewed five different theories of change that someone using appreciative inquiry could operate from in an organization development intervention. These are the social construction of reality, heliotropic hypothesis, the organizational inner dialogue, paradoxical dilemmas and appreciative process theories of change. In an earlier paper I argued that the development of AI as an OD intervention would depend on creation of new theory and that good practice would follow (Bushe, 1995). I am even more convinced of it now as I increasingly see evidence of attempts to do appreciative inquiry simply by asking people for "best of" stories with little theoretical or practical consideration of how this will lead to change in the systems being studied. Appreciative inquiry can be a truly revolutionary way in which we study and change social systems. Being someone, however, who believes that balance is where we find the "natural good", I think appreciation needs to be balanced with critical thinking to lead us there.

References

Barrett, F.J. (1995) Creating appreciative learning cultures. *Organizational Dynamics*, Fall 24:2, 36–49.

Barrett, F.J., Thomas, G.F. and Hocevar, S.P. (1995) The central role of discourse in large-scale change: A social construction perspective. *Journal of Applied Behavioral Science*, 31:3, 352–372.

Bushe, G.R. (1998) Appreciative inquiry with teams. *Organization Development Journal*, 16:3, 41–50.

Bushe, G.R. (1995) "Advances in appreciative inquiry as an organization development intervention". *Organization Development Journal*, 13:3, 14–22.

Bushe, G.R. and Coetzer, G. (1995) "Appreciative inquiry as a team development intervention: A controlled experiment". *Journal of Applied Behavioral Science*, 31:1, 13–30.

Bushe, G.R. and Pitman, T. (1991) "Appreciative process: A method for transformational change". *Organization Development Practitioner*, 23:3, 1–4.

Cooperrider, D.L. (1990) Positive image, positive action: The affirmative basis of organizing. In S.Srivastva and D.L. Cooperrider (Eds.), *Appreciative Management and Leadership* (pp. 91–125). San Francisco: Jossey-Bass.

Cooperrider, D. L. (1996). The "child" as agent of inquiry. *Organization Development Practitioner*, 28:1 and 2, 5–11.

Cooperrider, D. L., and Srivastva, S. (1987). Appreciative inquiry in organizational life. In W. Pasmore and R. Woodman (Eds.), *Research In Organization Change and Development* (Vol. 1, pp. 129–169). Greenwich, CT: JAI Press.

Smith, K.K. and Berg, D.N. (1987) *Paradoxes of Group Life*. San Francisco: Jossey-Bass.

PART II

Case Stories, Resources for Appreciative Inquiry Practice and Empirical Testing

Chapter 5

Advances in Appreciative Inquiry as an Organization Development Intervention

Gervase R. Bushe, Ph.D.
Simon Fraser University

Since Cooperrider and Srivastva's (1987) original article on appreciative inquiry there has been a lot of excitement and experimentation with this new form of action research. The technology of appreciative inquiry as a social research method and as an organization development (OD) intervention are evolving differently. Here I will mainly focus on it as an OD intervention. Currently there is no universally accepted method for doing an appreciative inquiry and it is premature to offer a "recipe" for how to do it. There is, however, a fairly well accepted set of parameters for distinguishing between what is and is not a legitimate appreciative inquiry. In this paper I will describe the basics of this technique and report on some innovations I and colleagues have experimented with to extend the appreciative approach. First, however, an introduction to the theory behind the technique.

What is Appreciative Inquiry?

Appreciative inquiry (Cooperrider and Srivastva, 1987), a theory of organizing and method for changing social systems, is one of the more significant innovations in action research in the past decade. Those who created action research in the 1950s were concerned with creating a research method that would lead to practical results as well as the development of new social theory. It was hoped that action research would be an important tool in social change. A key emphasis of action researchers has been on involving their "subjects" as co-researchers. Action research was and still is a cornerstone of organization development practice.

OD Journal, Vol. 13, No. 3, Fall 1995.

While always controversial as a scientific method of inquiry, action research has recently come under criticism as a method of organizational change and as a process for developing new theory. In their seminal paper Cooperrider and Srivastva criticize the lack of useful theory generated by traditional action research studies and contend that both the method of action research and implicit theory of social organization are to blame. The problem is that most action research projects use logical positivistic assumptions (Sussman and Evered, 1978), which treats social and psychological reality as something fundamentally stable, enduring, and "out there". Appreciative inquiry, however, is a product of the socio-rationalist paradigm (Gergen, 1982, 1990) which treats social and psychological reality as a product of the moment, open to continuous reconstruction. Cooperrider and Srivastva argue that there is nothing inherently real about any particular social form, notranscultural, everlasting, valid principles of social organization to be uncovered. While logical positivism assumes that social phenomena are sufficiently enduring, stable and replicable to allow for generalizations, socio-rationalism contends that social order is fundamentally unstable. "Social phenomena are guided by cognitive heuristics, limited only by the human imagination: the social order is a subject matter capable of infinite variation through the linkage of ideas and action". (Cooperrider and Srivastva, 1987, p. 139). Socio-rationalists argue that the theories we hold, our beliefs about social systems, have a powerful effect on the nature of social "reality". Not only do we see what we believe, but the very act of believing it creates it. From this point of view, the creation of new and evocative theories of groups, organizations, and societies, are a powerful way to aid in their change and development.

Like most post-modernists, Cooperrider and Srivastva argue that logical positivistic assumptions trap us in a rear-view world and methods based on these assumptions tend to (re) create the social realities they purport to be studying. Further, they argue that action researchers tend to assume that their purpose is to solve a problem. Groups and organizations are treated not only as if they have problems, but as if they are problems to be "solved". Cooperrider and Srivastva contend that this "problem-oriented" view of organizing and inquiry reduces the possibility of generating new theory, and new images of social reality, that might help us transcend current social forms. What if, instead of seeing organizations as problems to be solved, we saw them as miracles to be appreciated? How would our methods of inquiry and our theories of organizing be different?

Appreciative inquiry "refers to both a search for knowledge and a theory of intentional collective action which are designed to help evolve the normative vision and will of a group, organization, or society as a whole" (Cooperrider and Srivastva, 1987, p.159). Cooperrider makes the theory of change embedded in appreciative inquiry explicit in a later paper on the affirmative basis of organizing (Cooperrider, 1990). In this paper Cooperrider proffers the "heliotropic hypothesis"—that social forms evolve toward the "light"; that is, toward images that are affirming and life giving. In essence his argument is that all groups, organizations, communities or societies have images of themselves that underlay self-organizing processes and that social systems have a natural tendency to evolve toward the most positive images held by their members. Conscious evolution of positive imagery, therefore, is a viable option for changing the social system as a whole.

One of the ironies Cooperrider helps us to see is that the greatest obstacle to the well-being of an ailing group is the affirmative projection that currently guides the group. To affirm means to 'hold firm' and it "is precisely the strength of affirmation, the degree of belief or faith invested, that allows the image to carry out its heliotropic task" (Cooperrider, 1990, p. 120). When groups find that attempts to fix problems create more problems, or the same problems never go away, it is a clear signal of the inadequacy of the group's current affirmative projection. Groups, therefore, do not need to be fixed; they need to be affirmed and "every new affirmative projection of the future is a consequence of an appreciative understanding of the past or present" (p. 120).

Appreciative inquiry, as a method of changing social systems, is an attempt to generate a collective image of a new and better future by exploring the best of what is and has been. These new images, or "theories", create a pull effect that generates evolution in social forms. The four principles Cooperrider and Srivastva (1987, p.160) articulate for an action research that can create new and better images are that research should begin with appreciation, should be applicable, should be provocative, and should be collaborative. The basic process of appreciative inquiry is to begin with a grounded observation of the "best of what is", then through vision and logic collaboratively articulate "what might be", ensuring the consent of those in the system to "what should be" and collectively experimenting with "what can be". One significant published research study that used an appreciative inquiry methodology looked at the processes of organizing that are used by international non-governmental organizations (Johnson and Cooperrider, 1991).

Appreciative Inquiry as a Method of Change

An appreciative inquiry intervention can be thought of as consisting of these three parts:

> Discovering the best of . . . Appreciative interventions begin with a search for the best examples of organizing and organization within the experience of organizational members.

> Understanding what creates the best of . . . The inquiry seeks to create insight into the forces that lead to superior performance, as defined by organizational members. What is it about the people, the organization, and the context that creates peak experiences at work?

> Amplifying the people and processes who best exemplify the best of . . . Through the process of the inquiry itself, the elements that contribute to superior performance are reinforced and amplified.

The emphasis in my approach is on designing inquiry methods that amplify the values the system is seeking to actualize during the all phases of the inquiry process. I believe this is one key feature that distinguishes appreciative inquiry from other interventions. How to actually do that in practice is not so easy but as the pace of environmental change accelerates, we must find more rapid change processes for organizational renewal. The great promise of appreciative inquiry is that it will generate self-sustaining momentum within an organization toward actualizing the values that lead to superior performance.

The original form of appreciative inquiry developed by David Cooperrider involved a bottom-up interview process where almost all organizational members were interviewed to uncover the "life-giving forces" in the organization. People were asked to recall times they felt "most alive, most vital, most energized at work" and were then questioned about those incidents. The interview data were then treated much the same as any qualitative data set; through content analysis the consultants looked for what people in the organization valued and what conditions led to superior performance.

This analysis was fed back into a large planning group which was charged with developing "provocative propositions". Provocative propositions were statements of organizational aspiration and intent, based on the analysis of the organization at it's very best. These propositions were then validated by organizational members along two dimensions: (1) how much does this statement capture our values? and (2) how much are we like this? Nothing more was done with the data, analysis or propositions. John Carter of the Gestalt Institute of Cleveland, one of the early implementors of this approach, counsels against using the propositions as a set of standards or goals to then begin problem-solving around (Carter, 1989). Using the gestalt therapy notion of figure-ground, John argues that most inquiry methods make something figural, focusing attention.

Appreciative inquiry, he claims, creates ground. By coming to agreement on a set of provocative propositions, people have a compelling vision of the organization at its best and this in itself motivates new behaviors. People will take initiative and act differently without an action plan because the provocative propositions align organizational vision with employee's internal sense of what is important.

As a planned change technique, this approach lacked focus and didn't do as good a job of amplification as many of us would like. I continue to experiment with new techniques for generating discovery, understanding, and amplification. Here is a brief rundown on my current thinking.

Discovering

The initial appreciative inquiries attempted to study organizations as a whole. More recent interventions have begun to limit themselves to a few issues. This appears to make the process more manageable and understandable to others. Now, unless we are trying to help a company develop a future vision for the entire organization, appreciative inquiries focus on strategic human resource issues like empowerment, teamwork, leadership, customer service. Appreciative inquiry may have applications for other, non-HR issues but I don't know of anyone who has tried it (e.g., how to best organize an information system). One of the more interesting recent applications has been with gender issues in organizations. Marjorie Schiller of Quincy, Massachusetts has been working with corporations that found that traditional approaches to dealing with sexual harassment in the workplace (e.g., hire a harassment coordinator, gather survey data, do a lot of training) only resulted in more reported sexual harassment! Using an appreciative inquiry approach, teams of men and women are studying what co-gender work experiences are like at their very best and this seems to be having remarkable results.

After a couple of failures I learned that doing an "appreciative interview" is not as easy as it looks.

Simply talking about one's "peak" experience can easily degenerate into social banter and cliché-ridden interaction. The hallmark of successful appreciative interviews seems to be that the interviewee has at least one new insight into what made it a peak experience. I have noticed a bundle of behaviors that seem to distinguish those who are good and poor at appreciative interviewing (Bushe 1997). The key seems to be suspending one's own assumptions and not being content with superficial explanations given by others; to question the obvious and to do this in more of a conversational, self-disclosing kind of way than is normally taught in interviewing courses. There seem to be real limits to who can do this well and I have not been able to train people quickly (1 day) to be able to attend to others appreciatively. It appears that one of the early assumptions, that we could teach organizational members to run the data collection process by themselves, does not work as well as we'd hoped. People who have the basic ability to listen to others "generously", however, can be taught appreciative inquiry in about a day and a half. I have found the best results from teaming insiders with outsiders and doing paired interviews. David Cooperrider has noticed that using younger insiders to interview organizational elders results in a very special energy and the quality of images and data seems better.

I've come to the conclusion that getting the stories that people have about the topic is what is most important. Researchers and other linear thinkers have a tendency to want to generate abstract lists and propositional statements out of the interviews and this needs to be curtailed during the interview process or the same old lists and propositions get recycled. Fresh images and insight come from exploring the real stories people have about themselves and others at their best.

We've also found that people love to be interviewed appreciatively. Recently a team I was leading completed a series of appreciative interviews about leadership with the senior executives of a major telecommunications company. As you can imagine, many were loath to give up any time in their busy schedules to be interviewed. We asked for an hour. Most interviews actually lasted two and a half hours, with the executives canceling their appointments and just wanting talk on and on.

Understanding

It has been necessary to find ways of making the data useful for group interpretation. Large data sets on organizational peak experiences required more time and effort than busy managers could afford. We've experimented with structuring the data collection and reporting to reduce the ambiguity of the data and make it easier for large groups to work with. The main innovation has been the inquiry matrix (Bushe and Pitman, 1991). Prior to data collection, senior managers decide what elements of organizing they want to amplify in their organization (e.g., teamwork, quality, leadership), and an organizational model that they feel best captures the major categories of organizing (e.g., technology, structure, rewards, etc.). A matrix is then created of elements by categories. For example, there would be a cell for teamwork and technology, teamwork and structure, quality and technology, quality and structure, and so on. The data collection effort focuses on each of the cells. More importantly, the matrix focuses the analysis of the data and the generation of provocative propositions.

I have found that the quality of new understandings and insights created during an appreciative inquiry is strongly effected by the quality of stories and insights generated during the interviews.

Unless new understandings arise during the initial appreciative interviews, later analyses may simply recreate the initial mental models people come to the analysis with. Without important new insights, the process loses energy fast and leads to cliched propositions. Appreciative inquiry really challenges those doing the analysis to leave their preconceptions behind and approach the data with "the eyes of a child".

Write-ups of the interviews are very important. I've found that detailed recounts of the stories and most interesting quotes are what is needed and that these are best written in the first person. The output of appreciative interviews are a series of stories and quotes written in the language of those who told them.

What is normally the "data analysis" stage of action research needs to be done totally differently in an appreciative inquiry. I no longer call it "analysis". I haven't found a great term for it yet but I've used 'proalysis' and 'synergalysis'. At this point in an appreciative inquiry I want to get as many people as possible reading the most important interviews and stories in order to stimulate their thinking about the appreciative topic. Then I try to orchestrate one or more meetings where organizational members and consultants try to go beyond what they were told by the interviewees to craft propositional statements about the appreciative topic that will capture people's energy and excitement. We're not trying to extract themes from the data or categorize responses and add them up. We're trying to generate new theory that will have high face value to members of the organization. What makes this legitimate research, I believe, is that we go back to those we interviewed with these propositions and ask them if we have captured the spirit, if not the letter, of the meaning of the interviews. If they say yes, then I believe we have generated new theory based on something more real than simply imagination and good intentions.

Amplification

I believe that as a social intervention device, the quality of the dialogue generated is much more important than the "validity" of the synergalysis of the data. Studying the best of what is creates excitement and energy and this is a key part of the amplification process. I and others have been trying to find ways to further amplify what is exciting and energizing for people and effective for their organizations.

The number of people involved in all phases of the appreciative inquiry has obvious implications for this. I would like to experiment with getting very large numbers of people into something the size of a hockey arena to do consensual creation and validation of provocative propositions but to date have not found a client system willing to do this.

Once a set of propositions have been developed, they can be "tested" through a survey in the organization. The survey can ask to what extent they believe the proposition to be an important component of the topic under study and to what extent they believe the organization exemplifies the proposition. Simply filling out such a survey can do a lot toward spreading the ideas throughout the organization. Then communicating the results of the survey showing the strength of consensus about the importance of each proposition gives organizational members license to do more of it in their everyday work.

One major innovation has been to create thematic feed-back documents that identify who is giving the "quote" and the context the quote was given in. Instead of lists of anonymous quotes to illustrate themes found in conventional feedback reports, people get to read what their fellow employees are saying about their best experiences. You can imagine how much more dialogue and energy this creates.

Tom Pitman of Grand Rapids, Michigan and Geoff Hulin of Santa Cruz, California have experimented with video-taping the interviews and editing them into short, focused pieces on different themes. As a feedback device, videotape clips have proved to generate a great deal more energy and shared imagery than written reports. Again, the goal here is to create appreciative dialogues about the issues under study that result in new affirming images. The opportunities here continue to increase as new applications that marry video and computer technologies proliferate.

Where to next

We may find that the notion of "appreciative process" (Bushe and Pitman, 1991) as a consulting and change strategy has a larger and more lasting impact than large scale appreciative inquiries. My personal consulting style has undergone a radical transformation in the past 6 years as I have struggled to adopt an appreciative stance in my work. Now I pay attention to what is working well, the qualities of leadership or group process that I want to see more of, and try to amplify them when I see them. This is in direct contrast to my training where I learned to see what was missing and point that out. In the past I focused on understanding the failures and pathologies of leadership and organization. I thought that awareness was the first step in development and so I felt it was my job as an OD consultant to make people aware of just how bad things really were. Now I am focusing on helping people become aware of how good things are, on the genius in themselves and others, on the knowledge and abilities they already have, on examples of the future in the present. From this stance I am finding that change happens more easily, people don't get as bogged down in uncertainty or despair and energy runs more freely.

The appreciative lens has opened up a new vista for viewing and understanding the process of change in human systems. For example, I developed a form of appreciative inquiry for team building, experimentally tested it, and found it significantly improved a team's process and performance (Bushe and Coetzer, 1995). The method, as used in the experiments, goes as follows:

First, group members are asked to recall the best team experience they have ever been a part of. Even for those who have had few experiences of working with others in groups, there is a 'best' experience. Each group member is asked, in turn, to describe the experience while the rest of the group is encouraged to be curious and engage in dialogue with the focal person.

The facilitator encourages members to set aside their clichés and preconceptions, get firmly grounded in their memory of the actual experience, and fully explore what about themselves, the situation, the task, and others made this a "peak" experience. Once all members have exhausted their exploration, the facilitator asks the group, on the basis of what they have just discussed, to list and develop a consensus on the attributes of highly effective groups.

The intervention concludes with the facilitator inviting members to publicly acknowledge anything they have seen others in the group do that has helped the group be more like any of the listed attributes

This research has stimulated new group theory and new change theory. Graeme Coetzer, at Simon Fraser University, and I are working on a theory of "group image" that may offer insights into how groups function and dysfunction. I believe that the most important next steps for appreciative inquiry will be theoretical breakthroughs in understanding leadership, facilitation, and change processes in social systems. After this will come new techniques.

References

Bushe, G.R. (1997) *Attending to Others: Interviewing Appreciatively*. Vancouver, BC: Discovery and Design Inc.

Bushe, G.R. and Coetzer, G. (1995) Appreciative inquiry as a team development intervention: A controlled experiment. *Journal of Applied Behavioral Science*, 31:1, 19–31.

Bushe, G.R. and Pitman, T. (1991) "Appreciative process: A method for transformational change". *OD Practitioner*, September, 1–4.

Carter, J. (1989) Talk given at the Social Innovations Global Management conference, Weatherhead School of Management, Case Western Reserve University, Cleveland Ohio November 13–17.

Cooperrider, D.L. (1990) Positive image, positive action: The affirmative basis of organizing. In S.Srivastva and D.L. Cooperrider (Eds.), *Appreciative Management and Leadership* (pp.91–125). San Francisco: Jossey-Bass.

Cooperrider, D.L. and Srivastva, S. (1987) "Appreciative inquiry in organizational life". In R. Woodman and W. Pasmore (eds.) *Research in Organizational Change and Development: Volume 1* (pp.129–169). Greenwich, CT: JAI Press,

Gergen, K. (1982) *Toward Transformation in Social Knowledge*. New York: Spring-Verlag.

Gergen, K. (1990) Affect and organization in postmodern society. In S. Srivastva and D.L. Cooperrider.

Cooperrider (eds.), *Appreciative Management and Leadership* (pp.153–174). San Francisco, Jossey-Bass.

Johnson, P.C. and Cooperrider, D.L. (1991) Finding a path with heart: Global social change organizations and their challenge for the field of organization development. In R. Woodman and W.Pasmore (eds.) *Research in Organizational Change and Development: Volume 5* (pp.223–284). Greenwich CT: JAI Press.

Sussman, G.I and Evered, R.D. (1978) An assessment of the scientific merits of action research. *Administrative Science Quarterly*, 23, 582–603.

Chapter 6

THE "CHILD" AS AGENT OF INQUIRY

David L. Cooperrider
Case Western University

> The sense of wonder, that is our sixth sense. And it is the natural.
> —D. H. Lawrence

What is the role of wonder in OD? What creates a sense of wonder as we inquire into organizational life, and what spoils it? What are the varieties of wonder? What is the connection of wonder to knowledge? To the imagination? To the flowering of relationships? What happens to the storyteller, for example, when the room is filled by people sitting forward, listening, even smiling, with a sense of wonder? Why is uninhibited wonder something we generally restrict to children? If doing good inquiry is at the heart of OD, why then so little talk of things like awe, curiosity, veneration, surprise, delight, amazement, and wonder—in short, everything that serves to infuse what OD has traditionally referred to as the "spirit of inquiry".

Presented here is a thesis, a proposition, regarding the future of OD. It is a stand which I take with some hesitation, even with some tentativeness. It is a proposition I will illustrate with an "N" of one, hardly a proof. But it has, I think, some wisdom in it; one might even argue the idea was modeled in the lives of early pioneers like Kurt Lewin, Mary Parker Follett, Herb Shepard and others. The thesis emerges from years of experimenting with what my colleagues and I have termed "Appreciative Inquiry". It goes something like this: We have reached *"the end of problem solving"* as a mode of inquiry capable of inspiring, mobilizing, and sustaining human system change, and the future of OD belongs to methods that affirm, compel, and accelerate anticipatory learning involving larger and larger levels of collectivity. The new methods will be distinguished by the art and the science of asking powerful, positive questions (soon there will be an "encyclopedia of questions" that brings together classic formulations like Maslow's interview protocols on peak human experience and Vereena Kast's exceptional studies of joy, inspiration, and hope). The new methods will view realities as socially constructed and will therefore become more radically relational, widening the circles of dialogue to groups of 100s, 1000s, and perhaps more—with cyberspace

OD Practitioner, Vol. 28, Nos. 1 and 2, 1996.

relationships into the millions. The arduous task of intervention will give way to the speed of imagination and innovation; and instead of negative, criticism, and spiraling diagnosis, there will be discovery, dream, and design. Social construction will mean constructive constructing. And the metaphor speaking best to our primary task and role—"the child as the agent of inquiry"—is one where wonder, learning, and the dialogical imagination will be modus operandi.

Let's Illustrate: Imagine OD With a Whole City

I want to tell you about a successful businesswoman—a corporate banking executive for 16 years at First Chicago—who one day decided to leave it all to devote her next 10 years to transforming the city's future. Trained in OD, savvy in action–research methodologies, and a visionary in her own right, Bliss Browne asked the question: "What might happen if all of Chicago's citizens were mobilized to give public expression, continuously, to their imagination about a healthy future for the city as a whole, and were invited to claim their role in bringing that vision to life?" Could it be, she paused, "we human beings create our own realities through imagination and conversational processes, and *the creation of positive images on a collective basis in our three million person city might well be the most prolific activity* that individuals and organizations can engage in if their aim is to help bring to fruition a positive and humanly significant future?

Preposterous? "Perhaps", commented a Chicago Tribune journalist: "But Browne is the sort who thinks big and takes unorthodox action. . . . She's used to challenges. Browne was in the first class of 125 women who graduated from Yale University in 1971, and she was among the first women ordained into the priesthood of the Episcopal Church in 1977 (and then her career as corporate executive).[1]

It began, then, with a conference where community and business leaders met to discuss how imagination, economics, and faith could make the city a better place. But there were major concerns: surveys for example, showing 85% of Americans losing faith in both the future of our cities as well as the institutions that govern them, images of cities as hellholes (just look at the demonized picture of urban America in our movies and the nightly news); and the malaise of our young where the negative images have been correlated with apathy, cynicism, fear, discrimination and other damaging behavior. Ways are needed, agreed the participants, to rebuild essential connections, to renew hope, to reinvigorate human creativity and leadership at all levels. "How one conceives of the city shapes how one lives in the city," argued Browne. Even more, "Cities echo creation. They are a living symbol of our ability to imagine and create, to turn our visions into tangible products. They are an inventory of the possible, and incarnation of human capacity and diversity. Cities concentrate forces of darkness and light, and hold the world in miniature."

IMAGINE CHICAGO, now four years old, located at 35 E. Wacker Drive, was born out of that and subsequent meetings. IMAGINE CHICAGO is a catalyst for civic innovation, working to bring people who live and work in Chicago to the realization that they are the owners and creators of Chicago's future.[2] The MacArthur Foundation funded the first several years' pilot. And when theories and practices of change were sought out, Appreciative Inquiry (AI) was selected as the approach most likely to help serve as "a catalyst for civic innovation".[3]

The outcomes have been dramatic. The "pilot" included more than 800 individuals in more than 40 neighborhoods with involvement of more than 100 community organizations and schools. For example, IMAGINE CHICAGO, in collaboration with Barbara Radner, Director of The Center for Urban Education at DePaul University, developed a citizenship curriculum now being used by 4000 Chicago public school students (more on these exciting results later). Though only a young organization, IMAGINE CHICAGO has already attracted broad recognition: a national award in 1995 from Eureka Communities in Washington D.C. for its "exemplary work on behalf of children and their families"; citation by the Mayor's Youth Development Task Force in 1994, and perhaps the most profound recognition, that of being emulated. . . . There is now an IMAGINE DALLAS organization, as well as plans in other cities and in other parts of the world, namely an initiative called IMAGINE AFRICA.

A Most Extraordinary Learning

One of the important logistical questions for IMAGINE CHICAGO had to do with scale: How to create an appreciative "action research" cycle with such a large system. When I first met with the design team they asked about "mass mobilization" methods for each of the phases (see Figure 1) in appreciative inquiry. Discovery, Dream, Design and Destiny.[4]

There was talk, very early on, of wanting to conduct appreciative interviews with one million people—at least one interview for every household in the city. Now it appears, as the whole thing is blossoming, that many more than that will happen as new requests, programs, opportunities, and technologies are multiplying. But more important than scale was the other key question: *Who* should do the interviews? Should data collection be done by professors? OD consultants? Doctoral students from University of Chicago?

This is where the remarkable learning happened. It is one that continues to leave me breathless. The pilot's very best interviews—resulting in the most inspiring stories, the most passion filled data, the most textured and well illustrated examples, the most daring images of possibility—were all conducted by *children* of Chicago. The most powerful interviews were when children of all races and cultures did interviews with the city's "elders"—priests, CEOs, school principles, parents, entertainers, artists, activists, mystics, scientists. It was the *intergenerational dynamic of the dialogue*

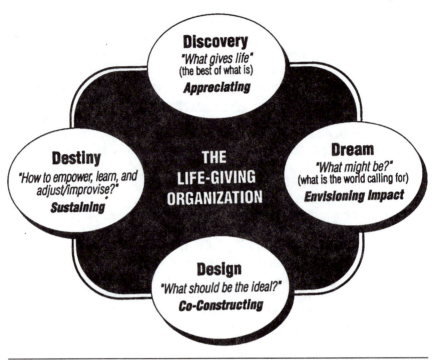

Figure 1.1. Appreciative Inquiry 4 "D" Cycle.

that made the data collection stage soar. One is reminded of Margaret Mead's hypothesis that the best societal learning has always occurred when three generations come together in contexts of discovery and valuing—the child, the elder, and the middle adult. Let's look further.[5]

Appreciation and Wonder

An observer described the chemistry in the interviews as "magical". One 72-year-old respondent said at the conclusion of his interview: "I really thank you for this conversation. You got all of me. That hasn't happened too often in my life. You forced me to share my visions, and crystallize them into clear images. This has given me tremendous hope. Now that I can articulate clearly, I know they are do-able."

In the classic interview, for example, a 13-year-old requests a time to meet with his principal. As interviewer he raises many questions: "As you reflect on your career, can you tell me the story of a highpoint, a time you felt most alive, most impactful, most successful in terms of contribution to this school and community?" The principle scratches her head even starts a bit slowly, but soon is in full voice. The youngster, listening to the drama, gets so excited with the story of courage and conviction that he cannot sit quiet. He interrupts the flow and blurts out—"so what was it about you that made it a high point . . . what are your best qualities . . . can you tell me what you value most about yourself?" A little later the topic switches to more volatile topics, like race relations. Again the positive query: "Thinking about your school's contributions to building higher quality multiracial and/or multicultural relationships, what have you done in this area that has made the biggest difference? What one thing are you most proud about?" The stories are told, one after the other. The interview lasts an hour longer than planned.

Later, an evaluation team follows up with the school principle to get feedback on the dynamic of the interview. Typical comments included:

- "I've never been asked these types of questions by youths in this school. When I do converse with the students it is *usually* for disciplinary reasons."

- "That night, after the interview, I laid wide awake. I could not sleep. I kept replaying the conversation. I got back in touch with a lot of things important to me.

- "You know, during that interview I really felt like I was on the pulpit. I got animated. I was literally looking into the face of the future, exploring the essential elements of the good society. This conversation *mattered*.

Barbara Radner's studies are now showing that when the appreciative civic inquiry methods are brought into the curriculum (in 13 Chicago Public Schools) children's achievement in all areas including math, reading, writing, etc., rises significantly in comparison to controls. In doing the interviews, children are hearing stories they would never hear on the news, on TV, or even in the more common cynical discourse of society at large. They are developing their own images of possibility and hearing experiences where change has happened for the better. One young person, Willie J. Hempel, was so excited and moved by his experiences he started volunteering his time to IMAGINE CHICAGO every day after school: "It was during my interview with Ed Brennen, CEO of Sears, that my dreams and hopes were ignited. You find you have so much in common in terms of hopes for our city. And you find out people like Ed really care, not just about money but social justice causes, about me as a young person and about our future . . . my ideas about people like Ed and the politicians I interviewed all changed, and so has my life. That is why I want to volunteer my time now; it is all about making change happen." *Where appreciation is alive and generations are re-connected through inquiry, hope grows and community expands.*[6]

Today, IMAGINE CHICAGO is taking the lessons of its pilot into five major project initiatives: The Urban Imagination Network, City Dialogues, Creating Chicago: A Citizens Guide, City Connections, Citizen Leaders, and Sacred Places. In all of these, the spirit—if not the actual process—of the intergenerational inquiry and change methodology will guide the way.

Dag Hammarskjold once said, "but we die on the day when our lives cease to be illuminated by the steady radiance, renewed daily, of a wonder, the source of which is beyond all reason." The *child as the agent of inquiry* is something I think all of us in OD need to reclaim and aspire to: openness, availability, epistemological humility, the ability to admire, to be surprised, to be inspired, to inquire into our valued and possible worlds, to wonder. In my own work in OD I have found that it does not help, in the long run, to begin my inquiries from the standpoint of the world as a problem to be solved. I am more effective, quite simply, as long as I can retain the spirit of inquiry of the everlasting beginner. The only thing I do that I think makes the difference is to craft, in better and more catalytic ways, the *unconditional positive question*.[7]

Unfortunately, and this is true of myself, it is not often that I begin a new OD inquiry feeling a profound state of wonder; what William James so aptly called the state of "ontological wonder". For me, the doorway into wonder is more matter-of-fact. Pragmatically, it is not so much a process of *trying* romantically to go back to the state of being a child; nor is it the same path as taken by the person in spiritual retreat. It begins in ordinary circumstances of discovery, conversation, and the deepening relationship all endowed by the positive question. *Inquiry itself creates wonder. When I'm really in a mode of inquiry, appreciable worlds are discovered everywhere. The feeling of wonder is the outcome. Of course it also cycles back. A good positive question, like Karl Weick's notion of "small wins", can change the world.*

IMAGINE CHICAGO, as a nascent example of one, is hardly enough to say that it provides answers for the future of OD. But there are clues, insists Browne: "My job, our job, is to be a home to the mysteries of city and its future . . . it is not about having answers." Albert Einstein put the option best, "There are only two ways to live your life. One is as though nothing is a miracle. The other is as though everything is a miracle."

References

[1]*Chicago Tribune*, "Imagine Shaping a Better Chicago" by Terry Wilson, section2, page 2. Tuesday, June 13, 1995.

[2]Browne, Bliss, "Imagine Chicago: Executive Summary", 1996 (for more information call 312-444-9913).

[3]Cooperrider D.L. and Srivasta, S. "Appreciative Inquiry Into Organizational Life" in Pasmore and Woodman (eds.) *Research in Organization Change and Development*, Vol. 1, pp. 129–169.

[4]Cooperrider, D. et. al. *Appreciative Inquiry Manual*. Unpublished Notes. Case Western Reserve University, 1996.

[5]Barrett, Frank "Creating Appreciative Learning Cultures", Vol. 24, *Organizational Dynamics*, Sept. 1995, pp. 36.

[6]Ludema, James. *Narrative Inquiry*, Unpublished Ph.D. Dissertation, Department of Organizational Behavior, Case Western Reserve University, Cleveland, Ohio, 1996.

[7]Wilmot, Timothy, *Inquiry, Hope and Change*. Unpublished Ph.D. Dissertation, Department of Organizational Behavior, Case Western Reserve University, Cleveland, Ohio, 1996.

David L. Cooperrider is Associate Professor of Organizational Behavior and is Co-Chair of the Centerfor Social Innovation In Global Management (SIGMA) at Case Western Reserve University's Weatherhead School of Management. David has taught at Stanford University, Katholieke University in Belgium, and several schools in the U.S. Beyond his teaching David has been elected as Chairman of the National Academy of Management's Division of Organization Development and Change, and is the Principal Investigator of a $3.5 million grant working with international organizations dealing with global issues of human health, environment, and development.

Dr. Cooperrider has served as researcher and consultant to a wide variety of organizations including, BP America, NYNEYXC, U.S. Agency for International Development, World Vision, Nature Conservancy, The American Hospital Association, Cleveland Clinic Foundation, Kaiser Permanente, Technoserve Inc., Omni Hotels, Federation of African Voluntary Development Organizations, and the World Mountain Forum. Currently, as part of the grant, David and his colleagues have organization development projects going on in 57 organizations working in over 100 countries. Most of these projects are inspired by the "Appreciative Inquiry" methodologies for which David is best known.

David's ideas have been widely published in journals such as *Human Relations, Administrative Science Quarterly, Journal of Applied Behavioral Science, Contemporary Psychology* and in research series such as *Advances in Strategic Management, Research in Organization Development and Change*, and *Inquiries in Social Construction*.

Chapter 7

Resources for Getting Appreciative Inquiry Started: An Example OD Proposal

David L. Cooperrider

Case Western Reserve University

Over the past several years people have been asking more and more for practical tools that will help them transform their OD consulting practice away from the diagnostic problem solving approaches toward more appreciative inquiry methods. One of the most common requests (when I do workshops on Appreciative Inquiry) is for examples of proposals—proposals that set the stage for OD contracting. This article presents a "composite picture" of several actual proposals that have led to major OD work. The "AMX" proposal represents the best of several projects that combine Appreciative Inquiry and Future Search. The corporate names used in this composite proposal are fictitious.

What I like most about the "whole system" change process spelled out here is that it completely lets go of problem solving. In my view, the problem-solving paradigm, while once incredibly effective, is simply out of sync with the realities of today's virtual worlds. Problem solving is painfully slow (always asking people to look backwards historically to yesterday's causes); it rarely results in new vision (by definition we say something is a problem because we already implicitly assume some idea, so we are not searching to create new knowledge of better ideals, we are searching how to close gaps), and, in human terms, problem solving approaches are notorious for generating defensiveness (it is not my problem but yours).

Organizations are centers of human relatedness, first and foremost, and relationships thrive where there is an appreciative eye—when people see the best in one another, when they can share their dreams and ultimate concerns in affirming ways, and when they are connected in full voice to create not just new worlds but better worlds. Douglas McGregor was convinced of the power of positive assumptions about human beings. The AMX proposal is an example of an OD proposal that, in practical ways, mobilizes the appreciative process to the fullest extent I know how. The proposal was written the week Congress passed legislation that

OD Practitioner, Vol. 28, Nos. 1 and 2, 1996.

would deregulate the telecommunications industry, changing the rules that guided the industry for over 60 years. AMX, one of the organizational giants, was literally in chaos with thousands being laid off. Facing the largest whole system transformation in their corporate history, the CEO asked, "How can we connect everyone to the adventure of creating the new century telecommunication organization?"

The AMX Connects! Proposal

Accelerating Organizational Learning For Winning the New Century

Background. During the past several years, AMX has positioned itself to take advantage of what may prove to be the greatest single business opportunity in history: the creation and management of the Information Superhighway. Part of this positioning has been the clear articulation of the new strategic "ABC" vision and reaffirmation of the goal of being the most customer responsive business in the industry. Along with the vision has come action. There are literally hundreds of successful new initiatives—reengineering, product innovations, new alliances, public relations campaigns, employee empowerment strategies, etc.—all combining to give birth to the new AMX. The entire system is in the thick of fundamental organizational transformation, and exists in a world where the economic, technological, and regulatory foundations of the business have radically changed. It simply is not the same business it used to be.

Important questions, therefore, are many: How can leaders accelerate positive transformation where the process of corporate change is revolutionary in result and evolutionary in execution? How can people reduce the time lag between exciting organizational innovations (initiatives, large and small, that illustrate what the new century AMX organization can and should look like) and organizational storytelling, sharing, advocacy, and mass learning from those innovations? How will employees sustain, over a period of years, corporate confidence and faith in

---

[1]According to recent surveys by Yankelovich, 85% of Americans have lost confidence in the future. People report little confidence that current institutions and leaders will do the job. They see the gap between promised rhetoric about a better future and the continued breakdown, in the present, of many systems. Likewise the negative discourse and storytelling which dominates the media, politics, and the popular culture at large, is associated with increased levels of apathy among young and old, cynicism, fear, discrimination, and other damaging behavior. What is happening throughout society obviously has a spillover effect in our corporations. Especially during times of major transition, ways are needed to rebuild essential connections, to renew hope, and to reinvigorate human creativity and leadership at all levels.

AMX's abilities to make fundamental change even in the midst of inevitable set-backs? How can AMX complement its problem-solving culture with an apprecia-tive mindset that selectively sees, studies, and learns from every positive new development? Can AMX develop and reclaim an oral tradition of storytelling that connects people across corporate generations and that propels the speed and spread of good news? How can AMX leaders decisively connect people throughout the system to the Future Search, and engage everyone in a "can do" way as social architects of the new century organization—a transformed organizational entity that lives its vision in all its structures, systems, strategies, management behav-iors, job designs, partnerships everything that the company does.'

Purpose

- The mission of AMX Connects! is to accelerate positive whole system trans-formation by actively connecting people to the "ABC" vision through the practice of Appreciative Inquiry.

Objectives

- To bring the "ABC" vision alive for 67,000 people at AMX by engaging a critical mass of people in an Appreciative Inquiry into the most positive and compelling organizational innovations, practices, and traditions that (1) best illustrate the translation of the "ABC" vision into transformational action and (2) provide an anticipatory glimpse into the kind of organization AMX should and might become in the new century.
- To deliver tangible follow-up to the 1995 Leadership Workshop (which builds on the momentum of the Aspen, Colorado success where 140 regional and corporate executives were introduced to the theory of Appreciative Inquiry), and tie together executive education with real-time organization transforma-tion. By co-leading the Appreciative Inquiry/Future Search process at the re-gional and corporate levels, the "action learning" design will contribute as much to leadership development as it does to organization development.
- To augment AMX's problem solving culture with an appreciative mind set that provides a paradigm shift in ways of looking at managerial analysis of all kinds—e.g., new options for approaching organization analysis, customer fo-cus groups, strategic planning methods, reengineering studies, employee sur-veys, performance appraisal processes, public affairs methodologies, diversity initiatives, benchmarking approaches, merger integration methods, and many others.
- To build an affirmative atmosphere of hope and confidence necessary to sus-tain, over the next several years, the largest whole-system transformation in the company's history.

- To discover and pioneer connections between Appreciative Inquiry/Future Search Conference methodologies (often involving hundreds of people interactively) and the voice, video, and data capabilities of AMX's advanced teleconferencing technologies. The potential for building connection and commitment to the future directions of the company are enormous: corporate visioning, advocacy, and good news telling will not be isolated to a few technical gurus, senior visionaries, or communication messengers, but will engage potentially thousands. When it comes to bringing vision alive, process is just as important as product. People want to be listened to and to be heard. The large group conference methodologies discussed below are truly impressive in their ability to cultivate the thrill of being a valued member in the creation of new and exciting futures.

Leadership

- AMX Connects! will be led by President Sheldon Abrahms; Susan Taft, Vice President Public Affairs; John Williams, Vice President of Organization Development, and the 140 individuals involved with the recent Leadership Conference. David L. Cooperrider and Associates from Case Western Reserve University's Weatherhead School of Management will provide outside guidance.

Timing

- The appreciative organizational inquiry and learning process will be formally inaugurated in 1996 with a workshop on Appreciative Inquiry. Participants will be the leadership group of 140 through 1996 and 1997. Appreciative Inquiry will be introduced and Future Search Conferences completed in every region of Operations. Results from each of these will form the basis of a synthesizing corporate-wide Future Search in the spring of 1998 and will culminate with a future report—images of The New Century AMX Organization—to be issued by the "think tank" group of 140.

---

²For an overview of the social constructionist theory behind the approach, see Cooperrider D.L. and Srivastva S. "Appreciative Inquiry Into Organizational Life" in Pasmore and Woodman (eds.) *Research in Organization Development and Change*, JAI Press, 1987. Also for more on the scientific studies of human behavior that provides a deeper logic for the appreciative approach, see Cooperrider D. "Positive Image, Positive Action: The Affirmative Basis of Organization" in Srivastva and Cooperrider's *Appreciative Leadership and Management: The Power of Positive Thought in Organizations*. Jossey Bass Publishers, 1990.

The ABCs of Appreciative Inquiry

In a typical Appreciative Inquiry, the process will lead up to a major Future Search Conference, two or three days in length, where a whole organization or representatives of the whole (anywhere from 100 to 1,000 people) will come together to both construct images of the system's most desired future and to formulate creative strategies to bring that future about. Often, an organizational model like the 7-S framework will serve as a template for building "possibility propositions" in each of the key organizational design areas—for example, what will the ideal organizational structures or systems look like in the future (the conference organizers will specify how far into the future to think . . . usually 3–5 years out). The stages for bringing the whole thing off productively typically follow the ABC sequence:

A. Appreciative understanding of your organization (from the past to present);

B. Benchmarked understanding of other organizations (exemplary models to learn from); and

C. Creative construction of the future (sometimes called the Future Search Conference).

One possible design would be to launch, in each of the regions, a broad-based set of Appreciative Inquiry interviews leading to a regional Future Search conference. The design of the interviews would stress storytelling and study into the "ABC" vision in action—examples of being "the easiest company to do business with"; times when people feel truly "empowered", examples of new forms of "servant leadership"; illustrations of how AMX is "winning in the new world"; etc. All of these interviews would be done face-to-face by AMX managers and employees within the region. All the best quotes, stories, and illustrations would be compiled into a regional report and used to inspire a regionally based Future Search Conference into "AMX In the New Century: Images of Organizational Possibility". At the Future Search Conference, with 100 to 2,000 people, participants meet for two or three days to design the organization's most desired future and formulate creative strategies to bring that future about. The key product is a planning

---

[3]See Wilmot, Tim (1995) "The Global Excellence in Management Program: A Two Year Evaluation of 25 Organizations Using Appreciative Inquiry" Case Western Reserve University For detailed analysis of large group methods and outcomes—from Ford Motor Company, First Nationwide Bank, SAS, Mariott, and Borning—see Jacobs, R. (1994) *Real Time Strategic Change: How to Involve an Entire Organization In Fast and Far Reaching Change*, San Francisco: Berrett Koehler Publishers. For ten case studies of the Future Search methods see Weisbord, M. (1992) *Discovering Common Ground: How Future Search Methods Bring People Together To Achieve Breakthrough Innovation, Empowerment, Shared Vision, and Collaborative Action*, San Francisco: Berrett-Koehler.

document made up of "possibility propositions" describing the collective hopes and dreams people feel inspired to bring about. In the search conference mode, people learn to think of the future as a condition that can be impacted and created intentionally out of values, visions, and what's technically and socially feasible. Such purposeful planning greatly increases the probability of making the desired future come alive. What is unique about the Future Search Conference method as described here is (1) its Appreciative Inquiry Foundation (often experienced as a liberating personal paradigm shift for people); and (2) the broad base of authentic participation that is demanded.

We live in a world of relentless economic change, based on 21st century technologies. Now we struggle to discover management methods equal to the complexity. The power of Appreciative Inquiry and the whole system focus of Future Search combine, our experience shows, to both accelerate and sustain change. Transformation happens faster, at lower cost, and with more inspired collective follow-up than older, more piecemeal or fragmented approaches. Studies show that one well facilitated Future Search with "everybody"—a metaphor for a broad cross-section of stakeholders—will produce more whole systems learning, empowerment, and feelings of connection around business vision than hundreds of fragmenting small group meetings.

The Future Search Conferences, held in each of the regions, would then be capped off with a corporate-wide Future Search of the top 140, the leadership group and key stakeholders representing the whole. If held concurrently in each of the ten regions, the potential for linking up via teleconference for positive storytelling across regions might add a creative and powerful integrative dimension. Literally thousands could be involved in real-time inquiry and transformational planning around the "ABC" vision. Each Future Search would involve something like the following:

1. A conference coordinating committee at the regional level of 4–6 people would meet to plan dates, time, location, meals, group meeting tasks, and who should attend. The goal is to get "the whole system" in the room, or at least strong representation of all those that have a clear stake in the future of the organization. Often then, this includes people "outside" of the organization like customers, community members, partner organizations, etc. The ground rule is that whomever comes to the Future Search must be there for the whole meeting and has the opportunity for full voice in the deliberations.

2. Participants (from 100 to 1000 people) sit in groups of eight to ten, with flip chart paper or a chalkboard available. Depending on the focus and assigned tasks, groupings may vary during the conference. All output from small group discussion is recorded, all ideas are valid, and agreement is not required to get ideas recorded.

3. The conference has four or five segments, each lasting up to a half day Each segment requires that people (a) look at or build a data base, (b) interpret it together, (c) draw conclusions for action.

4. The first major activity focuses on macro-trends likely to affect the organization in the future. Each group is asked to make notes on significant events, changes, and trends they see merging by looking at each of the past three decades from three perspectives: significant changes and events that happened at the world, personal, and institutional /industry levels over each of the past three decades. Each table reports to the total group, and a facilitator notes trends. The total conference then interprets the most positive macro-trends—those trends that indicate opportunities for building a better organization, society, or industry. Even the macro trends that appear negative or threatening often generate creative thinking on hidden opportunities or possibilities for creating the future people want.

5. The second major activity focuses on the appreciative analysis of the organization. Each group has a copy of the Appreciative Inquiry report that was compiled earlier, with quotes, stories, and comments from all the appreciative interviews. Three questions are then posed to each group:

    (a) What are the most outstanding, moments/stories from this organization's past that make you most proud to be a member of this organization?

    (b) What are the things that give life to the organization when it is most alive, most effective, most in tune with the over-arching vision, etc. (make a list of up to ten factors)? and

    (c) Continuity: What should we try to preserve about our organization—values, traditions, best practices—even as we change into the future? Again, consensus is not needed as the results are displayed and discussed by the whole conference.

6. The third major activity focuses on the benchmark understanding of the best practices of other organizations. Each group is given the report from benchmarking studies and is asked to make a list of the most interesting or novel things being done in other organizations. The list should include things that are interesting, novel, or even controversial and provocative. The list is not an endorsement of any of the practices—it is simply a compilation of interesting or new ideas and practices. There is to be no discussion of whether or not to adopt the practices in the present organization. If benchmark studies have not been done as part of the pre-conference Appreciative Inquiry process then group members should generate the list from things they have seen in other organizations have heard or read about. Reports are made to the whole conference and people are asked to comment on the most interesting or novel ideas.

7. The fourth major activity focuses on the future, especially the creative construction. New groups are formed and are given a half day to develop a draft of a preferred, possible future. The focus is on translating the business vision into inspired organizational vision. The focus is on the organizational dimensions of the future. Using a model like the 7-S model or a homegrown model

of organizational design elements, groups develop a set of "possibility propositions" of the ideal or preferred future organization (3–5 years into the future).

8.   The fifth major activity focuses on the next action steps. Groups are then
     asked to reflect on what has surfaced and, depending on the nature of the
     groupings, to make three lists of suggested action steps: commitments they
     want to make as individuals to move the vision forward; action steps their
     region, and work unit, might take; and things the organization as a whole
     might do. Action proposals are shared in a total group session and a steering
     committee is formed to discuss proposals for the total organization, prioritize
     themes, and prepare a report to be presented at the capstone Future Search.

Whole System Involvement

In a comprehensive study of successful habits of visionary companies, Stanford
University researchers Jerry Porras and James Collins put it simply:

It's become fashionable in recent decades for companies to spend countless
hours and sums of money drafting elegant vision statements, values statements,
purpose statements, aspiration statements, mission statements, purpose statements,
objective statements, and so on. Such pronouncements are all fine and good—indeed, they can be quite useful—but they are not the essence of a visionary company.
Just because a company has a "vision statement" (or something like it) in no way
guarantees that it will become a visionary company! If you walk away from this book
thinking that the most essential step in building a visionary company is to write such
a statement, then you will have missed the whole point. A statement might be a good
first step, but it is only a first step. (Taken from *Built to Last*, 1994.)

Translating core vision into everything the company does requires ways of
connecting everyone—evoking ownership, commitment, understanding, involvement, and confidence in the vision's promise. This proposal provides a doable
way to proceed: it is logistically possible and financially feasible to design a process where all of operations (67,000 people) are involved. Everyone, at a minimum, would be a participant in the Appreciative Inquiry as an interviewer,
interviewee, or both. And up to 10,000 would participate in at least three other
engaging activities of learning and doing: workshops on Appreciative Inquiry (one
day long); conducting the interviews (doing 5–10 interviews); and one or more
Future Search Conferences (three days in length). The working assumption, at the
regional level, is that approximately 1,000 people would participate in a day long
introduction to Appreciative Inquiry. They would subsequently be charged with
completing 5–10 interviews apiece, and then would serve as delegates to the regional Future Search Conference.

Measuring for Results

AMX Connects! will measure its results by asking how each step, and the whole process, achieves discrete, agreed upon objectives. This is a demanding approach that will force everyone involved to focus on how the method of Appreciative Inquiry actually affects the way people think, communicate, and act in relation to the process of whole system transformation. Some of the areas of expected impact include:

- Reduction in the time lag between organization innovations (innovations that are consistent with the "ABC" vision) and their spread throughout the corporation.
- The strengthening of a "can do" climate of hope and confidence in the corporation's ability to manage the transition and realize its transformational goals.
- Significant increase in the corporation's positive internal dialogue about the future (e.g., less cynical and deficit oriented discourse, less fear; less negativity; more vocabularies of positive possibility; more rapid spread of good news developments).
- Development of a more appreciative leadership mindset and culture which provides managers with new options for dealing with corporate and customer surveys, re-engineering, strategic planning analysis, team-building, merger integration, performance appraisal and others.
- Significant increase in the feeling of connection to the corporation's "ABC" vision at all levels and regions of AMX Operations.

Sustainability

The telecommunications industry is going through a profound change that involves reassessment of economic foundations, technological infrastructures, organizational forms and processes, and managerial mindsets. The whole-system transformation being called for is both comprehensive in scope and fundamental in nature. There are a number of things, therefore, that must not be overlooked. First, we must not overlook the reality of people's resistance to such profound change—to even thinking about it—since it involves challenge to the inner assumptions which have become an inherent part of the culture and individual ways of constructing the "way things ought to be". Nor should we fail to note that the coming changes will bring about a great deal of fear and uncertainty; in fact, keeping down the fear is probably the greatest challenge of all, since only with low levels of fear can people see clearly and take the right actions. But perhaps most important is the need to address questions of sustainability. What will make the appreciative inquiry/future search methodologies as outlined earlier more than just a one-time high? What will be done to sustain learning's at regional, corporate, and individual levels? Our own evaluations of Appreciative Inquiry and the evaluation studies of large group Future Search Conferences suggest the following five strategies for long term sustainability.

1. Skillbuilding: The Process of Organizational Transformation is a School for Leadership Development. In many respects, there is really no such thing as organizational transformation, there is only individual transformation. Because of this, especially with the leadership group of 140, every major session will involve both organizational analysis and personal planning as well as skillbuilding modules around all the phases of appreciative inquiry and the methods of facilitating interactive, large group meetings. In GE's recent whole system "Workout Program", for example, it was found that the most important outcome of the initial large group Workouts was managerial skill development—the Workout conference methodologies have become a way of life for almost two-thirds of the work units. Of course, Chairman and CEO John F. Welch played a major role in making the new participatory methods a priority. He was notorious in his surprise appearances at local Workout sessions and was consistent in his message: "building a revitalized 'human engine' to animate GE's formidable 'business engine'."

2. Extending Appreciative Inquiry Into Change Efforts Where There Will Be High Value-Added. Already there are plans being made by various AMX staff to use the appreciative methodologies to re-think and revitalize organization development practices like corporate surveys, customer focus groups, public affairs projects, etc. These efforts at extending Appreciative Inquiry should be made more systematic and priority driven. Our suggestions is that we should prioritize no more than five major extensions of Appreciative Inquiry—for example AIs contributions to merger integration methods, organizational surveys, process re-engineering, and diversity initiatives. Each of these efforts should be carefully documented and written up later in the form of a practitioner manual (e.g., a merger integration manual, or a customer focus group manual). Appreciative Inquiry involves a paradigm shift that will vitally transform, for example, how mergers or diversity initiatives are approached. The key, early on, is to prioritize several areas where there will be a high value added contribution and, in those areas, take the appreciative approach to the hilt.

3. Customized Regional Follow-up Consultation. In preparation for the Future Search Conferences, and in response to needed follow-up at the regional level, there will be a consultant/facilitator team made up of internal AMX professionals (e.g., OD, HR, PA) and a specialist from Cooperrider and Associates. This consultant team will commit, up front, to ten days of consulting follow-up at the regional level to tailor-make a response to the initiatives generated at

the Future Search Conferences. By definition, the customized response is un-known at this time, but our experience shows that the commitment to ten days of follow-up consultation is the single most important thing that can be done to ensure sustainability. In a recent study of Appreciative Inquiry with 25 organizations, it has been found that ninety percent of the organizations are continuing with the appreciative methodologies, some two years after the start (see Wilmot, 1995). An essential attribute of the sustainability was that in each case, all ten days of promised follow-up consultations were in fact used. Likewise, the follow-up was completely at the initiative and request of the organizations themselves. Each organization had to "apply" in writing for the follow-up: what were the goals, what kind of support did they need (e.g., facilitation, training, outside evaluation, retreat design, organization analysis, one-one personal counseling). The lesson is simple: we must plan for sustainability from the beginning, and the commitment to the customized fol-low-up opportunity is critical.

4. Advanced "Internal Consultant" Learning Partnership. Each year, there will be two special sessions among all internal AMX change agents that are in-volved with Appreciative Inquiry and the Future Search Conferences. The learning partnership will deal with advanced theoretical and practice issues, and will use clinical/field-based modes of learning. The purpose will be to build internal skills and competencies, to build a support network among AMX units and regions, and to make good use of the program's evaluation studies for advanced professional development.

5. Appreciative Inquiry "On-line". Already there have been discussions with specialists at AMX about how to accelerate the spread of innovations and good news storytelling by adding an Appreciative Inquiry protocol to the new AMX on-line suggestion program. An analogy here is useful: an ongoing Appreciative Inquiry will be to the "whole system transformation" what time-lapse photography is to the visible blossoming of an otherwise imperceptible flower. Putting Appreciative Inquiry on-line is a very exciting venture that has yet to be done anywhere. There is no question the time is ripe for this to happen; and it makes sense that it would be inaugurated at AMX, where lead-ership in the positive human impact of advanced technology lies at the fore-front of the corporate mission. One way to introduce the on-line approach would be to conceive of the 67,000 interviews as mini-training sessions in Appreciative Inquiry After each interview, people would be given a short booklet with simple instructions on how to use the internal on-line "web page". Stories and new images would be made available on a continuous basis. An award could even be established for the stories that best anticipate and give a glimpse of the new AMX, living its vision today. The implications of Appreciative Inquiry on-line are far reaching and exciting indeed. We are infants when it comes to our understanding of the power of this kind of non-hierarchical information sharing and whole system dialogue. The results could be revolutionary.

In the course of developing the ideas described above, it has become clear that people at AMX have this hope that there's a little window of opportunity for really responding to a radically changed business environment. That window of opportunity, and the current season of hope being expressed, is going to last about as long as Sheldon Abrahms, in the early days of his new presidency, uses this occasion to boldly enroll everyone in the positive transformation. To make it all work we (as an internal/external team) will not only need to work collaboratively, responsively, and flexibly as a "learning organization," but we also will need to be united around a shared revolutionary intent.

Conclusion

The relational, large group, participatory methods outlined here fly in the face of old hierarchical, piecemeal problem-analytic approaches to change. Likewise the appreciative paradigm, for many, is culturally at odds with the popular negativism and professional vocabularies of deficit that permeate our corporations and society at large. Most important, however, there are people, many people throughout AMX, that feel the time has come to make the "positive revolution" happen. These are the individuals that are just waiting to step forward and lead. The constructive, creative, and indispensable voices of the new AMX already exist. But their critical mass has yet to be legitimized. AMX Connects! is about mass mobilization; it is about the systematic creation of an organization that is in full voice. It is about transformation of the corporation's internal dialogue. It is about creating, over the next several years of discovery and transition, a center stage for the positive revolutionaries.

Chapter 8

An Appreciative Inquiry into the Factors of Culture Continuity During Leadership Transitions: A Case Study of LeadShare, Canada

Mary Ann Rainey
ComEd

LeadShare (LS), a partnership of nearly 350 accountants and management consultants in Canada, embodies a unique blend of tradition and innovation which has proved successful, often placing it at the forefront of change. LeadShare's inception dates back to the mid-nineteenth century, close to the time Canada became a country. Within the past 25 years, LeadShare has expanded its spectrum of client services and reshaped itself for double-digit growth, currently ranking among the top accounting firms in Canada.

Human Resources is a critical function at LeadShare. The firm values human capital and recognizes the need to hire the right people to produce and deliver quality products and services. Today, individuals recruited by LS have far more complex qualifications because competition for competent people is intense. The need for professional development is just as urgent.

More than ever, LS people have to be futurists. The firm must be capable of looking ahead, discerning what is on the horizon, and preparing for it. The goals LS has for itself are the same as those of its clients: do the best today and anticipate and be poised to do even better tomorrow As a partnership of shared management, preparation for tomorrow is a collective effort.

OD Practitioner, Vol. 28, Nos. 1 and 2, 1996.

Roundtable

In anticipation of transitions in two key executive positions within the span of three years, the organization set in place a succession plan to ensure minimum disruption and to prepare for leadership entering the next millennium.

LeadShare launched the "Roundtable" initiative; Roundtable to suggest leadership without hierarchy, shared resources, and cross-functional networks. The objective of Roundtable is to enlighten the next generation of leaders about the firm's history and tradition and their ingredients of success. A desired outcome for Roundtable participants is to develop a group of agents of culture who sustain the firm's traditions, practices, and behaviors while multiplying the factors of success.

Using current values, assumptions, and motivations as stepping stones to new ones requires knowledge of what the current ones are. Unfortunately, cultural assumptions are usually taken for granted and therefore difficult to see (Schein, 1985). LeadShare realizes that it must find ways to articulate the implicit aspects of its culture if it expects to grow in new directions. A move in that direction is to provide a venue for partners to talk about their experiences and views about what is different, special, and valuable about the firm. Freud (1921) spoke of five "principle conditions" for raising collective life to a higher order: (1) some degree of continuity; (2) some definite idea; (3) interaction among the group; (4) traditions, customs, and habits; and (5) definite structure. These principles serve as a useful preamble to the methodology that guided Roundtable. That methodology is Appreciative Inquiry.

Appreciative Inquiry

Appreciation is a *selective perceptual process* which apprehends "what is" rather than "what isn't." It represents a capacity to be selectively attentive to the lasting, essential, or enlivening qualities of a living human system. Appreciative management, as a process of valuing, consists of a rigorous ability to disassociate all seeming imperfections from that which has fundamental value (Cooperrider 88, p.4).

According to the theory's creators, David Cooperrider and Suresh Srivastva, in its most basic meaning, Appreciative Inquiry is a form of organizational study that selectively seeks to locate, highlight, and illuminate the "life-giving" forces of a firm's existence (1987).

There are two essential questions behind any appreciative study:

1. What makes organizing possible; and
2. What are the possibilities of newer and more effective forms of organizing.

Four basic principles guide Appreciative Inquiry:

1. Exploring the life-giving forces of the firm should be *appreciative* in nature. The appreciative approach looks for what "works"; those peak aspects that serve to activate partners' energies and competencies.

2. Exploring the life-giving forces of the firm should be *applicable*. It should lead to knowledge that can be validated and used productively

3. Exploring the life-giving forces of the firm should be *provocative*. Appreciative knowledge is, by nature, suggestive of what might be. Looking at the best of "what is" kindles the thought of "what might be"; it also challenges the firm to become the best of "what is possible".

4. Exploring the life-giving forces of the firm should be *collaborative*. It should foster healthy dialogue about the way things were, the way things are, and the way things can be.

Several dimensions of the AI process contribute to its uniqueness as a tool for succession planning (see Table 1). Foremost is the shift from the traditional "great man" approach to succession to one that emphasizes collectivity and collaboration. Harlow Cohen argues that managerial high performance is a function of collective effort (Cohen, 1986). Cohen believes that managerial work is characterized by (1) high dependence on others; (2) continuous ongoing activities with no defined beginning or end; and (3) a preponderance of time spent in face-to-face interaction. Collaboration is defined in terms of consciousness, choice, caring, and commitment. Collaboration operates within a relational system characterized as a just system based on fairness, mutuality and responsibility (Appley and Winder, 1977).

The primary objective of AI in the Roundtable program is to assist LeadShare in envisioning a collectively desired future, and then collaboratively carrying forth that vision in ways which successfully translate intention into reality and belief, and then into practice.

The Roundtable was a component in a major organization development intervention that spanned two decades at LeadShare. Roundtable itself was a multiyear intervention with core activities occurring during a six-month period (see Table2). Work included development of the AI interview protocol, data collection, thematic analysis of data, data feedback, and identification of future direction.

Collection of Data

Over 700 pages of data were collected throughout an 18-month period using common social science methods which included:

1. **Interviews.** The 40 partners who were selected to participate in Roundtable conducted open-ended formal interviews with the entire population of partners

Table 1. Comparison of Traditional Approaches to Succession and AI

	Conventional	Appreciative Inquiry
Unit of analysis	Primacy on individual	Primacy on group
Type of analysis	Problem and organization diagnosis	Embraces a solution
Source of vision	New leader, the 'Messiah'	Three generations of current leaders
Pre-succession succession	Psychological trauma disruption	Valuing, visioning, dialogue creating the vision
Post-succession	Alienation	Culture continuity

in the firm. Each interview lasted about two hours and covered questions about their experience in the firm and six topic areas; (1) partnership; (2)determination to be winners; (3) diversity; (4) Consensus decision making; (5)possibilities/positive thinking; and (6) conditions for people to excel. The topics and interview questionnaire were created by external consultants in collaboration with members of the organization's Management Committee. Roundtable participants were instructed by video on how to conduct an Appreciative Inquiry.

2. **Historical Documents.** Reports, articles, speeches, newsletters, unpublished papers, and memoranda were reviewed and content analyzed.

3. **Observations.** Office visits, committee meetings, and retreats were attended which provided a firsthand experiential basis for understanding the culture of the firm.

4. **Survey.** In a second phase of the research, a survey was conducted at the Annual Meeting of the partners to provide convergent validity to the interview data. Developed by the 40 Roundtable participants, the survey summarized the six topic areas based on the "7 S framework" (see Peters and Waterman, Jr., 1982). The partners gave two ratings on a 7-point Likert scale: (1) the extent to which they felt the survey statement represented an important "ideal" to continue to be pursued by the firm, and (2) the extent to which the survey statement was reflected in practice.

Analysis of Data

For purposes of reliability and objectivity, the raw data was analyzed by two independent researchers in addition to the author. Word counts and interpretations were consistent among the three. The qualitative data and results from the survey provided a set of descriptive themes. From these themes emerged a preliminary description of a set of characteristics around the concept of "culture continuity".

Table 2.   Roundtable/AI Design

May	• Data collected to identify affirmative topics to be explored • Affirmative topics identified • Affirmative topics discussed with Management Committee and modified
June	• Questionnaire developed
June/July	• Roundtable participants conduct interviews
July	• Interview data summarized
August	• Roundtable participants and staff receive samples of data from interviews
September	• Roundtable participants and staff receive summarized version of interview data • Roundtable session: Retreat at Mt. St. Marie, Ontario • Roundtable session focused on: 1. Reaffirming the affirmative topic choices and creating a common base of data for all participants 2. Stating provocative propositions about the life-giving properties in the firm 3. Consesus validation of propositions using force-field analysis and debate 4. Identifying the next steps for experimenting with provocative propositions
October	• Administration of Consensus Validation Survey at Annual Partners' Meeting

The following are the major themes of our analysis:

1. **The Feeling of Unity.**   This refers to general solidarity. Unity is exemplified through shared decision making, partner support, working and playing together, the annual meeting, other meetings and anniversary celebrations.

2. **Respected, Responsible, Inspirational Leadership.**   Partners focused on "success generating success" and confidence in the courageous and responsible leadership of the firm. Service to the client is not sacrificed through the commitment to success, growth, and profitability. Automatic committee rotations increase understanding and appreciation of various factors in the firm and provide continuity. Communication and participation before action and major changes build consensus and strengthen the feeling of "partnership". Deliberation guards against hasty decision making and the potential loss of things absolutely critical to the success of the firm.

3. **Justice and Equality.**   The consensus building process, the "one partner, one vote" decision making structure, the development and partnership system. The financial and remuneration structure, the commitment to diversity and autonomy, and the partner exit counseling program breed an environment based on fairness, choice, appreciation, openness, and care.

4. **People Development and Professional Competence.**   Constant learning and the development of partners are priorities. Partners should not only be

competent in their respective skill areas, but they must also have the ability to attract and retain top quality people and instill in them personal pride.

Major Themes with Selected Data

The following are the major theme areas with selected representative data. These examples are provided to build some sense of clarity around the thematic framework.

1. The Feeling of Unity
   - LeadShare does a very good job of making all the offices feel that they are a part of the whole. There is an ongoing feeling of unity among the partners, most likely from day-to-day experience. The partnership seems to work well. When you come away from the annual partners' meetings, you walk with a spring in your step.
   - Different specialties are encouraged to combine forces. Also, there is the "one firm" attitude, which fosters cooperation. Different groups are combined with a unified top management team and national profit sharing, which allows the success to be shared.
   - The managing partner's monthly memos are very important. It is clearly evident that he puts a lot of thought and time into them and through them the feeling of one firm is created. The feeling that we as a firm and as individual partners are very valuable, i.e., the feeling of "wholeness" comes through.

2. Respected, Responsible, Inspirational Leadership
   - The leadership does not dictate. It sacrifices quick decisions for gathering a majority view. This is the way it should be.
   - Through the whole process of choosing our leaders, we provide for continuity within the firm for building consensus.
   - Communication is the key word. It's letting partners know what the issues are prior to final decisions and obtaining feedback and input from them. Obviously, where partnership is so large, it may be difficult to do this on all issues, but we have found it beneficial at annual partners' meetings to have breakout groups where partners are able to have input on things of national concern.
   - No matter how small your office is or how far away you may be from the center of Canada, you still have very good feeling that you are making a contribution. Someone is listening to what you are saying. Your input counts.

Justice and Equality

- At LeadShare, it's equality: it's one pot, one partner, one vote.
- There is a great sense of pride among partners that LeadShare, against heavy odds, turned a challenging region into a success story. The managing partner spared no expense for translations and set an example by learning French.
- I've been involved in two or three instances where we have counseled partners out—it's a difficult process; and without a doubt, the firm has been fair with these, maybe more than anyone else would have been.
- We started out being autonomous, and organized into a national firm later. Our roots through the merged units are to be autonomous, so we centralized. The main thrust was to keep the autonomy of the local offices.
- Merger issues with [a particular firm] where certain outstanding merger issues were settled through cooperation in a manner that was most fair.
- When the firm lost a lawsuit, the manner in which the partners rallied around the individual partner involved was quite impressive.

People Development and Professional Competence

- In recognition that we are in a knowledge business, our leaders direct and the partners accept responsibility for significant self development—including personal, professional and people management skills.
- We feel that management of continuity is prepared well in advance so that when a change does occur, it is not disruptive. The confidence is in younger partners. There are efforts to develop the management potential of younger partners.
- The Roundtable. It's an interesting process in worrying about continuity from one leadership to the next. This process involves a number of perspectives from different partners as well as getting in touch with our strengths so that we don't move too quickly to change things that are absolutely critical to our success.

The Factors of Culture Continuity

Following are eleven propositions that emerged when the thematic framework was taken to a higher level.

1. Commitment to the concepts of "partnership" through communication, consensus building, "one partner, one vote," face-to-face interaction, partner development and evaluation, profit sharing, and confidentiality of unit allocation, all which supports a feeling of fairness and trust.

2. The firm continues to provide high quality, personalized, prompt, and diversified services as well as offering clients the best value for their money

3. The vision of the firm is communicated through everyday behavior and performance.

4. The concept of shared ownership demands that each partner be responsible for the future of the firm.

5. The concept of leadership goes beyond professional services and management processes—it includes the ability to inspire and nurture talent and innovation.

6. People at all levels are developing professional and client service skills. These skills include technical competence in their respective disciplines and a knowledge of current technology.

7. The firm attracts, recruits, and retains the best people across disciplines to develop as professionals.

8. The partnership attracts, develops, and retains people who are intelligent, hard working, energetic, possess good interpersonal skills, and have the courage to change barriers into opportunities.

9. The firm aggressively pursues specialty mergers, acquisitions of service firms and hires recognized experts to expand the diversity of services, skills and people, all to expand the firm's base.

10. The basic strategy for obtaining profitable growth in both the domestic and international environments is through harnessing positive and innovative thinking and using the most current technological and communications capabilities available.

11. Each partner is responsible for leaving a legacy in terms of building firm assets, which includes people, clients, and services.

Conclusion

To the extent that organizations want to maintain internal effectiveness and external adaptability, they need to know what their fundamental values are so they can build a template by which to juxtapose people. Appreciative Inquiry is one technique that can highlight values and help build consensus around what is important to individuals in a firm. AI can help an organization know where it is and where it wants to go, by defining criteria and identifying people who can get them where they need to go.

Appreciative Inquiry highlights the values individuals stand for and allows for rearticulation and reprioritization of those values. In this context, it is a process in pattern enhancement. Values are not simply rearticulated through AI, they are rearticulated more profoundly. Appreciative Inquiry is designed to elicit the ideals of the organization and to give substance to those ideas through a concrete interactive process. It also is designed to make sure people see the connections between their values and the system's.

Beyond this, we found that Appreciative Inquiry builds culture. By taping both common ground and shared values, AI mobilizes the maximum amount of commitment and increases members' confidence in what it is doing. It helps individuals clarify what it is they want to do and promote solidarity that represents a key source of rejuvenation as hard work depletes people's energies.

We also found that Appreciative Inquiry permits adaptation to the environment. In a professional organization, where the likelihood is high that new employees will bring with them the latest techniques, expertise, and knowledge necessary for keeping pace with emerging environmental demands, AI is likely to lead to the cementing of values that are indeed adaptive. If recruitment and development is from good schools and brings individuals with good sensors, and the system allows for learning and adaptation, then sharing values will be a growth process for the organization.

On the other hand, in those organizations displaying low recruitment and turnover, AI may prompt inbreeding and reinforce values that are behind the times, and therefore, threatening to organizational survival. Organizational culture may be very satisfactory for its members but not very adaptive to its environment. Consequently, Appreciative Inquiry could reinforce old, outdated systems values, thereby cementing blindness to the environment.

When AI is used as a succession technique, there is always the threat of demotivating persons not identified as fast trackers. There also is the very legitimate question of: *Are those who are identified as leaders of the future really managers or are they heretics?* To the extent that the system reflects the ideals of the membership, the organization may be down the path of its greatest ignorance. Other approaches to the succession process that introduced actors who backed the prevailing values may represent better guards or protection against this drawback.

Finally, it's clear that Appreciative Inquiry provides many contributions to collective and collaborative efforts and may be most ideal in those settings. It also appears that Appreciative Inquiry may be better suited to environments where fundamental changes have a low probability of occurrence because as much effort is required to maintain specialized cultures as is required to create them. Who should know that better than the partners of LeadShare, Canada.

References

Appley, D.G., and Winder, A.E. (1977). "An Evolving Definition of Collaboration and Some Implications for the World of Work." *Journal of Applied Behavioral Science*, 13, 297–91.

Cohen, Harow (1986). The Social Construction of Managerial High Performance. Unpublished Ph.D. dissertation; Case Western Reserve University, Cleveland, OH.

Cooperrider, D. (1986). "Appreciative Inquiry: Toward a Methodology for Understanding and Enhancing Organizational Innovation. Unpublished Ph.D. dissertation; Case Western Reserve University; Cleveland, OH.

Cooperrider, D. (1987). "Appreciative Inquiry in Organizational Life." *Research in Organizational Change and Development*, Vol. 1, 129–69. JAI Press.

Freud, S. (1921). *Group Psychology and the Analysis of the Ego.* 1922, London: Hogarth Press. Complete works, Vol. 18.

Gephart, Jr., R.P (1978). "Status Degradation and Organizational Succession. An Ethnomethodological Approach." *Administrative Science Quarterly*, 23, 553–581.

Gerth, H., and Mills, C. (1946). From Max Weber: *Essays in Sociology.* New York: Oxford University Press.

Gorden, G.E., and Rosen, N. (1981). "Critical Factors in Leadership Succession." *Organizational Behavior and Human Performance*, (27), 227–254.

Grusky, 0. (1963). "Managerial Succession and Organizational Effectiveness." *American Journal of Sociology*, 69, 21–31.

Jacobs, B. (1986). "Heir conditioning." *Public Relations Journal*, (3), 24–28.

Lieberson, S. and O'Connor, J.F (1972). "Leadership and Organizational Performance: A Study of Large Corporations." *American Sociological Review*, 37, 117–130.

Pfeffer, J. (1977) "The Ambiguity of Leadership." *Academy of Management Journal*, 2, 104–112.

Schein, E. (1985) *Organizational Culture and Leadership.* San Francisco: Jossey-Bass.

Schwartz, H. and Davis, S. (1980). "Corporate Culture and Business Strategy." *Harvard Business Review.*

Smith, J. E., Carson, K. P and Alexander, R.A. (1984). "Leadership: It Can Make a Difference." *Academy of Management Journal,* (27, 765–776).

Weick, K. (1979) *The Social Psychology of Organizing.* New York: Random House.

Chapter 9

Survey Guided Appreciative Inquiry: A Case Study

Rita F. Williams

The purpose of this article is to explore Appreciative Inquiry (AI) as a powerful example of one of the most often used Organizational Development (OD) methods, survey guided development. To date, survey guided development has been wedded almost exclusively to a problem-solving view of OD. However, Wendell French and Cecil H. Bell, Jr., in *Organizational Development* (1995) describe second generation OD methods which includes nontraditional interventions.

The context for the application of OD approaches has changed to a more turbulent environment. While there is still a major reliance on OD basics, considerable attention is being given to new concepts, interventions, and areas of application. Second generation OD includes interest in organizational transformation, organizational culture, the learning organization, teams and their various configurations, total quality management, visioning, and the whole system in the room.".

This article proposes a radical rethinking of the survey-guided method from the perspective of AI. Appreciative Inquiry is a form of organizational analysis first developed by Dr. David Cooperrider of Case Western Reserve University. The purpose of survey guided AI is to invite whole system exploration into an organization's highest human values. Instead of problem diagnosis, there is inquiry into hopes, dreams and visions. Instead of the survey itself being a "mirror of what is" it is an intervention into what "might be." (see Table 1).

Background

The Appreciative Inquiry process was successfully used as an intervention in an organization that was in a serious crisis. It served as a catalyst for change and as a vehicle for focusing an entire organization on a collective vision of the future. The site was an $11 billion regional commercial banking institution located in the Midwest which will be referred to as First Peoples Bank (FPB). The organization evolved from a rich history that consistently reflected dedication to serving its

OD Practitioner, Vol. 28, Nos. 1 and 2, 1996.

Table 1. Notes on Appreciative Inquiry

Problem Solving	Appreciative Inquiry
"Felt need" Analysis of Causes	Appreciating valuing the best of "What is"
Analysis of causes	Envisioning "What might be"
Analysis of Possible solution	Dialoguing "What will be"
Action Planning (Treatment)	Envisioning "What will be"

customers and their communities. The company's roots go back to 1893, when the bank was founded. In the decades that followed, the company established its strength in the industry through financial stability, asset growth, and product development. It was one of the few institutions to guarantee funds to its customers following the stock market crash of 1929 and to remain open throughout the Great Depression. Key highlights include:

- **1950s.** the branch-banking network grew
- **1960s.** the addition of a new building, and new automation for operations
- **1970s.** among the first banks in the Midwest to introduce automated teller equipment and cards; the company name changed reflecting a constantly broadening position
- **1980s.** gained a presence in 11 states with significant operations in Ohio, Indiana, Michigan and Texas

After deregulation went into effect in the late 1980s, the banking industry became unstable. Crisis and change had become a way of life as acquisitions, mergers, and problems with foreign loan portfolios created an unstable environment. In the late 1980s, FPB was beginning to feel the strain. An organization that had previously set an aggressive course for the future with confidence and without hesitation, suddenly had an air of uncertainty about its future business strategies. The leaders feared that the wrong decision would have long-term negative consequences. In the early 1990s the organization began to experience even more difficulty. Some of the Strategic Business Units (SBUs) at FPB were very profitable while others lost money and became a drain on profits. There was a hostile takeover attempt, major loss in profits for the year, all occurring within two consecutive years of record earnings. Loan losses from a risky foreign loan portfolio were balanced by drastic cost cutting measures including a corporate-wide downsizing, which involved laying off over 850 of FPB's 8,000 employees.

As Vice President of the organization, I was the project manager on the cost-cutting program. The project deliverables involved the development and implementation of a detailed plan for downsizing, including a resource guide and training method for the management team. Aggressive employee relation plans and programs were needed to stabilize the organization. Outplacement assistance was put in place for laid off staff along with comprehensive communication strategies to keep everyone informed. Uncertainty surrounding the downsizing created concern about retaining the high quality staff needed to move the organization forward.

Because managers were affected by the downsizing, a vision and statement of values was created by the organization's leaders and reviewed with each staff member. A more sincere effort was deemed necessary by managers because of the seriousness of the situation. There was a growing consensus about the need for a powerful intervention which would identify the organization's values and commit the staff to a vision of the future.

The process of Appreciative Inquiry (AI) could help in the identification of a common vision and values. However, there was concern that most of the previous AI applications had included healthy and/or growth oriented organizations. There were many unanswered questions about the potential impact of engaging an organization that was experiencing difficulty in the AI process.

The corporate human resources communication plan called for an aggressive employee relations campaign. The major focus of the campaign was on the construction of a common vision of the future around which employees and managers could align their efforts. It was critical that the vision statement be based on the values and ideals contributed by staff and that an opportunity for employees be available at all levels to develop an agreement and buy-in to this vision. Despite the risk, it appeared that Appreciative Inquiry was the best tool for accomplishing this goal. In the initial stages of this intervention, it was difficult to predict how far the process would go. The typical AI process included five phases (see Table 2). At FPB, a pilot was developed that involved one-on-one interviews with 250 randomly selected employees.

Table 2. Key Phases of the Process

An Overview	
Phase 1	Affirmation topic choice (Definition)
Phase 2	Inquiry into the "life-giving properties" (Data collection and discovery)
Phase 3	Articulation of possibility propositions (Visioning the Ideal—dreaming)
Phase 4	Consensual validation/agreement (Design through dialogue)
Phase 5	Co-construction of the preferred future (Destination)

Appreciative Inquiry Intervention

Phase 1: Affirmative Topic Choice

An interview protocol was created by using primarily open-ended questions which were designed to help people identify the best of "what is" and to allow the topics to emerge. Unlike traditional surveys that focus on participants' opinions, AI focused on the participants' experiences and observations and promoted storytelling of positive and significant events during their careers. An example of an interview protocol is shown in Table 3.

Phase 2: Inquiry Into 'Life-Giving Properties'

The data collection and discovery phase was handled by 20 of FPB's senior human resources staff who, altogether, interviewed 250 bank employees. Each interview was designed to inquire into the life giving properties of the organization as perceived by these employees. The interviewees represented a cross section of staff across the corporation at all levels in the organization. The HR interviewers received training on theory, practice, and application of AI through workshops and practice sessions. The 250 interviews took approximately three weeks to complete. Overall responses were extremely positive, and they generated powerful stories and examples of situations when the organization was functioning at its best:

- "We have a billing clerk that has taken ownership of her job. She says, "We can make it better if we do things differently." She is not afraid to initiate. And she gets recognized. She is a change agent. To be an owner is to be in the business of making continuous improvements.

Table 3.   Sample Interview Protocol

1.   What attracted you to FPB?
   - What were your initial excitements and impressions when you joined the company?
2.   Without being humble, what do you value most about yourself, the organization, your work?
   - What is the single most important thing the company has contributed to your life?
3.   Looking at your entire experience, can you recall a time when you felt most alive, most involved or most excited about working at FPB?
   - What made it an exciting experience?
   - Who were the most significant others?
   - Why were they significant?

- "Throughout my career here I have had the fortune to work with people who were for me. I've been given every opportunity imaginable. There were times when I was given opportunities that were such a stretch that I didn't even know if I was capable. I have worked for people who could somehow see things in me I couldn't even see in myself. Without that confidence, I don't think my career would have unfolded as it has."

Comments from employees interviewed about the AI process included:
- "We need to do this throughout the organization."
- "This is the Perfect time for us to be working towards generating a common focus."
- "I feel better just being interviewed. The questions were hard, but they made me think, and showed me why I stay here and why I want to be a part of FPB's future."

Phase 3: Articulation of Possibility Propositions/ Emerging Themes

The collected data was analyzed and summarized into a report that identified ten emerging values. The values were fashioned from the interviewee's actual experience and reflected the culture of FPB as they understood it from an appreciation of its proven strengths. They also represented a bold extension of those strengths—a focused vision to which people said they aspire as an organization.

The major themes were stated as provocative propositions which bridged the best of "what is" with the understanding of "what might be". They were provocative because they stretched the realm of the status quo, and helped suggest a course of action for the future. Because of this, the values reported were stated in the present tense, not because they had been totally attained, but because people were saying this was their present "ideal" based on experiences when the organization was at its best. In the report, each proposition was supported by actual employee quotes that detailed specific events and/or experiences (Table 4 briefly describes the ten themes).

A summary of the report was reviewed with FPB?s CEO and President. They were surprised by the depth and breadth of the employees? responses. One commented that it was exciting to know that among tellers, clerks and managers there were common values and collective commitment to the future.

The information was so compelling that they felt the entire executive management team should review it. A two-day off-site planning conference was held to present the findings and to develop a plan to move the process forward.

Table 4.   Core Values Emerging Themes

We value people
The company flourishes because each individual is valued as a precious resource.

Responsive performance
FBP is a corporation made up of people who take pride in their work, and who consider responsive performance as modus operandi.

Service and caring
"To serve others"—our unifying purpose. We provide excellent and innovative products that add value and exceed the expectations of those we serve.

Unifying structures
The formal structure is clearly understood but not constraining. FPB supports the use of networks, project teams, and task forces to manage issues that cross formal boundaries.

Honesty
Integrity is expected. It is a way of life. And it begins and ends with example, not procolomations.

Ownership
Employees act as Owners. Owners do things that hired hands will not see.

Being a significant corporation—rock solid
FPB's rock solid stability is a core value that gives life to the organization. People stay because of the stability. customers stay because FPB has been steady. Steady, Sturdy and Stable.

Community
FPB's image in the community is precious. The involvement and commitment has been consistent. It is one of the most important legacies we have inherited.

Being in full voice
When FPB is in full voice, three things occur: (1) new ideas are given full consideration; (2)information is openly shared; and (3)participation in decision making is pushed to the lowest possible level.

Servant leadership
Leadership at FPB is a process of serving others. It involves seeing potential in people in ways that they cannot even see themselves. It involves removing obstacles, coordinating, educating, listening, and coaching.

Phase 4: Consensual Validation Agreement

The senior management team decided that all employees in the organization should participate in the process and have an opportunity to give their input. The call for action included a plan to administer a written survey to all 8,000 employees over a 30-day period. Unlike traditional "off the shelf documents" this survey was internally developed, reflecting the emerging themes identified in the pilot and exploring values, ideals and practices of the organization. The questionnaires allowed all employees to: (1) have a voice in identifying what is important to the company and to them as individuals; (2) evaluate how well they practice those ideals today; and (3) indicate how much they have experienced their values in their career.

Employees were asked to think about times when they were really excited about FPB, where they thought it was going, what it was doing and what they were doing at the time that made it exciting (see Table 5). This vitality was the life and

Table 5.   Examples of consensus validation survey

Employee survey—confidential
Building on our proven strengths

Instructions: What follows is a series of statements about the way our organization should work, works, or has worked. For each statement, consider these three ratings:

- Important to me as an IDEAL. How important, on a sacle of 1 to 7, do you think the statement should be an ideal for FPB to pursue?
- Practied NOW in the Present. Using the scale of 1 to 7, how well do you think FPB lives the statement today?
- To what extent have you EXPERIENCED THIS IN YOUR CAREER AT FPB? Again using the scale.

1. FPB has been recognized as progressive—even ahead of its times—in the treatment of people.

• Important to me as an ideal	1	2	3	4	5	6	7
• Practiced now	1	2	3	4	5	6	7
• Experienced in my career	1	2	3	4	5	6	7

2. We have high expectations of ourselves. We deliver the best.

• Important to me as an ideal	1	2	3	4	5	6	7
• Practiced now	1	2	3	4	5	6	7
• Experienced in my career	1	2	3	4	5	6	7

3. Employees at all levels are aware of our customers' needs and are committed to responding with first-class service. We put ourselves in our customers' shoes and remember that—from the phone calls we answer to the paperwork we process—the way we do our jobs and work together significantly affects our customers' lives.

• Important to me as an ideal	1	2	3	4	5	6	7
• Practiced now	1	2	3	4	5	6	7
• Experienced in my career	1	2	3	4	5	6	7

4. FPB has a reputation as being a rock solid, secure and prestigious financial institution. FPB maintains its reputation through good business decisions and sound business practices.

• Important to me as an ideal	1	2	3	4	5	6	7
• Practiced now	1	2	3	4	5	6	7
• Experienced in my career	1	2	3	4	5	6	7

5. We recognize the value of each employee's contribution and eliminate the obstacles to get the job done.

• Important to me as an ideal	1	2	3	4	5	6	7
• Practiced now	1	2	3	4	5	6	7
• Experienced in my career	1	2	3	4	5	6	7

strength of the organization; it was the proven strengths that they would build upon. That inspection was important to all.

The data was collected so that a statistical analysis could be performed to review it for the organization as a whole and by SBU. The following coding system aided in the development of reports, feedback and action planning:

- Exempt or Non-exempt Status
- Years of Service
- Location (City and State)
- Strategic Business Unit (SBU)

The fixed response questionnaire made it easy to conduct a quantitative analysis in a short period of time. In addition to the fixed responses, the survey included a section with blank space that asked for additional comments and posed the following open-ended question: If you could develop or transform FPB in any way what would you do to heighten its vitality and overall health?

The data collection phase of the process was conducted in orientation meetings with employees in each SBU, kicked off by the senior executive. A videotape, featuring a message from the Chairman and President, described the goals of the project, and the steps of the "Call for Action" initiative. Participation was voluntary and each employee was encouraged to give his/her input.

Approximately 6,500 of the 8,000 employees participated in the survey This was an exceptional response. Even more surprising was the response to the open-ended questions that asked for their ideas and comments. Of the 6,500 surveys, 4,000 contained extensive responses. Many wrote suggestions and comments, some as long as two and three pages. It seemed that a safety valve had been opened to release constructive energy and thoughtful responses creating a collective hope and vision for the future. A team of HR professionals analyzed the data and prepared detailed reports for the entire organization and SBU.

The data was fed to the management team and employees through meetings across the organization. Of the ten themes included in the survey, the following topics emerged as values and strengths:

- Rock Solid Business Practices
- Exceptional Customer Service
- Honesty

In the thematic analysis of the open-ended comments at the end of the survey the value of teamwork emerged as a strength.

Phase 5: Construction of the Preferred Future

Team leaders were trained to facilitate brainstorming sessions with focus groups of employees throughout the organization. The goal of these sessions was to identify ways to build on the identified strengths and to take action in their work group to improve productivity and performance. These brainstorming sessions provided an opportunity for ongoing dialogue, action and commitment to change. A workbook was developed so that the data was uniformly collected and reported to Corporate Human Resources. Opportunities identified included both organizational and SBU specific initiatives. (See Table 6 for using the theme exceptional customer service.)

Impact of AI Process on FPB

The AI process powerfully impacted the nature of the conversations in the organization, causing a fundamental shift in the daily dialogue. Employees began to view problems as opportunities and the optimism inherent in the conversations led to feelings of empowerment; employees were ready to take action in the face of possibility rather than staying frozen in the face of problems and circumstances.

The exceptional response of the staff reinforced the fact that an intervention like AI can breathe life, strength and a proactive response to a crisis. A consensus and shared vision allowed the organization's leaders to move forward aggressively to stabilize the situation. Within one year of the AI interviews, the organization merged with another bank forming a large national holding company. It appeared that understanding its strengths made it easier for the organizations to honor those things that should be preserved. Part of the merger negotiation included selling a group of branch offices to another bank. The management of the

Table 6. Putting our valued commitments to work

Discussion workbook for focus groups

Customer service
FPB provides first-class customer service.
    We go the extram mile to provide excellent service
    We provide caring, responsive service
    We exceed customer expectations
    We have high expectations of ourselves
    We work together
    We deliver the best

Team discussion
A. What we do best and should keep doing.
    What do we have in place that shows great customer service? ("Customers" can be fellow employees, too.) Why does it work well?
B. What we should begin or start doing.
    What new things should we introduce to improve customer service?
C. What we should change or stop doing.
    What are we currently doing that we should question, change, or stop doing?

new bank commented on the positive and productive outlook of the FPB staff. They felt that their attitudes made the transition easy and that they were more receptive than their own staff members. The FPB case is a true example of the positive impact AI can have in the most negative situations.

Conclusion

The AI process in FPB served both as a catalyst and invitation. This was an invitation to participate in an organization-wide process where everyone at each location had the opportunity to think strategically and imaginatively about the future of the organization. As a catalyst, the report provided inspiring snapshots of the future. The information revealed the many strengths of the organization when it was working at its best. There, it must be acknowledged, is an undeniably positive quality about AI. Some of this stems from the nature of the questions that are asked and the responses that are collected. Equally important, much of this quality comes from tapping into the real sense of optimism people feel about the company and its prospects for the future.

In retrospect, several distinguishing features make this case unique. First, the AI intervention was spontaneously initiated by the HR department without the customary rigmarole of top management clearances. The self-sustaining enthusiasm of the employees generated a momentum of its own resulting in over 8,000 employees being surveyed in thirty days.

Second, the AI process collapsed the customary distinctions between leader and follower or between manager and employee by providing everyone in the organization with a meaningful sense of engagement in the organizational renewal process during a prior acute crisis.

Third, the case is an eloquent testimony to the power of AI as a transformative force; the survey questions generated powerful stories that unleashed the collective imagination of the workforce generating boundless optimism that stabilized the situation. AI, in the ultimate analysis, provided a powerful paradigm shift that led employees to view their current situation through a completely interpretive lens wherein problems were viewed as possibilities and the best of "what is" stimulated imagination of "what can be". It provided a new mode of consciousness akin to what Einstein alluded to when he said, "No problem can be solved from the same level of consciousness that created it."

Chapter 10

INITIATING CULTURE CHANGE IN HIGHER EDUCATION THROUGH APPRECIATIVE INQUIRY

Robert L. Head, RODP
Benedictine University
Michele M. Young, Ph.D.
Benedictine University

Abstract

The purpose of this paper is to describe an attempt to initiate culture change in the faculty of Benedictine University utilizing Appreciative Inquiry as the intervention. The traditional academic culture, dating back to the medieval period, is ill-equipped to respond to the public's demand for change and increasing accountability. The fragmentation and alienation which persists in the academy cries for the development of shared purpose and common values if it is to survive. Appreciative Inquiry is designed to articulate and affirm the positive values of an organization. This paper presents a summary of the process utilized, the outcomes of the intervention and the learnings we derived from this experience.

The State of Higher Education

Higher education is in trouble. This sentiment can be heard both without and within the academy today. Whether the focus is the relationship between cost and value, curricular inclusiveness or increasing competition from without, or shrinking resources and balancing priorities from within, change is required and, in fact, long

OD Journal, No. 2, Summer 1998.

overdue. The demand for change in higher education has taken many faces, including cost-cutting, outsourcing, business partnerships, faculty retrenchment and curricular redesign, among others.

In 1971, Sanford observed "We find in our institutions of higher learning widespread unhappiness and cynicism." (p. 357). This view was echoed by Jensen (1995) 24 years later when he speaks of the disaffection and cynicism pervasive in our colleges and universities. In a recent research project, Wilger and Massy (1996) interviewed faculty at 20 higher educational institutions. They found the prevailing theme to be one of atomization and fragmentation.

These findings, and others like them, illustrate that the current academic culture is not providing an environment in which faculty can find meaning and fulfillment in their work. The resultant bitterness can sound a death-knell to an organization besieged on all sides.

If the culture of an organization is the sum of the attitudes, beliefs and behaviors of its people, cultural change can only be accomplished by impacting those variables. Cultural assessment and change has long been housed in the discipline of organization development. However, organization development rarely has been utilized in colleges and universities (Boyer and Crockett, 1973).

One possible explanation for this is that the academic culture, with its foundations in rational thought and dialogue, is ill-suited to the feeling and relationship focus of OD. Or, it may be that the autonomy so strongly defended by faculty prevents the collaboration needed to engage in organizational change. A third explanation may be that colleges and universities rarely invest the financial resources necessary to engage in a system-wide OD effort (Bergquist, 1992).

The traditional academic culture is grounded in philosophy, ritual and practice that can be traced back for hundreds of years. In this culture, loyalty to the discipline transcends commitment to the institution. Tradition and custom serve as the bedrock of the professorial identity (Freedman, 1979). Subcultures confuse the issue further, as faculty can be divided by discipline, level of development (Freedman, 1979) and educational philosophy (Bergquist, 1992).

The resistance and complexity generated by these realities requires any OD effort to utilize processes designed to gain the faculty's active support and involvement for experimenting and modeling new behaviors (Boyers, 1973). Since it is anathema to faculty for anything to be imposed from without, the process of change must generate from the voice of the faculty. An OD intervention which seems uniquely designed to fit the academy is Appreciative Inquiry.

Appreciative Inquiry

Appreciative Inquiry (AI), developed by David Cooperrider and Suresh Srivastva, "is a philosophy, it's a methodology for working with organizations, and it's an intervention theory," (Cooperrider, cited in Gotches and Ludema, 1995). The theory of AI is grounded in five principles (Cooperrider, 1994):

1. **Constructionist Principle.** Our capacity for imagination and creation of images of the future allows for human systems (including organizations) to be altered or reconstructed.

2. **Simultaneity Principle.** Seeds of change are planted in the first question asked. Therefore, inquiry and intervention are interrelated and simultaneous.

3. **Poetic Principle.** Organizations are like an open book or poetry. They are open to multiple interpretations and conclusions.

4. **Anticipatory Principle.** An image of the future precedes the actual change.

5. **Positive Principle.** The more positive the question, the more positive the data. The more positive the willingness to participate, the more lasting the change process.

Unlike traditional problem-solving which seeks to identify and analyze problems in systems and relationships, AI seeks to appreciate and dream about their possibilities. Where problem-solving views organizations as a series of problems to be solved, AI looks at organizations as mysteries to be embraced. The Appreciative Inquiry model is constructed in four phases (Cooperrider, 1996):

1. **Discovery.** Determining what it is about an organization that should be appreciated and valued. What gives life to the organization? What in the organization is exceptional?

2. **Destiny.** What we learn in the process of inquiry should lead to sustainable change and growth.

3. **Dream.** Envisioning possibilities for the organization's future. What might be?

4. **Design.** What is the ideal? What is the human potential of organizational life?

Cooperrider (cited in Gotches and Ludema, 1995) states, "AI is a deliberate attempt to look at what gives life to organizations, and use the power of positive questioning to develop a data base out of which we can envision more provocative and positive futures" (p. 7). Barrett (1995) describes the appreciative process as a combination of emotional and cognitive energy which creates a positive image of the future and uncovers the core values of an organization.

There is a growing body of research to indicate that core values lead to organizational effectiveness. Collins (1995) reported on a study of exceptional organizations in the corporate arena. Those firms included Hewlett-Packard, 3M, Disney, Marriott and Motorola, among others. The firms had an average age of nearly 100 years, and combined they outperformed the stock market 15–1 since 1926. The key finding of the research was that these firms, all high-performing organizations, were "guided more by a core ideology—core values and a sense of purpose—than comparison organizations." (p. 84).

Schroeder, Brief and Guzzo (1996) identify two factors that are important in creating sustainable organizational change. The first is changing what members of the organization believe, while the second refers to the degree to which members understand what the organization values. We contend that mutual trust is an outcome of the convergence of these factors. Allowing Benedictine University to identify and commonly agree upon its core values would generate the framework for a shared purpose. This shared commitment will assist the institution in building an environment of trust and fostering constructive responses to change (Policy Perspectives, 1996).

The Change Process

Early in the summer of 1996, key administrators of Benedictine University engaged in a process of updating the 1994 strategic plan which formulated initiatives designed to increase the competitive advantage of the institution. One of these initiatives was related to academic culture. There was tacit agreement that a culture change was integral to any effective improvement in the institution's functioning. Therefore, an initiative related to culture was included in the document. It stated: "Establish a long-term strategy that will address issues that negatively affect morale in an attempt to develop higher levels of trust, cooperation, teambuilding, and community across the campus."

While no formal assessment of culture had been conducted, substantial anecdotal evidence existed to validate a less than desirable culture and a need for a second-order change. To add validity to these impressions, a content analysis was conducted of the minutes of faculty meetings and memos generated through the previous two years. The results of the content analysis lent support to the initial diagnosis.

Generally, the culture could be characterized as one of fragmentation and mistrust. The lack of trust manifested itself in increasingly intense discussions around governance and participation. Also prevalent was a language of separation and perceived hierarchy between employee groups.

An initial tactical decision was to engage senior members of the faculty who shared in the desire to improve the culture at Benedictine University. The first outcome from this planning group's discourse was to target the fall opening faculty meeting for initiating dialogue around culture. The opening faculty meeting was selected for two important reasons:

1. It brought together all returning and new faculty, who tend to be energized with the prospects of a new year. The hope was to capitalize on the high

TABLE 1. The Benedictine Core Values

Learning Community	A community in which education is the central value where both the sharing and discovery of knowledge are valued and rewarded.
Benedictine Community	A community which shares the values reflected in the "Rule of St. Benedict." A community which seeks to integrate the growth of the mind, body and spirit in every member, while calling each one to discover the presence of God in their own unique life circumstances. A community which strives for openness to the process of change and growth within the context of faithful commitment to the stewardship of God's gifts.
Human Community	A community where diversity is sought and appreciated; where all members of the community are treated fairly in a supportive manner, and provided with the opportunity for meaningful growth and development. A community in which social justice is understood as a driving value which is taught, lived and modeled by members of the community.
Open Community	A community in which differences are dealt with in an open, constructive and appreciative manner free from the fear of retribution; a community which recognizes its relationship to the external community of which it is an integral part; is sensitivie to and appropriately responsive in fulfilling its responsibility to that larger community.
Effective Community	A community in which each member is working toward explicit objectives and valued for their contribution to the mission of the school; a community in which each member internalizes a responsibility for, and is accountable for the most effective use of the organization's resources.
Celebrative Community	A community where the achievements and accomplishments of the members are recognized and celebrated by all; one in which rituals affirming both tradition and change are widely shared.

energy level and positive outlook and to create a collaborative roadmap for change.

2. The meeting had traditionally been used to establish a theme and priorities for the year. Symbolically, it was important that a dialogue on culture occur at this meeting of the full faculty and with visible participation and support of the administration, most notably the president. After considerable discussion, the second outcome of the planning group's efforts was the selection of AI as

the appropriate intervention. The institution had some experience with AI but, to date, had not utilized it to engage the faculty.

The final choice of AI as the appropriate intervention for an academic environment was based on the following:

1. It requires a high level of participation that is not always realized in a traditional problem-solving intervention where there is an exploration of a problem (and, inherently, an identification of cause/blame).

2. It pursues a spirited, intellectual pursuit of an ideal, which is congruent with an academician's pursuit of understanding and truth.

3. Its principles are grounded in the research of Maslow, Lewin, and Gergen (Cooperrider and Srivastva, 1987).

Formatting the Appreciative inquiry intervention was the next task of the planning group. Should we utilize a Search Conference method capturing the energies of the entire faculty simultaneously? Would we have "trained" facilitators interview each faculty member? These are some of the questions with which we wrestled. Given the AI principle of simultaneity, the idea that inquiry and intervention occur together, we chose to have one faculty member interview another. Following the interview, the two individuals would switch roles.

The next task was to develop the AI protocol. A traditional AI model served as the framework covering concepts such as:

- organization and affiliation
- organization and personal high points
- visioning/common purpose
- collaborative processes/cooperation
- commitment/empowerment

Another tactical decision was to enlist a senior faculty member, also a member of the planning group, to deliver a brief explanation of AI, the purpose of the inquiry, and specific instructions. This introduction, delivered by a respected natural scientist who had become an enthusiastic supporter of AI's possibilities, was critical to engage the faculty in this intervention.

Of the 86 faculty present, all but one participated in the interview process. Interviews were alive with stories of Benedictine University's strengths which included its students, academic purpose, the diversity and dedication of its people, and the fundamental grounding in the traditions of its Benedictine heritage. For illustration, one comment is included here:

One of my most satisfying experiences at Benedictine University was working with science faculty from several disciplines to create a successful grant proposal. A novel feature of the proposal was the creation of an interdisciplinary laboratory course intended for all entering science majors. In doing so, faculty members from Biology, Chemistry, and Physics were able to put aside partisan interests and to transcend the traditional discipline boundaries. The Howard Hughes Medical Institute awarded this proposal $600,000.

The themes and stories that emerged from the interviews were shaped by a volunteer group of faculty into a set of Core Values (Table 1).

Conclusion

Although the adoption of the Benedictine University Core Values, which developed through this intervention and the entire organizational development process, is far from complete, the use of AI in our institution has yielded some promising results. Our assessment of the intervention produced the following learnings:

1. The all but universal (n-1) participation in the intervention lent support to our choice of venue and the content of the protocol.
2. The speed at which we were able to capture data from all faculty proved very economical.
3. The intellectual isolation inherent in the faculty role was bridged by the partnering of faculty and the sharing of values through the interview process.
4. The focus on the positive and the possible produced an upbeat tone rarely found in faculty meetings.
5. The AI intervention produced an environment where cynicism was set aside and faculty were able to transcend the problems and celebrate the strengths of our organization.
6. The themes which were developed from the interview data do reflect a sense of shared values and a commitment to a common purpose among the faculty.
7. The themes developed by the faculty were very similar to those developed in an AI intervention conducted previously with administrators and staff.

In the months that followed the AI intervention, a small group of faculty and administrators (Core Values Group) continued the work begun at the opening faculty meeting. Specific accomplishments of this group include: (1) the development of behavioral definitions for the core values; (2) the creation of a preamble to the core values document; and (3) the development of an implementation plan which will guide the incorporation of the core values into the activities and relationships of all members of the university community.

Of equal importance with the tasks accomplished during this period, the members of the Core Values Group identified several outcomes which were personal in nature. These included areas such as developing a working relationship with extremely committed members of the university community; increasing sensitivity to the environment and culture; identifying the areas of congruency and incongruency between the historical values of the institution and current behaviors; and serving as change agents to help make informed decisions about the future of the organization.

The refinement and adoption of these Benedictine Core Values continues to be a work-in-progress for Benedictine University. However, the successful engagement of the faculty in the AI process and the resultant core values document give evidence of a culture which can once again anticipate a more vibrant future through a shared language of affirmation.

References

Austin, S. (1990). Assessing academic climates and cultures. In W. Tierney (Ed.), *New Direcitons for Institutional Research*, 61–74. San Francisco: Jossey-Bass.

Barrett, F. (1995). Creating appreciative learning cultures. *Organizational Dynamics*. 24, 36–49.

Berquist, W. (1992). *The Four Cultures of the Academy*. San Francisco: Jossey-Bass.

Boyer, R. and Crockett, C. (1973). OD in higher education: Introduction. *Journal of Higher Education*. 44, 339–351.

Collins, J. (1995). Building companies to last. *Inc*. 17, 83–86.

Cooperrider, D. (1994). *A Constructive Approach to Organization Development*. Unpublished manuscript.

Cooperrider, D. (1996). *Appreciative Inquiry Manual*. Unpublished manuscript. Case Western Reserve University.

Cooperrider, D. and Srivastva, S. (1987). Appreciative Inquiry in organizational life. In W. Pasmore and R. Woodman (Eds.) *Research in Organizational Change and Development*. Greenwich, CT: JAI Press.

Freedman, M. (with Brown, W., Ralph, N., Shukraft, R., Bloom, J., and Sanford,N.) (1979). *Academic Culture and Faculty Development*. Berkeley, CA: Montaigne.

Gotches, G. and Ludema, J. (1995). An interview with David Cooperrider on AI and the future of organization development. *OD Journal*, 13, 5–13.

Jensen, E. (1995). The bitter groves of academe. *Change*, Jan-Feb, 8–11.

Sanford, J. (1971). Academic culture and the teacher's development. *Sounding*, Winter, 357–371.

Schneider, B., Brief, A., and Guzzo, R. (1996). Creating a climate and culture for sustainable organizational change. *Organizational Dynamics*, Spring, 7–19.

Shared Purposes. (1996). *Policy Perspectives*. Philadelphia: University of Pennsylvania, Institute for Research on Higher Education.

Wilger, A. and Massy, W. (1993). Prospects for restructuring: A sampling of the faculty climate. *Policy Perspectives*. Philadelphia: University of Pennsylvania, Institute for Research on Higher Education.

Chapter 11

AN APPRECIATIVE NOTE TO THE READER

This article, while not a comprehensive case study in Appreciative Inquiry, appeared in a January issue of *Training Today*, a publication of the Chicago Chapter of the American Society for Training and Development. Also, this article precedes the pioneering work by Dr. Chris Easley involving the use of appreciative inquiry with gangs. Easley's most recent research with gangs indicates that, with appreciative inquiry and search conference methods, youth in gangs are capable of generating alternative ways to view their world, and are then able to socially reconstruct more positive possibilities for their future.

Traditional inquiries into the lives of youth in gangs are focused on what's wrong, what's broken, and what's not working. The images and language surrounding gang members are negative—messages of violence, crime, destruction, and despair. If gang members are to change, they must be a part of the change process and must believe that they have control over their future. Most critical, however, they must be able to vision a different reality, one that is important to them as individuals and as a collective organization.

Through affirmation and vision-creating, youth in gangs, when included in the positive dialogue process, can begin to dislodge the deficit language and negative modes that previously permeated every aspect of their lives. By dislodging the negative modalities impeding any hopeful possibilities for their future, these children are able to begin the positive dialogue to dream, discover, and design the vision of their own more promising future (Easley, 1999).

We are concerned for our children's future. The media validates our fears that children, regardless of race or economic background, are dying from gang violence. Most recently, this fear was again stirred by the violent massacre in Littleton, Colorado.

By the time the [Littleton, Colorado] terror ended with the killers' own suicides, 12 students and a teacher were dead, and 23 students were wounded, several of them critically. Klebold and Harris hoped to get the last laugh; it took days for police to find and defuse about 30 propane tank

and pipe bombs they had planted in the school for maximum carnage. Many mysteries surround the most lethal school shooting in history.
Newsweek, Anatomy of a Massacre, May 3, 1999.

Therefore, with all youth in mind, and consistent with this book's theme, we provide a means by which to rethink human organizations toward a positive theory of change. For a more comprehensive case study involving the use of appreciative inquiry on youth please visit Chris Easley at CEOCHRIS@aol.com.

Saving Tomorrow's Workforce

Christopher Anne Easley
Benedictine University

Therese Yaeger
Benedictine University

Peter Sorensen
Benedictine University

Fact: The Chicago area is home to one of the largest gang populations in the world.

Question: You might ask: "Why such a topic for a training and development publication?"

Answer: Simply put, today's youth are tomorrow's workforce. For those in the training and development field, social concern for youth as well as adults should be our over-arching responsibility.

Worldwide, young people are dying at record rates from varying forms of violence. Domestically, we are losing far too many to gang violence. Gangs are a major problem in our society, and sociologists, psychologists, and researchers have been studying gang behavior for decades attempting to understand the underlying behavioral patterns that give rise to gang behavior.

Over ten years ago, Johnston and Packard shocked the nation with their "Workforce 2000" demographics (Johnston and Packard, 1986). These changing demographics indicate a significant percentage of youth are affected by gang violence. If we are to maintain and re-populate a viable, thriving work force, corporations cannot stay uninvolved with this gang issue. We are losing our youth, and if they are not physically dying, youth still may be mentally dying.

Current research suggests that our youth can articulate vision; however, many have lost hope in their future. Traditional researchers continue to study youth in gangs as a problem to be solved. In this problem orientation, the researcher develops knowledge by emphasizing a critical approach to social problems believed to arise from the social context (Tenkasi et al., 1994).

Training Today, Jan–Feb, 1999.

Gangs as Organizations

A recent gang report states that many "ethnic" gangs are forming complex organizational structures as they form alliances with other ethnic gangs. Hagedorn examined the structure of "People and Folks," and reported how various gangs have joined together to become "nation" structures. Specifically within the Midwest, the People Nation includes the Vice-Lords, El Rukins and Latin Kings, and the Folks, the Gangster Disciples, and Spanish Cobras (Hagedorn, 1988).

The Department of Justice also published survey results within this report. Of significance were answers to the question: "What do you believe is the biggest contributor to the street gang problem in California?" Respondents cited as issues: poverty; lack of education and job training; breakdown of the family unit; lack of parental control, supervision and family values resulting in the gang family replacing the traditional family; lack of positive role models; lack of community involvement; community apathy; perception that there is a lack of economic opportunity combined with increased economic problems; lack of employment opportunities and adequate jobs to earn a living.

Another question was: "What do you believe will be the most significant trend pertaining to street gangs in California by the year 2000?" The top reply was an increase in the sophistication of the gangs and better organization and structure (Gangs, 2000).

Some researchers are looking at the gang structure from an organizational perspective. Martin Sanchez Jankowski, an associate professor of Sociology at University of California Berkeley, conducted a 10-year study of 37 gangs of varying ethnic backgrounds. The research centered in low income areas, where gangs have been institutionalized for years. The ethnic groups studied included Mexican Americans, African Americans, Salvadorans, Nicaraguans, Puerto Ricans, Dominican Jamaicans, and Irish gangs. Jankowski reported these gangs are an organizational response to inequality and poverty that acts in an entrepreneurial manner (Lockwood, 1993).

While gangs frequently engage in criminal activity, Jankowski reported that crime is not the central issue. Jankowski's study focused on the organizational traits of gangs, which included the nature, dynamics, and impact of the gang's organizational qualities. He reported that one reason that society does not understand the gang phenomenon clearly is that there have not been enough systematic studies undertaken as to how the gang works as an organization (Jankowski, 1991). Sociologists associate the individual gang member with the organization, but do not have much evidence as to what it is about the organization and its macrodynamics that makes the gang member's behavior different from what it would be if he or she were not in an organization (Jankowski, 1991).

Pygmalion Effect

The Pygmalion effect was clearly evident during the early days of the intervention. Prior to the intervention, the students were unable to articulate alternatives to survival other than engaging in gang related activities. Youth in gangs need an alternative vision of the future that offers hope and change; change that they can see within their scope of accomplishment. They also need an alternative vision for acknowledging the skills that they posses; skills we find in mainstream society (Easley, 1999).

The greatest value of the Pygmalion research is that it begins to provide empirical understanding of the relational pathways of the positive image-positive action dynamic and of the transactional basis of the human self. To understand the self as a symbolic social creation is to recognize that human beings are essentially modifiable, are open to new development, and are products of the human imagination and mind. Like the placebo response, it appears that the positive image plants a seed that redirects the mind of the perceiver to think about and see the other with affirmative eyes (Cooperrider, 1987).

By the conclusion of the search conference, the students were able to articulate a more positive future. One student commented for the group:

> Before she [Easley] came, I did not think I was going to be anything; she gives us some umph; she uplifts us; she tells us there are other resources; if your parents are on drugs, you may not know there are other ways; some might want to commit suicide, but you have to know there are alternatives; we expressed somethings that we would not have done or talked to someone about; she let us think about ourselves in another way; it's hard to bounce back when someone for sixteen years has been telling me I am not anything. It's hard to bounce back; this class has given us even more—she brought to us to forget about the past, you can be anything you want; (to me the student said) Be proud of yourself, you just saved another life. I really mean what I said; I am thankful for us that she came here; we can achieve—she let us know that. What you don't see, you don't know.

Heliotropic Evolution

Humans, like organizations are heliotropic in character in the sense that organizational actions have an observable and largely automatic tendency to evolve in the direction of positive imagery. We tend to move more rapidly and effectively in the direction of affirmative imagery (moving toward light) than in the opposite direction of negative imagery.

Inquiry into organizational structures studies organizations as evolving, trans-forming, social constructions, malleable to human choice (Barrett and Srivastva, 1991). Therefore, before attempting to understand the behavior of youth in gangs, we must examine the human choices that individuals in the gang make and the underlying premises for those choices. We must also understand the imagery that drives their choices and the metaphors that they are exposed to.

Currently, research is being conducted using an Appreciative Inquiry (AI) mode of intervention with gangs that approaches "organizing" as a miracle of cooperative human interaction which needs to be affirmed (Cooperrider and Srivastva, 1987; Tenkasi et al., 1994). When using AI with gangs, we seek to locate and highlight the life-giving properties of youth when they function as indi-viduals as well as when they organize. Through affirmation, gang members are most likely to realize what makes them and their ability to work together unique, thus opening possibilities of using gang resources to change the economical and social decay in which they live. Through the use of AI, we are helping gang mem-bers seek out the best of "what they are" in order to provide an impetus of their imaging "what might be" (Tenkasi et al., 1994).

Helping Tomorrow's Workforce Today

Most critically, however, youths in gangs must be able to envision a different reality—one that is important to them as individuals and as an organization. With a new year comes a resolution: Let's resolve not to wait until the next millennium to save tomorrow's workforce.

Chris Easley is Director of the DuPage Center for Multiculturalism at Benedictine University where she teaches in the Business Administration and Master's in Management and Organizational Behavior Programs. As a candidate in Benedictine University's doctoral program in Organization Development, her dissertation title is "The Role of Appreciative inquiry in the Fight to Save Our Youth".

References

Barrett, F, and Srivastva, S. (1991). "History as a mode of inquiry in organizational life: A role for human cosmogony", *Human Relations*, vol. 44, pp. 236–244.

Cooperrider, D. and Srivastva, S. (1987). "Appreciative inquiry in organizational life." *Research in Organizational Change and Development*, pp. 140–145.

California Department of Justice. Division of Law Enforcement, Bureau of Investigation (March 1993), *Gangs 2000: A call to action.* The Attorney Generals report on the impact of criminal street gangs on crime and violence in California by the year 2000.

French, W. L. Bell, C. H. *Organization Development*, Englewood Cliffs, NJ: Prentice-Hall, Inc.

Golembiewski, R (1989). *Organization Development, ideas, and issues*, New Brunswick, NJ: Transaction Publishers.

Hagedorn, J., with Macon, P (1988). *People and Folks, Gangs Crime and the Underclass in a Rustbelt City*, Chicago, IL: Lake View Press.

Johnson, W. B. and Packer, A. H. (1987). *Workforce 2000: Work and Workers for the 21st Century.* Indianapolis, IN: Hudson Institute.

Lockwood, A., (1993). The professor of gangs." *Focus in Change*, n 10, p. 10–14.

Reason, Peter (1988). *Human Inquiry in Action, Developments in New Paradigm Research*, Newbury Park, CA: Sage Publications.

Sanchez-Jankowski, M. (1991). *Islands in the Street, Gangs and American Urban Society*, Berkeley: CA. University of California Press.

Srivastva, S., and Barrett, F. (1998). The transforming nature of metaphors in group development: A study in group theory," *Human Relations*, v. 41, Number 1, pp. 31–64.

Tenkasi, R., Thatchenkery, T., Barrett, F. and Manning, M. (1994). "The impact of schemes and inquiry on consultants' constructions of expectations about the client system." *CEO Publications* (G 94-13 (256), 1994) pp. 1–29.

Chapter 12

APPRECIATIVE INQUIRY WITH TEAMS

Gervase R. Bushe Ph.D.
Simon Fraser University

Executive Summary

This article describes the author's thoughts and experiences in trying to help people have conversations that generate new, affirming and generative images. A simple process for running an appreciative inquiry with a team is described. Differences in using appreciative inquiry with new teams and ongoing teams are discussed. Four different ways to use appreciative inquiry in team-building events run by an external facilitator are described. The author goes on to discuss the role of the consultant as wordsmith in an appreciative process with teams.

Introduction

The question I have been thinking about is how do people come to have conversations in groups that generate new, affirming and generative images of the group? By images I mean phrases, metaphors and stories that people invest with shared meanings. By affirming I mean that these images call to the best in us, capturing our heart's yearning and our spirit's intent. By generative I mean images that lead to developmental transitions or that constitute a more developed group identity.

OD Journal, Volume 16, No. 3, Fall 1998.

I have been experimenting with a form of appreciative inquiry (Cooperrider and Srivastva, 1987) that I think can help create those kinds of conversations and lead to productive, developmental changes in teams. Appreciative Inquiry is a form of action research that attempts to help groups, organizations and communities create new, generative images for themselves based on an affirmative understanding of their past. Working from a socio-rationalist theory of change, (Barrett, Thomas and Hocevar, 1995, Bushe, 1995, Cooperrider, 1990, Gergen, 1990) these new images are expected to lead to developmental changes in the systems in which they are created. The four principles Cooperrider and Srivastva lay down for appreciative inquiry are that action research should begin with appreciation, should be applicable, should be provocative, and should be collaborative. The basic process of appreciative inquiry is to begin with a grounded observation of the "best of what is", then through vision and logic collaboratively articulate "what might be", ensuring the consent of those in the system to "what should be" and collectively experimenting with "what can be."

In this article I will describe findings from my empirical and clinical (in the sense of Schein, 1987) research in using appreciative inquiry with teams. First I'll describe the "best team" method I have developed and impacts I have observed. I will share my thoughts on the use of appreciative inquiries with teams at different stages of their lifecycle and with some of the different issues they confront. I will look at how the "best team" appreciative inquiry can aid team development even when it doesn't generate new images. I will discuss other appreciative inquiries that can be more useful for team building and other uses for "best team" inquiries in addition to generating affirming images. I conclude by talking about the role of OD consultants in helping teams to craft affirming, generative images.

A "Best Team" Appreciative Inquiry

I developed a form of appreciative inquiry that can be used in small groups. In its simplest form it focuses on developing a shared, generative image of team work and goes like this:

First, group members are asked to recall the best team experience they have ever been a part of. Even for those who have had few experiences of working with others in groups, there is a 'best' experience. Each group member is asked, in turn, to describe the experience while the rest of the group is encouraged to be curious and engage in dialogue with the focal person. The facilitator encourages members to set aside their clichés and preconceptions, get firmly grounded in their memory of the actual experience, and fully explore what about themselves, the situation, the task, and others made this a "peak" experience. Once all members have exhausted their exploration, the facilitator asks the group, on the basis of what they have just discussed, to list and develop a consensus on the attributes of highly effective groups. The intervention concludes with the facilitator inviting members to publicly acknowledge anything they have seen others in the group do that has helped the group be more like any of the listed attributes.

In one business team I worked with one member talked about a group of young men he played pick-up basket ball with and described why they were, in his opinion, such an outstanding "team". He described their shared sense of what they were there to do, lack of rigid roles, easy adaptability to the constraints of any particular situation in the service of their mission. But what most captured the team's imagination was his description of how this group was both competitive and collaborative at the same time. Each person competed with all the rest to play the best ball, to come up with the neatest move and play. Once having executed it, and shown his prowess, he quickly "gave it away" to the other players in the pickup game, showing them how to do it as well. This was a very meaningful image for this group as a key, unspoken, tension was the amount of competitiveness members felt with each other at the same time as they needed to cooperate for the organization's good. "Back alley ball" became an important synthesizing image for this group that resolved the paradox of competitiveness and cooperation.

An appreciative inquiry like the one I described can have a useful impact on a group even if it does not result in any clearly articulated, shared imagery. In an experiment I found that project groups that received this intervention scored significantly higher on task outcomes and group processes than groups that didn't (Bushe and Coetzer, 1995). So there does some to be some benefit to sharing stories and stepping into an appreciative space without requiring highly specialized facilitation.

Sometimes simply creating an appreciative space is all a group needs to produce its own images. But more often than not the process does not simply unfold by itself. It takes some skill on the part of the facilitator to frame, shape and embellish the images group members generate into affirming and generative ones. These skills include a poetic ear, an eye for beauty, a keen sense of what others find inspiring and an open heart that can feel the unconscious yearning in the group.

As a team development intervention, there are times when a more focused inquiry is required than the "best team" inquiry described above. In these cases some subset of teamwork, like leadership or conflict management, is what members need to talk to each other about. So in addition to the skills mentioned above, the facilitator needs to have a good sense of timing and sense of what is called for in the situation.

New Teams

The "best team" appreciative inquiry is particularly appropriate for new teams and may help the team do some important "norming" without having to go through "storming". When teams are first formed, members are trying to establish their personal identities in the group. Much of the "forming and "storming" dynamics come out of the clash of establishing personal identity and the role complementarities these create (Srivastva, Obert and Neilsen, 1977). Role complementarity refers to the fact that for any person to take on a role (e.g., leader) others have to be willing to take on complimentary roles (e.g., followers). Attempts to assert identity in newly formed groups create the unintended effect of forcing others into role compliments, some of which they may not like. This leads to the "storming" phase of group development.

Having the opportunity to tell one's "best team" story provides individuals with an important opportunity to establish their identity in the group. It gives them a chance to tell others, in a somewhat indirect way, what is important to them in relating to other team members, what roles they prefer to occupy, what group characteristics they most value, and so on. This can greatly accelerate the team formation process.

Developing a joint statement of good group qualities makes some norms members want to operate by explicit. Generally, these lists are not much different from the list a group would develop without the first step of telling their stories. These lists, however, have much greater meaning for group members because each point is tied to one or more stories. So much time is spent in organizations writing up lists that I have found listing kinds of activities, by themselves, to have limited value. More often than not the list is soon forgotten. Lists generated after an appreciative inquiry, however, can stick a lot more if the process has real participation from those involved.

If an appreciative inquiry is conducted very close to the beginning of a group's life the last step, appreciating other's contributions, may not be appropriate. That step could be taken later as a way to reinforce the aspirations the group set for itself and provide a cohesion building intervention on its own. If the group has had more than 10 hours of meeting or work time together, however, the last part of the intervention is appropriate.

Sometimes members find it hard to think of anything to appreciate in others, especially right after the question is first asked. This is to be expected as we know that in early group dynamics, members are too focused on themselves to be paying much attention to other people's contributions. When we have finished making the list and I invite people to point out things others have done to help the group be more like the listed attributes, I pause for about 20 seconds and if no one is able to offer anything, I then alter the request. I point out that I am not asking them to describe actions that made the group like the listed attributes, just things that helped the group move in those directions. These could be little things, but small actions can, over time, have large consequences. I then ask them to spend ten minutes alone and think of anything they have personally done to help the group be more like the listed attributes and, if anything comes to mind, to note things others have done as well.

This last step is an important intervention into early group life. It allows for further differentiation of the members. It gives people a chance to describe the intentions behind their past behaviors, increasing the level of disclosure and giving each other more insight into each person on the team. Often, in doing this, people remember things others have done as well and this recognition is important in building group cohesion.

A common experience in newly formed teams is that people are looking for similar things from a good team. This can be a potent learning when one or more of the team members come to the team with a reputation that others are leery of. In one team that used this process, one of the members had a reputation for being cold, uncaring and rigid. At first she refused to take part in telling stories of good teams. After others had completed their stories, however, she said she was now willing to do so and told an extremely touching story of a wonderful team experience early in her career at this organization. By the end of it she (and others) were in tears. The story also described how this team was poorly treated by the organization and helped to explain her fear of getting close to others at work. This event radically altered members' perceptions of this woman, the quality of relationships that developed and the whole development trajectory of this group in very positive ways.

Ongoing Teams

Appreciative inquiry in ongoing teams is both more challenging and has the potential to be a more transformational experience. In newly formed teams a "best team" inquiry is always perceived as useful and appropriate. In teams that have worked together for some time and will continue to work together for the foreseeable future, this is not always the case. If the intervention is not well positioned and/or does not help deal with an important issue members may feel that it is a pollyannish waste of time. Like any action research project, for an appreciative inquiry to be an effective change process key decision makers need to be intimately involved.

I have found some success in using an appreciative inquiry intervention with on-going teams in four different ways, discussed below. Some of these interventions result in the kinds of processes and outcomes called for by Cooperrider's and Srivastva's theory. Others aid groups in different ways.

A) Team building retreat where the focus is to increase effective relationships.

One application of appreciative inquiry with teams is where the team, or team's manager, wants to spend some time building relationships amongst team members. This kind of team building request is often served by having members fill out a personality inventory and then learn about each other's styles and differences. Appreciative inquiry is a good alternative, especially if the team has already had a personality inventory type of workshop.

a personality inventory and then learn about each other's styles and differences. Appreciative inquiry is a good alternative, especially if the team has already had a personality inventory type of workshop.

In this case, it might be better to have members describe their "best experience in this organization" rather than their best team. This is a judgment call for the facilitator. In either case, the main point is to facilitate a dialogue between individuals and the team where the team gets to understand the interests and aspirations of it's members and where images that have a lot of power for the group are highlighted and played with so that they "stick". I do not recommend members talking about their best team experience in that particular group, however. Times I have done something like that I have found that members will recall a similar experience and after 2 or 3 people have talked about it the process loses steam and members who haven't spoken yet have little to contribute. The likelihood of all having the same "peak experience" probably depends on how long the team has been together.

One of the most powerful examples of this process I am aware of concerned the senior executives of a large utility. This group of eight spent a whole day simply listening to each other's stories about their peak experiences in the organization. Most of them had 30 or more years with the organization. Most of them had spent many years working together. Yet few of them had ever had such an intimate conversation with each other. Even the consultants were amazed at the level of intensity and focus in the group as each member physically went into the centre of the room, told his/her stories, and replied to the questions of their peers.

An inquiry that is appropriate to the issues the group faces

Appreciative inquiry can be a useful intervention when a team finds itself stuck in a rut and needs creative ways out. These can be task related or social process related ruts. When focused on task related issues appreciative inquiry can look a lot like benchmarking (and, unfortunately, poorly organized benchmarking). The difference is that benchmarking is an attempt to discover the best of what is in order to imitate it, while appreciative inquiry is an attempt to uncover the best of our experience in order to develop new shared meanings. It may be that benchmarking is a better process for task issues, especially when they are "closed ended" problems. Appreciative inquiry is, after all, a theory of how to develop social systems, not how to improve efficiency. A lot of things that look like "task issues", however, often have a social process component to them. I am not aware, however, of an example of effectively using appreciative inquiry to get a group out of a task related rut. I have, however, seen "appreciative process" (Bushe and Pitman, 1991) used effectively in this way.

Appreciative process is promoting change by amplifying the best of what is rather than attempting to fix what isn't working. It begins with faith-based positions like you can have more of what ever you want, that there is a genius in everyone, that there is more than enough for everyone. In this case, a consultant, identified and people are willing to put some energy into changing. Using the "best team" inquiry may or may not work well here. To the extent it takes the group away from what it needs to focus on, it will be less than useful and probably resisted. However, it is a good umbrella inquiry in that many different focal issues can be addressed within it. If there is some fear in the group around naming the dysfunctional issue, then "best team" can be a safe way to start broaching the topic. For example, if the relationship with the "boss" is a key issue for team members, but members are afraid to take this up directly, then it can be more safely broached by team members talking about "best team" experiences and the facilitator can ask questions about how the boss acted in each person's best team story. Then when listing the attributes of a good team, the facilitator can pay special attention to characteristics of a good boss of a team. The facilitator can ask the boss about his/her best experience of a boss. Others may be surprised to discover the boss values the same things they do. When it comes time to giving others appreciation the consultant can ask the boss how s/he feels s/he compares to the listed attributes and whether s/he is interested in getting feedback from others. This can be a very gentle and effective setup for a good round of disclosure and feedback.

More often than not, however, the appreciative inquiry will focus on the issue the team is facing. If the team feels there is a general lack of motivation and energy we can inquire into times people have felt most motivated and energized. If there is fear and distrust we can inquire into the biggest experience of trust building people have had. The result of the inquiry will be a new set of ideas and images for how to ameliorate the problem. Often, just the inquiry itself goes some way toward generating the kind of change people are looking for.

For example a senior team in one organization identified a "lack of leadership" amongst middle managers as a key problem. What they were not willing to tell themselves was that they also felt that lack of leadership amongst themselves was a key problem. As part of an intervention into the leadership development process in this company, this group was brought together to have an appreciative inquiry into leadership. They talked about the best examples of leadership within their company that they had witnessed. One key image that emerged for this group was that "great leaders love the people and love the work". As far as anyone could remember, this was the first time that the word "love" had been used at work to describe a manager's job. In fact it was the facilitator who introduced the phrase to summarize a number of stories but people in the group quickly accepted it as descriptive of their experiences. A whole discourse about what it really meant to "love the people" ensued, as well as a discourse about the barriers the organization created to managers "loving" their subordinates. This turned to a deep and intimate conversation about the barriers and fears they experienced in allowing themselves to love their subordinates. This intervention proved to have profound consequences for the entire leadership development process that was subsequently designed. It probably had an impact on these managers as leaders and as a team but I was not able to personally observe the after effects.

C) Paradoxical intervention into groups stuck in undisclosed resentment.

I have had a couple of experiences of consulting to groups where a major theme was undisclosed resentments members had toward each other. They were willing to tell me but were adamant that they were not willing to talk about this at a team building session. In these cases I believed that discussion of the resentments could lead to clearing up misconceptions and fuzzy expectations but I was not allowed to tackle these issues directly. I used to find these assignments very difficult and hadn't had much luck transforming such a group.

The first time I tried AI it was out of frustration and no better ideas to try. The results were a lot better than I expected. At the end of the first day of a two day retreat I led the group in the first two parts of the intervention: telling their stories and listing the attributes. I told them their homework that evening was to think of things that others had done to make the group more like the listed attributes and to come back tomorrow ready to share their appreciation's. The next morning members came into the group with a lot of nervous energy. Then one woman led off by saying that she had not been able to sleep all night because of how angry she was with the group and how little appreciation she was feeling. Others quickly agreed that they had found the exercise difficult for similar reasons. The issues that had been simmering under the surface came boiling up and the group spent the rest of the morning leveling and working through past hurts and resentments. It was a very cathartic session. A great deal of openness was restored. As the session wound down members felt that my intervention had failed and expressed some regret for not having done what I had requested. I thought that was pretty funny and we all had a good laugh as I described my undisclosed frustration of the previous day.

I look at this as a "paradoxical intervention" (Quinn and Cameron, 1988; Watzlawick, Weakland and Fisch, 1974). In this case the intervention does not result in new shared images. Rather it creates a cathartic release by forcing people into a paradoxical tension. By focusing on what they are not feeling (appreciation for each other) the issues that are causing the discordant feelings cannot be contained. This is a powerful intervention and not for the timid. But then so is stepping into the middle of a hostile, frustrated team.

D) Resolving Group Paradoxes

A perspective on groups that I find useful is that groups get "stuck" because they are enmeshed in a paradoxical dilemma (Smith and Berg, 1987). Paradoxes are endemic to group life and for the most part do not result in stuckness. Rather, they are experienced as "dilemmas" that frame a continuum of choice in decision situations (Billig et al, 1988; Hampden-Turner, 1990). For example, "staff up projects to best utilize the talents of the staff" and "staff up projects to provide staff developmental opportunities" is a common dilemma in project organizations. In most cases such dilemmas are dealt with on a project by project basis, with succeeding decisions balancing off these mutually exclusive values. But when a group becomes stuck, unable to make a decision or take action, it is often because such a paradox is operating at an unconscious level in the group. This does not mean that members are not conscious of it (some probably are) but that the group, for whatever reason, is not able to talk to itself about it.

The first example I gave in this paper described such a situation. The group's ability to develop further as a team was stuck because of the competition-cooperation paradox and the appreciative inquiry led to a new image the resolved the paradox for the group. This can be one of the most transformative results of an appreciative inquiry—the development of images that resolve underlying paradoxes for a group. If the facilitator is aware of the nature of the group's unresolved paradox then s/he can be paying particular attention to stories and images that have the potential to help the group find a way out. Let me give another example.

An "empowered work team" of analysts was stuck over what Smith and Berg (1987) call the paradox of authority. The issue was that people were not willing to authorize others to act on the group's behalf but at the same time some wanted authority to act on the group's behalf in dealing with others in and outside the organization. The group had not conceptualized the problem in this way. Rather, the group became paralyzed by the inability of members to take action without having to convene a meeting of the group to get sanction. This was experienced by all as very frustrating and a sense was developing that "this empowered work team stuff just won't work". During an appreciative inquiry into best team experiences one member told the story of working on a charity fund-raising drive with people who had been loaned, full time for 3 months, from their respective companies. Each person had pursued independent, creative initiatives in raising funds while at the same time fully supporting the initiatives of others. There was a program of activities to be done that had built up over the years and was fully documented for them. Over and above that, individuals pursued the group's core mission however they thought best.

The team I was working with reacted a little differently to this story than it had to others. Members were quieter and more withdrawn. It then dawned on me that this story offered a way out of the authority paradox (which, at the time, was one of a number of alternative explanations I had for their stuckness). I asked how the group was able to let others have free reign without fearing someone, due to inexperience or eagerness, would get them into a bind? He said "we decided we had no way of knowing if we could trust each other so we figured we had more to lose by not trusting than by trusting". At this another member piped in "so trust costs less".

The image of "trust costs less" blended this groups bottom-line business identity with the essential element for the resolution of the paradox. Because it was such a novel combination of those words, it opened up new gateways to emotional issues in this group. They were able to explore what the "price of distrust" was. Some were angry about how much other's distrust had cost them. People were able to admit that they hadn't felt trusted, hadn't been trusting others and that they believed trust would cost less. From there it was easy to decide on the "core program" and general objectives for individual initiatives.

This seems to be a common quality of generative images: they jostle conventional thinking by jostling up word combinations. In doing so they offer opportunities to find synthetic resolutions to paradoxical dilemmas. Groups stuck in a paradox may be where appreciative inquiry is the most effective OD tool available.

Culling or Crafting the Images: Beyond Facilitation

In a team building contract there is an expectation that something "significant" will happen in the designated time. In an appreciative inquiry, that presumably means generating new, affirmative images. In this last section I want to take up an issue with the method itself, applied to teams by a hired consultant.

In an appreciative inquiry it is usually one person who comes up with the image that the group then adopts. I suppose consulting practice might vary along a continuum from those who feel their job is mainly to cull images from the offerings of members to those who believe their job is to help craft the images. In practice I find myself working at highlighting the maps of those members who seem to have the most complex, developed, affirming and generative maps of groups. If they are not able to, I will try to frame, shape and embellish their stories into phrases members use to talk to each other in new ways. I'm not saying this is the "right" way to do appreciative inquiry—its just what I notice myself doing when I have been hired to do team-building and I am trying to help people have conversations that generate new, affirming, generative images. I think the power of appreciative inquiry as a change method relies on someone who can wordsmith these experiences and stories into pithy statements (provocative propositions). If a member of the group can provide that, great. If not, I try my best. It may be that part of the role of the consultant in an appreciative inquiry is "wordsmith".

I find myself paying attention to what most moves me in what others are saying, notice what moves others, and then work at helping people articulate it in "sticky language". That requires using moist, juicy poetic language, not dry, technical or precise language. It is not often that I stumble across a new idea or image of group health and vitality but people often find my ideas and images different from theirs. Am I putting words into their mouths or am I helping them to frame and embellish what is tacit in their stories? I suppose I'm doing both. Is that how appreciative inquiry works with a one consultant organization development intervention? I think so.

Conclusion

A simple process based on the principles of appreciative inquiry that I've referred to as the "best team" inquiry has been experimentally shown to effect groups positively. In this article I've tried to look at why. I tried to show how it helps members of new teams establish personal identity and differentiate themselves. New teams can also benefit from this way of generating "group guidelines" and appreciative recognition can help to build group cohesion. Ongoing teams can benefit from a "best team" inquiry in several ways. It can help to create a safe gateway into difficult issues for a group. When lack of appreciation is the issue, It can create so much tension in members that they deal up their resentments and expectations. It can aid the development of shared mental maps of group success. It can help create affirming, generative images that allow for a different discourse, a different set of understandings and opportunities to materialize for a group. This can be therapeutic for a group stuck in a paradox. In working with teams to develop affirming, generative images, an appreciative inquiry into something other than teams is often appropriate and can have very positive impacts on groups and their members. As a change process appreciative inquiry is a powerful "pull" strategy and can sometimes transform a relationship or a group.

References

Barrett, F.J., Thomas, G.F. and Hocevar, S.P. (1995) "The central role of discourse in large-scale change: A social construction perspective". *Journal of Applied Behavioral Science*, 31:3, 352–372.

Billig, M., Condor, S., Edwards, D., Gane, M., Middleton, D. and Radley, A. (1988) *Ideological Dilemmas: A Social Psychology of Everyday Thinking.* London, UK: Sage.

Bushe, G.R. (1995) "Appreciative Inquiry as an Organization Development Intervention". *Organization Development Journal*, 13:3, 14–22.

Bushe, G.R. and Coetzer, G. (1995) "Appreciative inquiry as a team development intervention: A controlled experiment". *Journal of Applied Behavioral Science*, 31:1, 13–30.

Bushe, G.R. and Pitman, T. (1991) Appreciative process: A method for transformational change. *OD Practitioner*, 23(3), 1–4.

Cooperrider, D.L. (1990) Positive image, positive action: The affirmative basis of organizing. In S.Srivastva and D.L. Cooperrider (Eds.), *Appreciative Management and Leadership* (pp. 91–125). San Francisco: Jossey-Bass.

Cooperrider, D.L. and Srivastva, S. (1987) "Appreciative inquiry in organizational life". In R. Woodman and W. Pasmore (eds.) *Research in Organizational Change and Development: Volume 1* (pp. 129–169). Greenwich, CT: JAI Press.

Gergen, K. (1990) Affect and organization in postmodern society. In S. Srivastva and D.L. Cooperrider (eds.), *Appreciative Management and Leadership* (pp.153–174). San Francisco, Jossey-Bass.

Hampden-Turner, C. (1990) *Charting the Corporate Mind*. New York: Free Press.

Quinn, R.E. and Cameron, K.S. (Eds.) (1988) *Paradox and Transformation*. Cambridge, MA: Ballinger.

Schein, E.H. (1987) *The Clinical Perspective in Field Work*. Newbury Park, CA: Sage.

Smith, K.K. and Berg, D.N. (1987) *Paradoxes of Group Life*. San Francisco: Jossey-Bass.

Srivastva, S., Obert, S.L. and Neilsen, E.H. (1977) Organizational analysis through group processes: A theoretical perspective for organization development. In C.Cooper (Ed.), *Organizational Development in the U.K. and the U.S.A.* (pp.83–111). New York: Macmillan.

Watzlawick, P., Weakland, J. and Fisch, R. (1974) *Change*. New York: Norton.

Chapter 13

A FIELD EXPERIMENT IN APPRECIATIVE INQUIRY

David A. Jones
Wendy's International

Abstract

Most studies or publications of Appreciative Inquiry focus on the process itself. Although this process emphasis has benefits, relatively little attention, from academicians or practitioners, has been addressed to Appreciative Inquiry use in a specific business setting tracking quantifiable results. In this study, a field experiment utilizing Appreciative Inquiry was conducted within 94 fast-food restaurants of a national Fortune 500 restaurant chain in a major metropolitan area. The purpose of this study was to determine if Appreciative Inquiry could be a useful intervention in enhancing salaried management restaurant level retention. Findings are significantly favorable in that the Appreciative Inquiry test group had 30–32 percent higher retention than the two control groups. Subjects in the Appreciative Inquiry test group expressed a decreased "Inclination to leave" as evidenced by the higher retention rate along with an enhanced appreciation of working within the much-maligned restaurant industry itself. This suggests further field studies using the Appreciative Inquiry methodology in order to expand its use from both an academic and practitioner oriented perspective.

Overview

There are literally thousands of articles and studies focusing on turnover within various organizations and industries. There is also a growing body of literature discussing Appreciative Inquiry. To the best of this author's knowledge, there

---

OD Journal, No. 4, Winter 1998.

have not been any studies with quantitative data analysis within the Appreciative Inquiry spectrum.

The closest study was completed by Carter and Johnson (1992), which conducted a study on a Big Eight accounting firm referred to as AK&G. David Cooperrider, founder of Appreciative Inquiry, participated in this study in the role of advisor. Even though this study's methodology was well thought out, planned and executed, it still lacked the presentation of quantifiable results preferred in the business world. The purpose of the following study then was to contribute to the field by attempting to address the central question of application—i.e., can upper management in the hospitality industry use Appreciative Inquiry to increase entry-level management retention?

Understanding Turnover

Employee initiated turnover has been a traditional problem for the hospitality industry. However, the problem has been routinely accepted as bothersome but manageable (Woods and Macaulay, 1989). Woods and Macaulay (1989) stated that employers have not sufficiently examined the problem since the labor pool has always exceeded the number of available jobs.

There are other issues that relate to the routine acceptance of turnover. Senior management has regarded entry-level management employees as temporary employees who would quickly resign when other employment opportunities became available (Powers, 1988). Many entry-level managers take the job as an "interim" position while waiting for an opening in the job or career they really want (Powers, 1988). It is this author's opinion that senior management has subliminally accepted the stereotypical negative image of entry-level hospitality management positions, thereby accepting turnover as a normal cost of doing business. This traditional view of entry-level management turnover has changed in recent years. Three reasons for this change have been a decrease in available employees, increased industry growth and intense competition within the industry (Withiam, 1989).

The Labor Pool

The decrease in the number of available employees partially has been the result of a declining, population growth rate in the United States (Meyers, 1990). The U.S. Department of Commerce has predicted that this trend will continue through the year 2005 (Sack, 1997).

A decrease in the future labor supply will result in the inevitable shortage of workers in many U.S. industries. Withiam (1989) reported that an analyst for the

National Planning Association has predicted that the labor demand in the U.S. service sector will grow at an annual rate of 1.3 percent during the 1990s, while the supply will increase at a rate of only 1.2 percent. The National Restaurant Association has forecast a shortfall of over 1.1 million workers by the year 2000 (Sack, 1997).

Another trend in the U.S. population has had a significant impact on the hospitality industry. The decline in the nation's population growth rate combined with an increase in longevity has greatly changed the demographic composition of the workforce (Ananth and DeMicco, 1991). While the number of individuals between the ages of 16 and 24 has decreased, the number of individuals over the age 55 has increased which is not the targeted age group for hospitality industry management. By the year 2030 the number of adults over the age of 55 has been estimated to be one in three (Ananth and DeMicco, 1991). The department of commerce has predicted that the number of Americans over age 65 will increase from 25 million in 1980 to over 35 million by the year 2000 (Meyers, 1990). The anticipated increase in this older population segment raises the ante for the hospitality industry to rethink its recruiting and hiring strategy. The typical entry-level management recruitment pool currently comes from the ages 18 to 30. Hiring older employees will require rethinking organizational policies concerning education, training, development, compensation, pensions and alternate work programs (Ananth and DeMicco, 1991).

Industry Competititon

Another factor that has changed the hospitality industry's view of management turnover has been intense competition. With increased growth, competition for both market share and human resources has resulted (Lee, 1987: Withiam, 1989). As the availability of employment opportunities increases, employee turnover also has been shown to increase (Huttin, Roznowski and Hachiya, 1985; Mobley, 1982).

Minimizing Employee Shortages

Two main concepts have been proposed as methods to minimize employee shortages in the U.S. hospitality industry. The two approaches consist of (1) a reduction in turnover by increasing employee retention (the focus of this study) and (2) a reduction in the number of required employees through organizational change. The concept of reducing turnover by increasing retention requires senior management to examine current human resource management practices and to make changes in those practices which impact retention (Krone, Tabacchi, and Farber, 1989; Sarabakhsh, Carson, and Lindizren, 1989, Withiam, 1989: Woods and Macaulay, 1989).

This concept has not been unique to the hospitality industry. Woods and Maulay (1989) and Withiam (1989) stated that retention management programs are driven by the following factors: organization culture and structure, recruitment strategy, pay and benefits philosophy, employee support programs and career development systems. They have incorporated these factors into recommendations directed specifically at the hospitality industry.

The second concept of reducing the number of employees through organizational change is a more drastic and long term approach. Advocates of this concept state that emphasis solely on human resource management practices such as recruitment and pay will have a limited affect on the problem (Withiam, 1989). Gregory and Laker (1990) have stated that the hospitality industry has developed a traditional "labor mindset." This mindset has restricted both the industry's definition of the problem and the identification of possible solutions. Overcoming this mindset will require reexamination of the problem using a four part conceptual framework. Parts of this framework include finding alternatives for changing the nature of the following operational variables: the delivery system, the product or service being offered, the production technology and the structure of the service organization (Gregory and Laker, 1990).

Purpose of this Research

The purpose of this study was to determine if Appreciative Inquiry could be a useful intervention in addressing some of these issues by enhancing salaried management restaurant level retention. The methodology will be presented first by discussing the study's value, and moving on to describe the organization, the sample groups, the Appreciative Inquiry process and other instrumentation, data analysis, and results/findings. The contribution to knowledge within this study comes in four forms:

1. Enhanced knowledge of the role of Appreciative Inquiry in entry-level management retention.

2. An Appreciative Inquiry study with specific data analysis.

3. Specific focus on the hospitality industry itself where comprehensive examination is not as prevalent or rigorous.

4. The author has detailed knowledge due to authority position within the study organization that will minimize the acknowledged problem in distinguishing voluntary and involuntary turnover (Mobley, Griffeth, Hand and Meglino, 1979: Muchinsky and Tuttle, 1979; Marsh and Mannari, 1977, Mirvis and Lawler, 1977, Waters, Roach, and Waters, 1976, Hinrichs, 1975; and Letkowitz and Katz, 1969). Only voluntary turnover was considered in this study.

It should be noted that the following Appreciative Inquiry methodology will be (to the best of this author's knowledge), one of only two published detailed articulations on Appreciative Inquiry, and the only one with specific data analysis as it relates to management turnover in the hospitality industry. David Cooperrider has resisted publishing such a "methodology," concerned that it would exacerbate the split between theory and practice if it was applied as an OD technology rather than as a thoughtful inquiry into the nature of organizational life for a particular client (Carter and Johnson, 1992). There is also the risk that in publishing a methodology, it may become reified and cast in stone. The validity of these concerns is shared, although the future value to the research and practitioner communities warrants some form of structure and definition. Therefore, this study is presented as only "one" example of a highly effective intervention and not as the "one" correct way to conduct Appreciative Inquiry, as that would not be congruent with the basic foundation or philosophy of Appreciative Inquiry in the first place.

Methodology

Study Population

For the purposes of this study, the study population included all fast-food restaurant level salaried management personnel within 94 restaurants in a major metropolitan area. This target population was divided into three test groups on a randomized basis. The Appreciative Inquiry test group consisted of 33 locations hereafter referred to as test group #1. Test group #2 consisted of 32 locations that experienced normal "problem-solving" approaches toward retention. Test group #3 consisted of 29 locations that simply went on with business as usual without any interventions targeted at retention. All three test groups were alike in their geographic and demographic composition as a whole. See Table 1 for detailed information on the three test groups.

This study excluded new restaurants opened during the test period of eighteen months to maintain the integrity of the methodology and study results. Specific geographic and demographic data on the test group participants is superfluous as the differences blend together for each of the test groups as a whole.

Instrumentation

The instruments used for this study were a survey, detailed turnover tracking data, an Appreciative Inquiry questionnaire used as a question guide for individual and group interviews, and the Appreciative Inquiry intervention methodology itself.

TABLE 13.1. Test Group Location / Numerical Specifics

Test Group	# of Locations	Salaried Base #	# / % in City[d]	#/% Suburbs
1 (AI)[a]	33	116	12/36%	21/64%
2 (PS)[b]	32	112	13/40%	19/60%
3 (O)[c]	29	102	9/31%	20/69%
Totals	94	330	34/36%	60/64%

[a]Appreciative Inquiry gorup
[b]Problem Solving group
[c]No Intervention group
[d]# of locations in City or Suburbs

Appreciative Inquiry Intervention Methodology

The primary instrumentation of this study was the Appreciative Inquiry intervention methodology. Appreciative Inquiry is the manipulated independent active variable in this study. The main body of this methodology was emulated from the approach taken by Carter and Johnson (1992) as shown in Table 2.

Early stages were spent resolving issues of design and logistics. The leadership team consisted of the author, six district managers managing restaurants within the test group #1, and six top performing general managers, one from each district.

The culmination of the project was the Appreciative Inquiry test group roundtable meeting. The Project Appreciative Retention Roundtable was a three and one-half day design. The initial challenge was to transform individuals into a community of inquiry with a common purpose and set of data. The Roundtable began in the evening of the first day. We decided to capture the individual experiences in the room during this time. To do so, we facilitated a discussion around four questions:

1. What one word best characterizes your experience of the Appreciative Inquiry group interviews/meetings?

2. What was the most exciting, surprising or humorous thing that occurred during your group interviews/meetings?

3. Based on the meeting, interview and survey data you have, what would be the most important outcome or message for senior management from the roundtable session?

4. What do you believe is the essence or life-giving force of the firm?

The Project Appreciative Retention Roundtable had five objectives as listed below:

1. Reaffirm affirmative topic choices and create a common base of data for all participants.

2. State provocative propositions about the life-giving properties in the firm.

TABLE 13.2. Stages in Appreciative Inquiry Intervention

1. Initial Appreciative Inquiry rollout and Survey #1
2. Initial meeting with test group #2 and Survey #1 (2 meetings)
3. Initial meeting with test group #3 and Survey #1 (2 meetings)
4. AI groupd meeting with leadership team.
5. 2nd and 3rd AI rollout and Survey #1 (2 meetings)
6. AI leader meeting on survey review and next steps
7. One AI meeting per month w/Author (15 meetings)
8. Two AI meetings per year w/DMs (18 meetings/6 DMs)
9. AI leadership team meeting-next steps
10. AI Test Group Roundtable Conference and Survey #2
11. Test Group #2 Survey #2 (2 meetings)
12. Test Group #3 Survey #2 (2 meetings)
13. Complete analysis of surveys #1 and #2
14. Project Completion and Communication to all 3 test groups
15. AI leadership team meeting-next steps

3. Consensus validation of propositions using force-field analysis and debate.

4. State realizable provocative propositions.

5. State personal commitments and plan next steps for acting on provocative propositions.

Data Collection and Analysis

Data for this study were collected throughout a two-and-a-half year time period using multiple social science methods including:

1. Historical Documents. Company documents, published articles, books, and unpublished papers.

2. Observations. Aside from the meetings scheduled as part of the Appreciative Inquiry intervention, numerous other committee and departmental meetings were attended providing a direct experiential basis for understanding and complementing the survey and Appreciative Inquiry meeting data. Author journal data provided assistance in "weaving" much of the data appropriate for presentation in the results / findings section.

3. Surveys and Group Discussion of Data. Pre and post surveys were given asking for demographic information along with other questions designed to provide data for retention and turnover analysis. The purpose of the survey was to provide convergent validation around the Appreciative Inquiry intervention. The purpose of administering the surveys in two time periods was to provide a "before and after" picture mainly from the Appreciative Inquiry test group perspective.

4. Turnover Tracking Data. This turnover data tracking tool was implemented
    one year prior to the study period in order to provide extensive information
    for analysis purposes. The format of the data allowed the author to minimize
    the acknowledged problem in distinguishing voluntary and involuntary turn-
    over (Mobley et al., 1979; Muchinsky and Tuttle, 1979; Marsh and Mannari,
    1977; Mirvis and Lawler, 1977; Waters, Roach, and Waters, 1976; Hinrichs,
    1975; and Letkowitz and Katz, 1969). The cited issues of inaccurate com-
    pany records, insufficient turnover categories, employees listed as voluntary
    when they were actually "allowed" to quit, and haphazard record keeping
    were minimized due to the detail of the turnover tracking data along with the
    author's ability to ensure detail and accuracy. Only voluntary turnover was
    considered for this study.

Results and Discussion

In general, the two primary and significant findings of this study were as follows:

1. Management retention at the restaurant level was 32 percent higher in the
    Appreciative Inquiry test group #1 than test group #3 and 30 percent higher
    than test group #2.
2. Survey results revealed that the Appreciative Inquiry test group #1 were less
    inclined to leave the organization than either test groups #2 or #3.

A 32 percent increase in management retention translates to $103,320 sav-
ings in hard training dollars alone for the Appreciative Inquiry test group. The
following steps below provide the detail for attaining this calculation:

1. The test group consisted of 116 management personnel.
2. 38% pre-test turnover equates to losing 44 people.
3. 26% test-period turnover equates to losing 30 people.
4. This 12% decrease in turnover translates to a 32% improvement.
5. Using an average weekly salary of $615 and a 12 week training period for all
    management candidates, this translates to $7,380 ($615 × 12) training cost
    per candidate. Multiply $7,380 by the reduction in turnover (14) and the re-
    sult is $103,320.

This $103,320 represents only the hard cost of training dollars associated
with the replacement of the management people. Lost productivity, recruitment
costs, benefits, morale issues, crew turnover caused by management turnover, crew
turnover training costs, sales loss due to lost productivity, and legal costs associated with turnover are not included. Using various forms of measuring these losses
could easily increase the hard cost tenfold.

Some broader scope and more qualitative results (e.g., Cooperrider, 1996) are presented in summary form below:

The metaphor speaking best to our primary task and role is one where wonder, learning and the dialogical imagination will be modus operandi.

The Future Search conference will produce more whole systems learning, empowerment, and feelings of connection around business vision than hundreds of fragmenting small group meetings.

There is a reduction of time lag between organization innovations and their spread throughout the organization.

The strengthening of a "can do" climate of hope and confidence in the organization's ability to manage the transition and realize its transformational goals.

Significant increase in the organization's positive inner dialogue about the future (e.g., less cynical and deficit oriented discourse; less fear; less negativity; more vocabularies of positive possibility; more rapid spread of good news developments).

Development of a more appreciative leadership mindset and culture which provides managers with new options for dealing with organization and customer surveys, re-engineering, strategic planning analysis, team-building, merger integration, performance appraisal and others.

Significant increase in the feeling of connection to the organization's vision at all levels.

Limitations

Although the findings reported above are meaningful and significant, this study does have some limitations. First, based on these data it is not possible to "prove" that the differences in results should be attributed to the Appreciative Inquiry intervention alone. Regardless of geographic, numerical and demographic similarity within the test groups, the one key factor not analyzed nor taken into account was leadership. The author was more involved with the test group (although limited to the Appreciative Inquiry intervention alone) than the other two which could be considered part of the reason for enhanced retention and financial results.

According to Daft (1995), another limitation is as quoted below quite succinctly:

What works in one setting may not work in another setting. There is not one best way. Contingency theory means, "it depends." For example . . . some organizations may experience a certain environment, use a routine technology, and desire efficiency. In this situation, a mechanistic approach to management that uses bureaucratic control procedures, a functional structure, and formal communication would be appropriate. Likewise, organic, free flowing management processes work best in an uncertain environment with a non-routine technology. The correct management approach is contingent upon the organization's situation.

According to Sorensen, Preston and Head (1997), the above may be minimized when working with Appreciative Inquiry. Appreciative Inquiry has proven successful all over the world, and with types of organizations. Appreciative Inquiry is not a "tool" like team building, grid management, or quality circle—rather it is a innovative approach to change management. Appreciative Inquiry's approach directly attacks one of the few "universal truths" of OD practice—successful OD requires overcoming resistance to change.

Another limitation is the sample size of the test groups in relation to the hospitality industry as a whole along with the geographic restriction of all being located in one major metropolitan area. There are other variables that affect turnover (although most of these were controlled for in the turnover tracking data instrument and subsequent author analysis) that may have not been taken into account.

Directions for Future Research

For the above reasons, further research should be pursued regarding data analysis of the Appreciative Inquiry action research intervention within organizations. There is a growing literature with a qualitative "grounded theory" (Glaser and Strauss, 1967) methodology that is proving the merit and value of Appreciative Inquiry, but inserting some quantitative research into the arena can do nothing but advance this exciting organizational intervention.

The following are specific recommendations for future research:

More multivariate research specific to the fast-food restaurant industry.

More longitudinal studies specific to the fast-food restaurant industry.

A thorough meta-analysis of all major turnover studies within the past ten years.

Clearly, Appreciative Inquiry is a powerful organizational intervention that does not end. It becomes self-sustaining as it creates energy and enthusiasm within the people that it touches.

References

Anath, M., and DeMicco, F.J. (1991). Strategies for Tomorrow's Hospitality Workforce. *FIU Hospitality Review*, 9 (1), 25–37.

Barrett, F.J. (1995). Creating Appreciative Learning Cultures. *Organizational Dynamics*, 24(1), 36–49.

Carter, J.D. and Johnson, P. (1992). *Institutionalizing Change Through Dialogue: The Round Table, An Appreciative Inquiry Organizational Intervention*. John D. Carter and Associates.

Cooperrider, D.L., and Srivastva, S. (1987). An Appreciative Inquiry in Organizational Life. In W. Pasmore and R. Woodman (Eds.), *Research in Organization Chanize and Development* (Vol. 1, pp.129–169). Greenwich, CT: JAI Press.

Cooperrider, D.L. (1996). Resources for Getting Appreciative Inquiry Started: An Example OD Proposal. *OD Practitioner*, 28, (1 and 2), 23–33.

Daft, R. (1995). Organization Theory and Design, 5th ed., Minneapolis: *Hospitality Research Journal*, 14 (2), West Publishing 155–162.

Glaser, G.G. and Strauss, A.L. (1967). *The Discovery of Grounded Theory: Strategies for Qualitative Research.* Reading, New York: Aldine de Gruyter.

Gregory, S.R., and Laker, D.R. (1990). Changing the "labor mindset" alternative solutions to the labor shortage. *Hospitality Research Journal*, 14 (2), 625–626.

Hinrichs, J.R. (1975). Measurement of Reasons for Resignation of Professionals: Questionnaire versus Company and Consultant Exit Interviews. *Journal of Applied Psychology*, 60, 530–532.

Hutlin, C.L., Roznowski, M., and Hachiya, D. (1 985). Alternative Opportunities and Withdrawal Decisions: Empirical and Theoretical Discrepancies and Integration. *Psychological Bulletin*, 97, 233–259.

Krone, C., Tabacchi, M., and Farber, B. (1989). Manager Burnout. *Cornell Hotel and Restaurant Administration Quarterly*, 30 (3), 58–63.

Lee, D.R. (1987). Why Some Succeed Where Others Fail. *Cornell Hotel and Restaurant Administration Quarterly* 28 (3), 33–37.

Letkowitz, J., and Katz, M.L. (1969). Validity of Exit Interviews. *Personnel Psychology*, 22, 445–447.

Marsh, R., and Mannari, H. (I 977). Organizational Commitment and Turnover: A Predictive Study. *Administrative Science Quarterly*, 22, 57–75.

Meyers, K.W. (1990). The Fast-Food Industry: Company Benefits and Stress.

Mirvis, P.H., and Lawler, E.E., 111. (1977). Measuring the Financial Impact of Employee Attitudes. *Joumal of Applied Psychology*, 62, 1–8.

Mobley, W.H., Griffeth, R.W., Hand, H.H., and Meglino, B.M. (1979). Review and Conceptual Analysis of the Employee Turnover Process. *Psychological Bulletin* 86, 493–522.

Mobley, W.H. (1982). *Employee Turnover: Causes, Consequences, and Control.* Reading, MA: Addison-Wesley.

Muchinsky, P.M., and Tuttle, M.L. (1979). Employee Turnover: An Empirical and Methodological Assessment. *Journal of Vocational Behavior*, 14, 43–77.

Powers, T. (1 988). *Introduction to Management in the Hospital Industry.* New York: John Wiley and Sons.

Sack, K.J. (1997). Industry Surveys: Restaurants. Standard and Poor's.

Sarabakhsh, M., Carson, D., and Lindgren, E. (I 989). The Personal Cost of Hospitality Management. *Cornell Hotel and Restaurant Administration Quarterly* 30 (1), 73–76.

Sorensen, P.F., Preston, P. F., and Head, T. (1997). Is Aprreciative Inquiry OD's Philosopher's Stone? Pre-publication handout.

Waters, L.K., Roach, D., and Waters, C.A. (1976). Estimate of Future Tenure, Satisfaction, and Biographical Variables as Predictors of Termination. *Personnel Psychology*, 29, 57–60.

Withiam, G.W. (I 989). The Labor Shortage Might Not Happen. *Cornell Hotel and Restaurant Administration Quarterly*, 30 (2), 4.

Woods, R.H., and Macaulay, J.F. (I 989). Rx for Turnover: Retention Programs that Work. *Cornell Hotel and Restaurant Administration Quarterly* (1), 79–90.

Chapter 14

APPRECIATIVE INQUIRY MEETS THE LOGICAL POSITIVIST

Peter F. Sorensen, Jr.
Benedictine University

Linda Sharkey
G.E. Capital

Robert Head
Benedictine University

Dale Spartz
Riverside Hospital

This article presents a brief summary and discussion of a series of studies illustrating the contribution of Appreciative Inquiry (AI) to the field of Organization Development (OD). The article discusses the integration of AI with existing mainstream OD interventions and reports the results of empirical studies, testing the effects of AI.

The integration of AI with existing approaches to OD is presented through a discussion of studies dealing with changes in organizational performance, team development, survey feedback and culture change. Team building and survey feedback have historically been core OD interventions. These two approaches are described by Cummings and Worley (1997) as the two earliest interventions in the field and are attributed to the initial work of Kurt Lewin. These approaches continue to be the two most frequently used interventions as cited by Joyce and Kilmann (1991), in their study of more than 300 large-scale change efforts. The central importance of team building and survey feedback is again confirmed by Head, Sorensen, Preston and Yaeger in their article later in this book (see Chapter 15). Their article reports that team building and survey feedback are the first and third most frequently used interventions in international and multinational organizational change projects.

Assessing AI based on empirical studies in the tradition of logical-positivist research methodology may appear to be inconsistent with AI and its social constructionist foundation. However several authors including Robert Golembiewski (1998) and Thomas Head (1997) have argued for the timeliness and appropriateness of such an evaluation. This article takes the position that an assessment based on traditional empirical methods serves to strengthen AI. There has been little such research to date. In fact, Bushe and Coetzer (1995) indicate that no empirical studies existed prior to their work.

Organizational Performance

The first study by David Jones deals with changes in organizational performance and is of special significance in that it represents a particularly rigorous field experiment with more than 90 work units. This study was a recipient of a "Best OD Paper Award" by the OD Institute and is reported more fully in this book (see Chapter 13). In brief, the study dealt with a situation of critical importance to the industry. The field experiment contrasted AI with more traditional human resource approaches to managerial turnover and a control group. The reported quantitative results indicate a clear superiority for AI, with significant organizational improvement. Qualitative findings reinforce the existence of positive change through the identification of such organizational changes as:

- Time reduction in the diffusion of innovations
- Greater confidence in the ability to manage change
- Increases in the organization's positive inner dialogue concerning the future
- Development of more appreciative leadership
- Increased feelings of commitment to the organization's vision

Team Development

Two experimental studies have been reported using Appreciative Inquiry in team development. The first study and probably the first experimental study (Bushe and Coetzer, 1995) reports the results of a controlled laboratory experiment with 96 undergraduate students in an introductory organization development course. The study compares the effects of Appreciative Inquiry on group development with task-oriented team development and lectures on group process. The study supports the effectiveness of Appreciative Inquiry as a team building intervention. The authors suggest that AI may be particularly appropriate for newly formed teams in facilitating team development through the creation of a positive group image. The authors also suggest that AI may be particularly helpful with highly fragmented, fragile groups, or teams in conflict. This observation is consistent with AI applications reported by David Cooperrider and Thomas Head. The application of AI to groups is discussed further in the Bushe article on Appreciative Inquiry and teams, also included in this book (see Chapter 12).

A recent study by Robert Head (1999) of team development incorporating several of the observations addressed by Bushe and Coetzer, is particularly significant in that it directly addresses one of the central principles of Appreciative Inquiry, namely the Anticipatory Principle. The Anticipatory Principle is described as:

> The infinite human resource we have for generating constructive organized change is our collective imagination and discourse about the future. One of the basic theorems of the Anticipatory view of organizational life is that it is the image of the future, which in fact guides what might be called the current behavior of an organism or organization. Much like a movie projector on a screen, human systems are forever projecting ahead of themselves a horizon of expectations (in their talk in the hallways, in the metaphors and language they use) that brings the future powerfully in to the present as a mobilizing agent, to inquire in ways that serve to refashion anticipatory reality—especially the artful creation of positive imagery on a collective basis—may be the most prolific thing any inquiry can do (Srivastva and Barrett, 1990).

The study by Head is also of interest in that it addresses the questions of the effectiveness of AI in facilitating the speed at which teams develop, and the use of the Anticipatory Principle for heterogeneous groups while bridging issues of diversity.

Similar to David Jones, Robert Head employs the methodology of the field experiment. The experiment is comprised of eighteen groups of managers and supervisors, totaling 124 participants from a large governmental agency. The results of the study support AI applications to team development, with the AI groups experiencing more positive group images and higher performance.

Survey Feedback

The final group of studies links Appreciative Inquiry to survey feedback and instrumented or databased change. Each of these studies employed a particular survey instrument, the Organization Culture Inventory (OCI). The OCI defines organization culture in terms of twelve cultural styles resulting in a profile of the organization culture. These twelve styles are clustered into three groupings. These three groupings are: Satisfaction cultures comprised of achievement, self-actualizing, humanistic and helpful styles; People/Security cultures comprised of approval, conventional, dependent, and avoidance; Task/Security cultures comprised of oppositional, power, competitive and perfectionistic styles.

The OCI is based on a number of central and familiar concepts in organizational behavior and organization development. For example, satisfaction styles are associated with Maslow's higher level needs while the two security cultures are associated with Maslow's lower level or security needs. In a similar fashion McGregor's TheoryY assumptions are associated with achievement, self-actualizing, humanistic and helpful styles. These same culture styles share conceptual foundations with such classic OD approaches as Rensis Likert's Systems Three and Four, and Blake and Mouton's Managerial Grid Style 9.9. These Satisfaction styles also appear to be associated with the characteristics of high involvement, high commitment and high performance organizations.

The studies discussed below draw heavily on the Positive Principle of Appreciative Inquiry. The role and meaning of the Positive Principle is defined by Cooperrider:

> Put most simply, it has been our experience that building and sustaining momentum for change requires large amounts of positive affect and social bonding—things like hope, excitement, inspiration, caring, camaraderie, sense of urgent purpose, and sheer joy in creating something meaningful together. What we have found is that the more positive the question we ask in our work the more long lasting and successful this change effort. It does not help, we have found, to begin our inquiries from the standpoint of the world as a problem to be solved. We are more effective the longer we can retain the spirit of inquiry for the ever-lasting beginner. The major thing we do that makes the difference is to craft and seed, in more catalytic ways, the unconditional positive question (Cooperrider, 1990).

The discussion here is based on interventions in five organizations: three private hospitals, a large financial institution and a government agency. In each of these cases participants were asked to respond to the survey instrument in terms of their peak experiences in their organization, the time at which they and the organization were at their best.

The experiences across each of the organizations are highly consistent.

- In each organization, peak experiences were clearly defined in terms of those styles comprised of achievement, self-actualizing, humanistic, and helpful.
- The appreciative patterns were frequently in sharp contrast with perceptions of the existing culture.
- The appreciative patterns were markedly consistent across organizational levels, which was frequently not true for perceptions of the existing culture.
- The appreciative question provided respondents with the opportunity to share common experiences as to when the organization was at its best.
- The AI process clearly facilitated the acceptance of the change process.
- The appreciative question and profile clearly created positive momentum, energy and support for continuing the change process.
- In the cases where the organization's appreciative profile was tracked over time there remained a high degree of consistency between periods.
- Stories relating to peak experiences were consistently about task accomplishment, collaboration, and shared effort.

- The AI experience created the foundation for exploring and developing sustainable positive organization norms.
- The AI experience created a positive image of the possible.

These experiences with AI clearly demonstrate that AI provides an important, perhaps critical, new way of approaching organizational change. It is a change strategy in and of itself, and at the same time, a powerful extension of existing OD technologies. Although AI departs from the problem-solving approach so deeply embedded in OD and management in general it is consistent with much of what we have learned of organizational change from the behavioral sciences over the last 50 years. Nevertheless, there is much that we need to understand. Appreciative Inquiry is very much in its embryonic stage as a comprehensive theory of change. Some of the issues that need to be better understood, for example, include:

What exactly is it about AI, which creates its unique power? and

Under what conditions is it the intervention of choice?

For example, although the Bushe and Coetzer study demonstrates the effective application to teams it was not the most effective intervention under the particular conditions of the study.

Clearly we have a way to go. We need verification provided by experimental studies but probably even more important is the understanding provided by longitudinal studies designed to explore the sustainability of AI-led interventions.

The full appreciation of AI continues to evolve. The need to more fully understand the nature and the role of AI in OD is probably best articulated in an article by Robert Golembiewski appropriately titled *Appreciating Appreciative Inquiry* (1998). The reader is recommended to this article for a comprehensive review, critique and important perspective on AI.

Summary

This article has dealt with the integration and effect of Appreciative Inquiry when combined with two of the foundation and core intervention technologies in OD: team development and survey feedback. Both methods continue to be the most frequently employed methods in the field both nationally and internationally. The article also viewed Appreciative Inquiry from the perspective of the logical positivist and begins to answer the question, "What happens when you test AI using traditional positivist approaches to evaluate its effectiveness?"

Cooperrider describes Appreciative Inquiry as a new paradigm in change management. But it also appears that AI does, in fact, do well by the *old* paradigm of traditional logical-positivist empirical research. Although systematic, empirical testing of AI continues to be limited, the studies that do exist support and strengthen the position of AI. It is our sense that AI has provided new paradigm ways of contributing in a critical manner to two of the most central and historically important approaches in OD as well as to the development of the OD field. AI should continue to be served well by its assessment by more traditional behavioral science methodologies.

References

Bushe G., and Coetzer, G. (1995). Appreciative Inquiry as a team development intervention. *Journal of Applied Behavioral Science*, 31, 13–30.

Cooke, R. and Hartmann, J. (1989). *Interpreting the Culture Styles Measured By the Organizational Culture Inventory: Organizational Culture Inventory Leader's Guide*, Plymouth, Michigan: Human Synergistics, Inc.

Cooke, R. and Lafferty, J. C. (1989). *The Organizational Culture Inventory*, Plymouth Michigan: Human Synergistics, Inc.

Cummings, T. and Worley, C. G. (1993). *Organization Development and Change*, 6th ed., Minneapolis: West Publishing Company.

Golembiewski, R. T. (1998). Appreciating Appreciative Inquiry: Diagnosis and Perspectives on How to Do Better. In R. Woodman and W. B. Pasmore (Eds.) *Research in Organizational Change and Development* (Vol. 11, pp. 1–45).

Head, R. (1999). "Appreciative Inquiry as a Team Development Intervention for Newly formed Heterogeneous Groups," presented at the International Association of Management.

Head, T. C. (1997). Why does appreciative inquiry work? Speculation and a call for empirical study. Working paper. Tennessee State University, Nashville, TN.

Head, T. and Sorensen, P. (1993). Cultural Values and Organization Development. *Leadership and Organization Development Journal*, 11, 3–7.

Joyce, T., and Kilmann, R., (1991). Profiling Large-Scale Change Efforts. *OD Journal*, Vol. 9, No. 2, Summer 1991.

Likert, R. (1962). *New Patterns of Management*, New York: McGraw-Hill

Likert, R. (1967). *The Human Organization*, New York: McGraw-Hill

Sharkey, L. (1999). Changing organizational culture through leadership development: A case in leadership transformation. *OD Journal*, Fall 1999.

Sharkey, L., Sorensen, P., Yaeger, T., "Integrating Traditional and Contemporary Approaches to Change: Culture, Survey Feedback and Appreciative Inquiry." Creating Healthy Organization Cultures Conference, Loyola University, Chicago, IL June 1998.

Sorensen, P., Head, T., Gironda, L., and Larsen, H. (1996). Global Organization Development: Lessons From Scandinavia. *Organization Development Journal.*

Sorensen, P., Head, T., Johnson, K. and Mathys, N. (1991). *International Organization Development*, Champaign, IL: Stipes.

Spartz, D. (1998) Creating Healthy Organization Cultures Conference, Loyola University, Chicago, IL June 1998. "Diagnosing and developing a management culture: A case study in health care"

Srivastva, S., & Barrett, F.J. (1990) Appreciative organizing: Implications for executive functioning. In S. Srivastva, D.L. Cooperrider, & Associates (Eds.), *Appreciative management and leadership*, San Francisco, CA: Jossey-Bass.

PART III

New Horizons

Chapter 15

Is Appreciative Inquiry OD's Philosopher's Stone?

Thomas C. Head
Roosevelt University

Peter F. Sorensen, Jr.
Benedictine University

Joanne C. Preston
Pepperdine University

Therese F. Yaeger
Benedictine University

Can Appreciative Inquiry (AI) be that alchemist's philosopher's stone OD has been searching for? AI, as an approach to organization transformation, has proven its effectiveness in a wide variety of organizations and cultures—from seeking solutions for Romanian orphanages to providing direction to Fortune 500 boardrooms. Regardless of national/corporate culture AI appears to be effective—so is it the "universal" approach to change that we have so long sought for (and taught against)? This paper will present a "stream of thought" which provides an explanation for AI's apparent universal success.

The Journey Begins: True OD Requires An Organization Culture Change

"OD involves both the creation and the subsequent reinforcement of change. It moves beyond the initial attention to implementing a change program to a longer-term concern for stabilizing and institutionalizing new activities within the organization." (Cummings and Worley, 1993, p. 2) It has long been accepted that legitimate OD's "end result" involves a culture change in the client organization. Rensis Likert (1962) supported this notion when he created his "Three-Variable Model" and placed what we now call "organization culture" firmly into the Causal Variable category. In essence, Likert suggests that interventions which fail to effect

217

the causal variables (culture) will only address "intervening level" variables—similar to a physician who only treats a patient's symptoms without eliminating the disease. The patient/client "feels" better but the problem is only masked. The patient is still sick and sooner or later new, and most likely more dangerous, symptoms will emerge.

Lewin's (1952) three-stage change model also supports the belief that "true" OD must involve a change in organization culture. Lewin's first stage, unfreezing, "involves reducing those forces maintaining the organization's behavior . . . sometimes accomplished by introducing information that shows discrepancies between behaviors desired by organizational members and those behaviors they currently exhibit." (Cummings and Worley, 1993, p. 53) Clearly a call for "attacking" the current corporate culture—showing the employees the faults in the present culture and the possibilities of a new culture. This interpretation is further supported by Lewin's final state, refreezing, which "stabilizes the organization at a new state of equilibrium . . . frequently accomplished through the use of supporting mechanisms that reinforce the new organizational state, such as organization culture, norms, policies, and structures." (Cummings and Worley, 1993, p. 53).

In a more contemporary view Tichy (1983) further reinforces cultural change's requirement for "true" change. Organization culture is one of the three "loosely coupled" systems—the others being the technical and political systems. Organization change requires first developing a vision of the organization which involves the three systems being aligned. To achieve this image the three systems must be "uncoupled" and each one, separately, receive intervention. Only after all three systems have been changed can they be "recoupled" to insure continued success.

Implicit in Tichy's model is the understanding that while successful change requires an organization culture modification, that cultural transformation does not have to be "radical", rather it can be incremental in nature (Meyer, Goes, and Brooks, 1992). Possibly Roosevelt Thomas (1990), in his discussion of managing cultural diversity, described the requisite culture change best. Thomas suggests that while sometimes a massive organization culture upheaval is needed, more typically subtle changes are called for. These subtle changes are similar to what a tree surgeon does—trimming a branch here, grafting a part there, and removing (or rerouting) a diseased root, all to reinforce what is "good" about the tree while removing the "bad". Generally employees like the organization's culture—that is often the reason why they remain employees. These people will recognize the need for subtle cultural modifications—retaining the "best" parts, changing the diseased elements, but only removing that which is malignant.

First Bend: Culture Change, Yes, But To What?

It is clear that successful organization interventions require the active alteration of the organization's culture. But a culture change to what? Some theorists have argued for a "universally desirable" culture—typically centering around employee participation. Rensis Likert (1962a, 1967, 1977) is one such individual—making strong arguments for the overwhelming desirability of the "System 4" organization. System 4 is "designed around group methods of decision making and supervision . . . fosters high degrees of member involvement and participation. Work groups are highly involved in setting goals, making decisions, improving methods, and appraising results." (Cummings and Worley, 1993, p. 247)

Blake and Mouton (1975), through their "9,9" (or Team Management) universally desirable Leadership style, also advocate one "all encompassing" organization culture. "9,9" organizations stress "understanding and agreement through involvement—participation—commitment as the key to . . . boss–subordinate (relationships)." (p. 164)

While the notion of a "universally desirable" corporate culture would make everyone's life much simpler the evidence clearly contradicts this belief. Cummings and Worley (1993), in their reviews, note that while Blake and Mouton's "Grid can be successful, but not in all situations." (p. 258), and "although there is evidence to support the effectiveness of system 4 (research and theory) suggests that such success may be limited to certain situations." (p. 251)

The reason for Likert and Blake and Mouton's failures to achieve universal applicability is quite simple. "Despite changes in the environment, organizations are not all alike. A great many problems occur when all organizations are treated as similar, which was the case with both the administrative principles and bureaucratic approaches (Scientific Management and Classical Management Movements) that tried to design all organizations alike." (Daft, 1995, p. 23). The basis for all modern management thought is contingency—the understanding that organizations must be designed for a "goodness-of-fit" with their own unique environment (Pennings, 1992). Daft (1995, pp. 24–25) illustrates the concept quite succinctly:

> What works in one setting may not work in another setting. There is not one best way. Contingency theory means, "it depends." For example, some organizations may experience a certain environment, use a routine technology, and desire efficiency. In this situation, a mechanistic approach to management that uses bureaucratic control procedures, a functional structure, and formal communication would be appropriate. Likewise, organic, free-flowing management processes work best in an uncertain environment with a nonroutine technology. The correct management approach is contingent upon the organization's situation.

Clearly there is no "universal" corporate culture. The concept is based upon false assumptions. So, the central question around implementing successful change becomes "Changing the culture, okay, but to what?" Daft has already answered this: the ideal corporate culture is contingent upon the unique influences the client organization faces.

Second Bend: Nation's Culture Influences Organization Culture

The ideal culture for a corporation is dependent upon the organization's internal and external environments. There is plenty of evidence that supports the belief that the socio-cultural (national cultural values) sector is a major influence on the organization's systems (Daft, 1995). Hofstede (1980) was one of first to empirically study the influence of a nation's culture on management practices. Hofstede found that most countries have a unique combination of four values: masculinity/ femininity, uncertainty avoidance, power distance, and individualist/ collectivist. With this evidence Hofstede speculated that management practices developed in one country (based upon its own culture) could not be useful in other countries.

While it is now apparent that Hofstede overstated his case (Sorensen, Head, Johnson and Mathys, 1991), his work has still proved to be an invaluable guide for change theorists. Central for this paper is the work of Jaeger (1986), who reanalyzed Hofstede's data with specific regards to the compatibility of national cultural values with organization development's core values (low uncertainty avoidance, feminine, low power distance, and moderate collectivist). Specifically, Jaeger was able to classify countries as "similar to OD", "somewhat different to OD" (different on 1 or 2 values), and "different to OD" (differing on 3 or all 4 values). Jaeger suggested that the closer a country's culture is to OD's values, the more successful OD interventions would be in that culture. Jaeger (1989) and Head and Sorensen (1993) empirically tested, and confirmed, this hypothesis. A corollary evolved from Jaeger's work—Organization Development interventions can be successful in incompatible cultures—but adjustments are required to achieve a cultural fit. For a detailed example of this corollary, see Head, Sorensen, Larsen and Nielsen (1993), which examines how an intervention (management development) takes on different characteristics in three distinct cultures: Denmark, U.S.A., and the Republic of China.

Recently, this body of research has specifically looked at the relationship between national cultural values and ideal corporate cultures. One example of this research stream is that of Sorensen, Head, Gironda, and Larsen (1996). Utilizing Cooke and Lafferty's (1989) Organization Culture Inventory, Sorensen et al. have been documenting national "ideal" corporate cultures. Before these results are presented, an understanding of the Organization Culture Inventory is needed.

The Organizational Culture Inventory (OCI) is a multi-level diagnostic tool developed by Robert Cooke and Clayton Lafferty. The OCI provides a standardized measure of corporate culture with regards to the behavioral norms and expectations associated with the more abstract aspects of organization culture such as shared values and beliefs. Responses to the OCI have been related to organizational outcomes such as member satisfaction, motivation, teamwork, the quality of products/services and other criteria of organizational effectiveness such as sales performance. Clearly, the OCI is an appropriate and useful instrument for facilitating culture change programs (Sorensen, Head, Gironda, Larsen, 1996). More importantly for this paper, the OCI has been used and adopted by various national and international organizations and completed by more than 200,000 respondents world-wide. The OCI has been reprinted in French, German and translation keys developed in Spanish and Russian.

The OCI measures an organization's ideal culture with regard to 12 different value styles (Cooke and Hartmann, 1989):

1. Humanistic-Helpful Culture: High priority is placed on constructive interpersonal relationships. Members are expected to be friendly, open and sensitive to their work group and also sharing feelings and thoughts.

2. Affiliative Culture: High priority is placed on constructive interpersonal relationships. Members are expected to be friendly, open, and sensitive to their work group and also sharing feelings and thoughts.

3. Approval Culture: Conflicts are avoided and interpersonal conflicts are pleasant—at least superficially. Members feel like they should agree with, gain the approval of, and be liked by others.

4. Conventional Culture: Conservative, traditional and bureaucratically controlled. Members are expected to conform, follow the rules, make good impressions and always follow policies and practices.

5. Dependent Culture: Hierarchically controlled and non-participative. Centralized decision making leads members to do only as they are told, clear all decisions with superiors, doing what is expected and pleasing those in positions of authority.

6. Avoidance Culture: Fail to reward success but nevertheless punish mistakes. The negative reward system leads members to shift responsibilities to others, avoid any possibility of being blamed, wait for others to act first, and take few chances.

7. Oppositional Culture: Confrontation prevails and negativism is rewarded. Members gain status and influence by being critical and thus reinforced to oppose the ideas of others, make safe decisions, pointing out flaws and are hard to impress.

8. Power Culture: Non-participative organizations structured on the basis of authority inherent in members' positions. Members believe they will be rewarded for taking charge, controlling subordinates while being responsive to demands of superiors.

9. Competitive Culture: Winning is valued and members are rewarded for outperforming one another. Members operate in a win-lose framework and believe they must work against, not with, their peers.

10. Competence/Perfectionist Culture: Perfectionism, persistence and hard work are valued. Members feel they must avoid all mistakes, keep track of everything, work long hours to attain narrowly defined objectives.

11. Achievement Culture: Do things well and value members who accomplish goals. Members set challenging but realistic goals, establish plans to reach them and pursue them with enthusiasm.

12. Self-Actualization Culture: Value creativity, quality over quantity and both task accomplishment and individual growth. Members are encouraged to gain enjoyment from their work, develop themselves and take on interesting activities.

These twelve values are arranged in a "clock" format recording progressive interrelationships and behaviors. The values at the top of the clock (11, 12, 1 and 2) indicate constructive cultures; values towards the bottom of the clock indicate passive, aggressive, and/or defensive cultures. For the sake of comparison the "clock" dimensions are standardized. The further away from the center point, the more prevalent a specific trait is for that organization's culture.

Sorensen et al. (1996), through surveys of fourteen countries' MBA students, have found dramatic differences in OCI profiles based upon the countries' cultural similarity to Organization Development values. Their findings are reported in Figures 1, 2, and 3. Each profile, as expected, is unique, and will be discussed below. One interesting and unexpected finding was that all three groups' profiles did have one similarity. The values of Conventional style (4 o'clock) and Dependent style (5 o'clock) were identified as the least significant in all three groups' profiles. Therefore the discussion of profile differences will focus on the opposite end of the spectrum: those values which are dominant in the profiles.

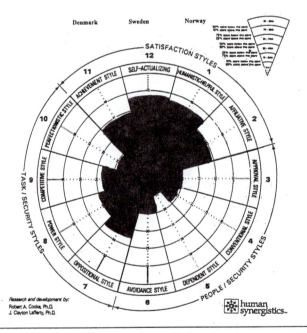

Figure 1. Organization Culture Inventory Profile for those countries whose culture is very similar to that of Organization Development.

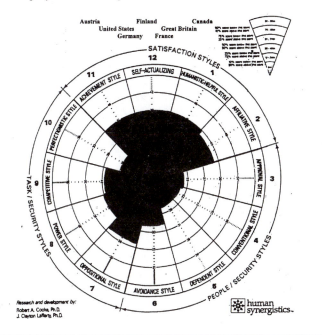

Figure 2. Organization Culture Inventory Profile for those countries whose culture is "somewhat similar" to Organization Development's.

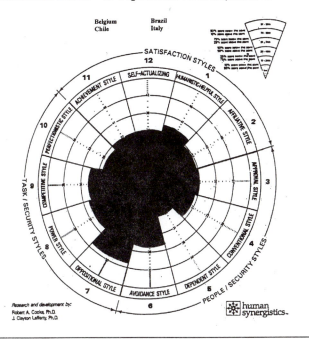

Figure 3. Organization Culture Inventory Profile for those countries whose culture is "very different" from those of Organization Development.

Figure 1 illustrates the ideal corporate culture profile of the three countries (Denmark, Norway, and Sweden) whose values are similar to those of organization development. The two "dominant" cultural values, not surprisingly, reflect the true nature of OD: Self-Actualizing (12 o'clock) and Humanistic-Helpful (1 o'clock). Figure 2 illustrates the ideal corporate culture profile made up of respondents from seven countries falling into Jaeger's "somewhat different from OD" category: Austria, Canada, Finland, France, Germany, Great Britain, and the United States. One distinguishing element of this profile is the lack of a clearly dominant set of values. While Achievement (11 o'clock) and humanistic (1 o'clock) values are dominant, they are not "overwhelmingly" so. Self-Actualizing (12 o'clock), Affiliative (2 o'clock), and Oppositional (7 o'clock) are all very close to having the same level of significance in these countries. Figure 3 illustrates the ideal corporate culture profile for the 4 countries whose values are "very different" from those of organization development (Belgium, Brazil, Chile, and Italy). Not unexpectedly, these countries' profiles indicate a set of dominant values, which are polar opposite of organization development's. Oppositional style values (7 o'clock) and Power style (8 o'clock) dominate in this profile.

While the "somewhat different" countries' profile muddies the interpretation, if one compares the profiles of "similar" and "different" countries, a clear conclusion arises. It does appear that countries with different value sets do indeed have different "ideal" corporate cultures. Countries whose values are similar to OD's will desire organization cultures dominated by "Top Of The Clock" values, while countries whose values are very different to OD's will prefer cultures which stress "Bottom Of The Clock" beliefs. Therefore, looking back to the earlier question, "Change—but to what," there is now an answer—successful change will reflect movement in organizational values towards the organization's "ideal". This "ideal" will be greatly influenced by the country's cultural values in which the organization is located. Therefore, with condolences to Likert and Blake and Mouton, for some countries the OD consultant's task is to change an organizations culture to emphasize oppositional and power values—exactly opposite of what these theorists suggest.

Third Bend: No Universal End Result. But What About Tools?

Clearly, there is no universal set of values, no universal culture, no universal end result—each consulting situation requires a culture change custom tailored for its own unique set of requirements. Most interesting is the fact that often times these culture changes, being brought about through organization development, will take the shape of OD's antithesis. One would think that OD tools could not function correctly to bring about such a "negative (from their design)" result. However, there is plenty of evidence showing that OD does work in countries with "very different" cultures (see for example Boss and Variono's description of OD in Italy (1987); Fuch's (1987) discussion of OD practices in Chile).

The next question, logically, becomes: "If there is no universal 'end result' for OD, is there a set of tools, or a tool, which can facilitate the culture change process regardless of what form that change will take? Head and Sorensen (1993) and Jaeger (1989), present two studies, which indirectly tests this hypothesis. Combined, they examined the use, and usefulness, of 15 different OD interventions, in 12 different countries. The combined results are found in Table 1. There were no "universally" used, or effective, tools. Team Building came the closest to universality, being used and effective in 8 countries (66%). MBO was the only other intervention used in more than 50% of the countries (7), but it was only reported effective in 33% (4) of the countries.

It is also important to remember, as mentioned earlier, that even those interventions which are utilized in a wide variety of countries will undoubtedly be adjusted in order to match the country's cultural values (Head, Sorensen, Larsen, and Nielsen, 1993). Such adjustments are required to avoid falling victim to the false assumptions often found in international/multinational organization development (Johnson, Head and Sorensen, 1989). Of specific interest here is the *Unity of Practice Assumption* (p. 310).

Organization Development techniques are clearly defined, as labeled. If there are subtle gradations and shadings from one application to another, and shifts in definition when the application takes place, then a central anchor point is lost in the understanding and evaluation of Organization Development techniques. In particular, adjustments which may take place in another culture, and which may be critical for the understanding of the adaptation of Organization Development to that culture, may go unrecognized and unmeasured.

Table 1. OD Interventions Reported Use and Effectiveness in 12 Different Coutries

Intervention	Number of Countries Reporting Use	Number of Countries Effective Reporting Effective
Team building	8	8
Management by objectives	7	4
Survey feedback	6	6
Quality of work life	5	2
Transaction analysis	5	2
Process consultation	5	4
Job design	4	4
Career development	4	1
Role Negotiation	4	0
Confrontation	3	3
Physical settings	3	0
Organization mirror	2	0
Force field analysis	2	2
3rd party consultation	2	2
Collateral organization	1	1

Fourth Bend: Okay, But What About A Different Kind of Tool?

Apparently there are no universal OD interventions which can facilitate organization culture change to a desired end result. Or is there? Recently, a new technique has been developed by David Cooperrider and associates known as Appreciative Inquiry (AI). AI has proven successful all over the world, and with all different types of organizations.

Appreciative Inquiry's (Srivastva and Cooperrider, 1990) approach to organization development is rooted in discovering the positive forces that give meaning to an organization, focusing upon what is right, not wrong. Attention is focused on remembering peak experiences when situations were positive and working well, and allowing those positive experiences to guide the change process. This contrasts with the problem solving approach which first identifies the problems and what is wrong with the organization. Appreciative Inquiry, by focusing on what is working right and how the challenges that the organization is facing can be addressed, creates a positive atmosphere for change and avoids the resistance and loss of hope for a better future encountered through the more traditional approaches.

Appreciative Inquiry assumes that the change process is guided by the first questions we ask of the participants. If negative questions begin the process, this will set a negative climate—if positive questions are asked, this will help the process move in a positive direction.

Typically, the first step in Appreciative Inquiry involves an interviewing process centering upon four key questions:

1. Describe a peak experience or high point
2. Describe things valued most about (a) yourself, (b) nature of one's work, (c) the organization
3. Describe Core Factor that gives "life" to the organization
4. Describe three wishes to heighten vitality and health of the organization.

These four questions guide the change process in a positive direction. From the interviews, common topics or themes typically emerge, i.e., quality, commitment, customer service. These topics are explored in detail, focusing on when the organization has experienced them at their best, not worst.

The four basic principles of Appreciative Inquiry (Cooperrider, 1990) are:

1. Inquiry into "the art of the possible", the appreciative approach gets inspiration from "what is" and aims at valuing, learning and understanding.
2. What's possible should be applicable, what is discovered in an organization should generate knowledge that can be used, applied and validated.
3. What's possible should be provocative, an organization should be open-ended, learning how to take part in its own evolution.
4. Human potential of organizational life should be collaborative.

This is very different from the assumption that "organizations are problems to be solved." This problem solving approach is one that is familiar and on which most interventions are based. Problem solving includes:

1. Identifying key problems (what is wrong?)
2. Analyzing key causes (whose fault is it?)
3. Analyzing solutions (what must be changed to correct it?)
4. Developing an action plan (what is politically feasible?)

Contrast these with AI's four steps:

1. Discovery and valuing
2. Envisioning
3. Dialogue
4. Co-construction of the future.

Journey's End: Why Appreciative Inquiry

Why might appreciative inquiry prove to be Organization Development's "philosopher's stone", turning every consulting project into golden success? AI is not a "tool" like team building, grid management, or quality circles, rather it is an innovative approach to change management. AI's approach directly attacks one of the few "universal truths" of OD practice—successful OD requires overcoming resistance to change.

Table 2 illustrates exactly how AI resolves the primary causes for employees to resist change. Aside from just removing change resistance, AI also accomplishes two other principle goals of OD consultants—regardless of what culture they operate in: acquiring employee ownership into the program, and maximizing employee input into the design of the new system.

Conclusion

We will take a somewhat different approach to this paper's conclusion. Rather than simply restate what has been written, we believe that an example of AI's universal potential will best support our thesis.

The client was a two-hospital "chain". Significant and constant conflict had ground the organization's progress to a halt. The bickering also began to be known in the community, negatively impacting the organization's image. The conflict was not centered around the differences between the two hospitals. Rather, as

Table 2. How Appreciative Inquiry Undermines Resistance to Change

Reason for Employee Resistance	How Does AI Reduce Resistance
Fear of the unknown—we know what we have, but we don't know what change will bring.	AI works from the known—the organization is trying to "recapture" the already experienced peaks.
Change can cause the employee to question his/her self-image—"Can I do the new task?"	AI begins with what employees like most about the existing system—making the peak experiences the norm. The implication is that at the same time non peak experiences will be adjusted/removed.
The employees feel imposed upon—they have to do all the work for the change, but only the "organization" will reap the benefits.	AI clearly puts the "gain" into personal terms. The process focuses on how to permit each employee tonstantly experience the personal satisfaction that occurred during the "peak experiences".
The employees feel imposed upon—they have to do all the work for the change, but only the "organization" will reap the benefits.	AI clearly puts the "gain" into personal terms. The process focuses on how to permit each employee tonstantly experience the personal satisfaction that occurred during the "peak experiences".
The employees view this change process as another "fad"—"why adopt anything new when management is going to forget it in a coupld of weeks anyway?"	AI does not appear to be a revolutionary concept. Its goal can be seen as making "what is going on now" better. It is logical, and fits into the current paradigms—managers are always trying to get the current system to be more effective and efficient.

many experienced in working with hospitals can identify with, the conflict centered upon the differences between the medical and administrative staffs.

The consultant was called in to help the organization find a resolution to the conflict at the executive level. While the tensions were felt throughout the hospitals it appeared that the source was at the management level. For the most part the two sets of combatants only interacted regularly at the executive level; lower level participants merely adopted the attitudes of their managers; thus spreading the problem throughout the organization.

The executive team had already tried everything, working with a wide variety of consultants to resolve the problems—nothing seemed to work. Why? It quickly became obvious that the organization was suffering from a split personality: there were two sets of very different corporate cultures. Simulations of the two OCI profiles can be found in Figures 4 and 5.

Faced with a situation where none of the "usual" tools would work, the "new" consultant turned to appreciative inquiry (he had just been exposed to it and AI intrigued him—enough to try it on his own without any formal training).

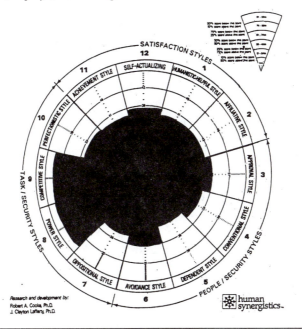

Figure 4. Organizational Culture Inventory Profile for the Hospital's Administrative staff.

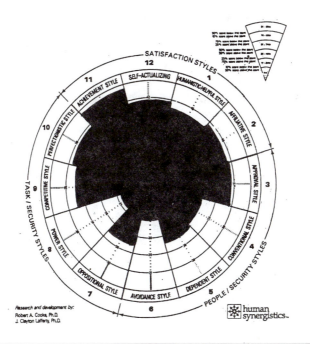

Figure 5. Organizational Culture Inventory Profile for the Hospital's medical staff.

Appreciative Inquiry seems to have worked—at least this is what the client reports about a year after the initial session (the consultant had several "sessions" over 6 months). The executive team has broken out of the "grid lock" and has worked well together—even initiating several projects that had been placed on "political" hold.

Appreciative Inquiry was immediately accepted by the team—it literally caught them unaware. The team was prepared for another "problem solving" session and were startled when asked to recall those times when things had worked well. Of course there were the initial comments which had to be dismissed, such as "things have never worked well", and "peak experiences—it's whenever the (other 'side's) members were absent." When pressed to come up with a few specific examples the group responded. Possibly the biggest break came when both "sides" identified several of the same experiences. This permitted specific analysis, perfect for both groups, with regards to why things worked well in these cases.

The end result of the sessions was to create a "rules of the road" set of behaviors and attitudes which would govern the inter "side" of interactions. These rules (named this way because many of the participants had a common interest in motorcycles, unknown to all before the sessions) were positive in nature—not a list of "thou shall nots". Some examples were "We will truly investigate a situation from several perspectives before suggesting possible solutions;" "While we might disagree with each other's ideas—we all have similar motives;" "Conflict can be our best resource—differences can lead to improvements;" and "Consensus does not have to mean unanimity".

What really happened? It was clear to everyone that the two "ideal cultures" could not be melded into one common—the differences were more related to the parties' professional values than anything else. So the organization has begun to create a "third" culture—specifically aimed at the executive team when they are interacting (as opposed to performing their individual tasks). This third culture was a direct result of tapping into the common peak experiences—when the group did function well. No one had to compromise their personal values and beliefs, or change what they "wanted"—only what they did in the old status quo situation. They were not trying to invent something new, only recapture what they had lost.

Appreciative Inquiry has proven successful in a wide variety of national and corporate cultures—even those with split personalities. Why? We argue, hopefully successfully, that a major reason is that it overcomes the universal problem—resistance to change. Are there other reasons? Possibly so. We encourage you to join us and explore the possibilities together.

References

R. Blake and J. Mouton, 1975, "An Overview Of The Grid", *Training and Development Journal*.

R. W. Boss, M. V. Variono, 1987, "Organization Development In Italy," *Group and Organization Studies*, 12, 245–256.

R.A. Cooke, J. Hartmann, 1989, *Interpreting the Culture Styles Measured By The Organizational Culture Inventory: Organizational Culture Inventory Leader's Guide*, Plymouth, Michigan: Human Synergistics, Inc.

R.A. Cooke, J. C. Lafferty, 1989, *The Organizational Culture Inventory*, Plymouth, Michigan: Human Synergistics, Inc.

D. Cooperrider, *Appreciative Inquiry, A Constructive Approach to Organization Development*. Cleveland: Case Western Reserve University.

T. G. Cummings and C.G. Worley, 1993, *Organization Development and Change, 5th ed.*, Minneapolis: West Publishing Company.

R. Daft, 1995, *Organization Theory and Design, 5th ed.*, Minneapolis: West Publishing.

C. Fuchs, 1987, "Organizational Development Under Political, Economic and Natural Crisis," *Organization Development Journal*, 5, 37–45.

T. Head and P. Sorensen, 1993, "Cultural Values And Organizational Development," *Leadership And Organization Development Journal*, 11, 3–7.

G. Hofstede, 1980, *Culture's Consequences: International Differences in Work-Related Values*, London: Sage.

A. Jaeger, 1986, "Organization Development and National Culture: Where's the Fit?" *Academy of Management Review*, 11, 178–190.

A. Jaeger, 1989, "Organization Development Methods in Practice: A 5-Country Examination," in *Advances In International Comparative Management*, 4, 113–130, Greenwich, CT: JAI Press.

K. R. Johnson, T. Head, and P. Sorensen, 1989, "Cross-Cultural Organization Development: Suggestions for Paradigm Development", *Academy of Management Best Paper Proceedings*.

K. Lewin, 1951, *Field Theory In Social Science*, New York: Harper and Row.

R. Likert, 1962, "New Patterns in Sales Management," in *Changing Perspectives In Marketing Management*, ed. M.R. Warshaw, Ann Arbor: University of Michigan Bureau of Research.

R. Likert, 1962a, *New Patterns of Management*, New York: McGraw-Hill.

R. Likert, 1967, *The Human Organization*, New York: McGraw-Hill.

R. Likert, 1977, "Management Styles and The Human Component," *Management Review*.

A. Meyer, J. Goes, G. Brooks, 1992, "Organizations in Disequilibrium: Environmental Jolts and Industry Revolutions," in G. Huber and W. Glick, eds., *Organizational Change and Redesign*, New York: Oxford University Press.

J. M. Pennings, 1992, "Structural Contingency Theory: A Reappraisal," *Research in Organizational Behavior*, 14, pp. 267–309.

P. Sorensen, T. Head, L. Gironda, H. Larsen, 1996, "Global Organization Development: Lessons From Scandinavia," *Organization Development Journal*, in print.

P. Sorensen, T. Head, K. Johnson, and N. Mathys (1991), *International Organization Development*, Champaign, IL: Stipes.

Srivastva, S., and Cooperrider, D., 1990. *Appreciative Management and Leadership*. San Francisco: Jossey-Bass.

R.R. Thomas, 1990, *Beyond Race and Gender*, New York: AMACOM.

N. Tichy, 1983, *Managing Strategic Change: Technical, Political, and Cultural Dynamics*, New York: John Wiley.

Chapter 16

Postmodern Principles and Practices for Large Scale Organization Change and Global Cooperation

Diana Whitney, Ph.D.
The Taos Institute

Globalization as Opportunity and Imperative

As the new millennium dawns in time as it has already in consciousness, possibilities for global cooperation emerge in ways never before imagined. Religious leaders around the globe are coming together to discuss the conditions of the world and how they and their religions can contribute to peace. Business, government and NGO leaders from opposite sides of the globe are meeting to share best practices for organizing and for creating global cooperation and social justice. People who may never meet in person are becoming friends and doing business via the Internet. And hundreds of people who care about the environment and culture of mountain regions around the world are meeting, in person and via the Internet, to envision possibilities, to share stories and to bridge resources.

The development of communication technology creates both possibilities and expectations. With the ability to communicate simultaneously around the globe comes a demand to do so.

Colleagues around the world no longer receive a summary of the meeting two days later; now they participate via teleconferencing, video conferencing or on-line networking. Global simultaneity is fast becoming the way of doing business.

With the ability to share information without imitation comes the expectation that needed information be available anytime of the day or night, anywhere in the world. Information is no longer a limit to cooperation. It is possible and expected that wherever we are in the world we have the same information in front of us as we meet and do business. Information accessibility, availability and equity are givens in the emerging business environment.

OD Journal, Vol. 14, No. 4, Winter 1996.

With the ability to organize large groups of people communicating online about areas of common interest comes the expectation to do so as a matter of practice. Intranets are now as important a business process as typing was two decades ago. Ongoing conferences and dialogues are commonplace on company Intranets as well as on the Internet. In the past few months I have participated in: an ongoing dialogue among academic colleagues around the world about dialogue, an ongoing conference as a member of The Mountain Forum, an ongoing meeting of founders of The Taos Institute and an ongoing meeting of the planning group for an Appreciative Inquiry Organization Summit. Each of these conversations among numbers of people ranging from 8 to 800 is ongoing. As an interested party I can participate as I like based upon whatever criteria I bring to the use of my online time and the management of relationships and responsibilities in multiple, diverse domains. Connections and conversations are there waiting to be engaged and supplemented. Large group conversations, online and face to face, are becoming primary means of organizing for global cooperation and impact.

The Unfolding Context for Life and Word in the New Millennium

As communication technology spreads around the world from urban center to rural village, from educational center to local craft cooperative, from Fortune 50 company to customers around the globe, we are discovering the essential relatedness of all members of our global village. The greater our exposure to the diversity of humankind; the stronger the realization that we are all related—different and related. What happens in one part of the globe effects the life of the whole. Communication technology enables this to be known and experienced.

The awareness of relatedness is unfolding in the physical sciences as well as the social sciences. In *Wholeness and the implicate Order*, David Bohm, a quantum physicist, outlines a general theory of the universe in which he suggests that everything is connected to everything else. The notion on essential relatedness goes beyond human relations to a connectedness of all life and consciousness.

As new communication practices emerge they create the metaframe within which life at work and at home exist. With information readily available, a premium is placed on processes of interpretation and meaning making. As larger and larger groups of people become engaged in information sharing there is created a demand for processes which engage larger and larger numbers of people in interpretation and meaning making. Sense making in organizations moves from the arenas of interpersonal and small group communication into the arena of public conversation. Organizing becomes a process of simultaneously, online or in person, engaging large numbers of people in inquiry and conversation about their collective possibilities.

And so human life in the new millennium organization is emerging as a technology assisted highly relational and interpretively rich flow of large-scale public conversations.

Modern Models and Methods of Organization Development

Methods of organizing to accomplish results in business, government, social service, education as well as religion in the past sixty plus years have been based on the physical and behavioral sciences of the early 1900s. The science of the modern era, like its organizational counterparts was organized around notions of relational objectivity, mechanistic efficiency and never ending progress.

The dominant metaphor for industrial age organizations was the machine. Efficiency of human effort was the means of achieving better productivity and hence greater profitability. Theories of Scientific Materialism led to time and motion studies aimed at describing human effort in machine like terms. Organizational Improvement rested on the ability to figure human action as coordinated with machine action; and to determine the most efficient patterns of action. Human behavior was studied as a means of improving industrial efficiency.

In response to this overly mechanized approach, organizational consultants and scholars began to put their views of "human" into human behavior. The T-Group evolved and The National Training Laboratory emerged as vehicles to help managers become aware of feelings. The dominant notions were that better people make better organizations; and that better people are those who are in touch with their feelings and can be appropriately sensitive to the feelings of others including co-workers. Human behavior was studied as a means of improving individual effectiveness and hence organizational effectiveness. As the behavioral sciences focused attention on individual development and psychology so too did organization behavior focus on the individual as the center of causality and change.

Organizational behavior, while individual centered, was conceptualized as operating on three levels—the individual, the group and the organizational. The study of group processes led to principles of organizing based on the process of group development and the experience of people in groups. Form, storm, norm and perform became code words for the story of how groups develop; and for the personal and interpersonal dramas of group work. People in groups were described as having varying needs for inclusion, affection and control. A group's effectiveness and hence organizational effectiveness was said to result from awareness of and attention to these varying needs. Other theories went beyond the notions of individuals in groups to a concern for group process itself. As group effectiveness became a focus for organization development group theories posited group goals, roles, responsibilities, leadership, relationships and helpful mechanisms as central to success.

Whatever the view of group behavior, there was one common thread — the potential for improvement through intervention by an objective external other— an organization development consultant. Processes for team building based on small group theories emerged as means of hastening business start-ups, product development and manufacturing efficiency. The total quality movement continues to build upon the focus on group effectiveness as a means to organizational effectiveness.

At the macro level theories of Action Research were being developed and enacted by organization consultants as agents of change. Organization Development was defined by French and Bell as,

> a planned, systematic process in which applied behavioral science principles and practices are introduced into an ongoing organization toward the goals of effecting organization improvement, greater organization competence, and greater organization effectiveness.

Action Research developed as a means of ensuring that change was data based and participatory. Data was important as the basis of good knowledge and good-decision making. Data in a modern scientific sense was objective and untainted by subjective views. There was an operational belief that information; meaning and the people involved and affected could be separated. Group theory began to suggest a crack in their belief as it showed that participation led to greater commitment and greater productivity. The degree and nature of participation influenced the meaningfulness of a given organizational effort. Organization development as a field became an advocate for participation in the workplace.

Action Research processes generally engaged organization members in some variation of four basic stages:

1. Data Collection
2. Feedback and Planning
3. Implementation
4. Monitoring and Revising

Action Research processes were based on the assumption that an objective outside party—consultants—could through interviews, interactions and observations develop an objective picture of the organization. It was thought that such an objective picture, when reflected back to organization members, might help them think about their organization in new and enhancing ways. Following a feedback session plans for change were created that generally initiated activities "top down". Change management was a leadership task to be driven from the top of the organization. In too many cases top management was a leadership task to be driven from the top of the organization. In too many cases top management became the drivers without asking themselves what they believed or without holding themselves accountable for demonstrable change. In other and generally more successful cases, the idea that change starts at the top meant that senior management engaged themselves in processes of learning and development.

Action Research while a process applicable to small group change, became the vehicle for total system change. The dominant metaphor for the organization shifted from machine to system. Organization theorists began writing about organizations as open systems (Katz and Kahn, 1966).

The challenge for the field of organization development became the question of how to effect change in organizations as large systems. Adding knowledge of the behavioral sciences, small group theory and cybernetic systems theory to practical wisdom based on years of experience in organization development have caused the bar to be raised in the field of organization development. Among them, Marvin Weisbord, Kathleen Dannemiller and Harrison Owen who with colleagues have pioneered large scale change in organizations.

Each of these theories of human behavior has left their mark on organizational life in the 1990s. Organization development has a rich past of theory and practice. The challenge we face as practitioners today is the development of theory and practice suited to the new millennium, and to organizing on a global scale. As with all successful social change, we must evolve our work by honoring the past, by recalling the best of what was, and by creating a context for a future richly woven with the successes of our past. We must do this while at the same time envisioning possibilities beyond what has been, and future scanning for the emerging edges of innovation and social transformation. On the horizon of theories of social change are notions of postmodern social science. I believe they hold potential for furthering the practice of organization development to the level of global cooperation.

Postmodern Principles for Organizing in the new Millennium

What we need in particular are not more effective procedures for the general will to have its way, but a real conversation. We must talk in the public forum about the things that finally matter and about common measures that will give these things a secure and prominent place in our midst.
—Albert Borgmann, Crossing the Postmodern Divide.

Much is being written about postmodernism and organizing (Bergquist, 1993; Borgman, 1992; Hassard and Parker, 1993). New ways of thinking about organizations and new theories and methods of management and leadership are emerging (Boje and Dennehy, 1993). They are growing out of postmodern principles in the social sciences and are now fertile ground for social innovation in the fields of organization development and global organizing. The following summary of an affirmative post-modem social science is quoted from Pauline Marie Rosenau's *Post-Modernism and The Social Sciences*. It is offered as one writer's overview of postmodernism and ought not be read as an inclusive or comprehensive description. Following each of her points I suggest implication for the field of organization development and especially for the arena of large-scale change and global cooperation.

1. "Yet, one thing seems clear, postmodernism in all of its forms, shakes us loose of our preconceptions, our 'normal' way of doing social science. It asks some of the most potent questions we are capable of phrasing."

This suggests that a postmodern organization development would emphasize the practice of inquiry and questioning. We would seek to understand the way inquiry operates as a means of social creation. And we would develop the theory and practice of inquiry as an organizing process. Data would be valued as a position in a story, an understanding determined by a relational rich context, rather than as a relational objective bit of information. Inquiry would be valued and enacted as a process of social meaning making rather than a process of data collection.

2. For these post-modernists the pursuit of knowledge results in a sense of wonder and amazement (Murphy, 1988). It is an encounter with the unexpected, a 'voyage into the unforeseen' (Graff, 1979).

The postmodern organizational consultant would see organizations as David Cooperrider suggests, as mysteries to be unfolded, rather than as problems to be solved. We would use wonder and delight as criteria for meaningfulness rather than the modern sentiments of concern and worry. Organization development would be propelled by a sincere sense of wonder and curiosity so great that it cannot be ignored, rather than by the all too familiar stories about problems of doomsday proportion.

Organization development consultants would engage with clients to learn and to explore possibilities for a better future, rather than to plan and to ensure predetermined results. Organization development consultants would become partners in the co-creation and conscious evolution of shared organizational destiny. Excitement, enthusiasm, wonder, and amazement would be signs of organizational success.

Notions of leadership shift dramatically from the leader as authority or one responsible for vision, action and organization, to leader who fosters public conversations among multiple stakeholders. Leadership becomes a process of ensuring relational meaning making, of ensuring that multiple, diverse voices are heard, of creating and holding space for stories to be shared and meaning to be made among globally disparate and diverse people.

Leadership must also be the process by which the voices of all of our relatives are honored, given space and heard. Leadership must learn to invite, create and celebrate organizations of full voice.

3. "The post-modern social science is process oriented. It leaves room for a so-cially sensitive, active human being, groping for a new postmodern politics, religion and life in general: New Age, New Wave, new post-modern social movements."

And we are groping for new postmodern forms of organizing—the network organization, the virtual organization, the eco-conscious organization, the agile organization. For the past decade we have been talking about the reinvention for the corporation (Nasbitt), the reinvention of government (Gore) and the reinven-tion of work (Fox). A postmodern organization development must help business, government, religious and social leaders not only to reinvent but also to create forms of organizing for the new millennium. We must attend to organizing via processes of social interaction through which personal and collective identities, meaning and destiny emerges. These processes are uniquely conversational at the interpersonal, small group and large-scale levels of change.

Organization development in the new millennium must focus on the processes for the mass mobilization of inquiry, dialogue and public conversation both on line and face to face. Postmodern organizations may be no more than ongoing conversations among interested parties. The notions of organizations as structures—buildings, organization charts, hierarchies, standard policies and procedures are giving way to notions of organizing as conferences—temporary, as well as ongo-ing, conversations among diverse people with common interests and dreams for the future.

4. "The affirmative (Postmodernists, would retain history as a form of story tell-ing, as a local narrative without privilege. . . . There could be as many differ-ent and conflicting histories as there are consumers of the historical text."

As we collectively tell stories of our past and interpret them through the val-ues of today, we not only make history meaningful but we also provide continuity to life. A postmodern organization development would honor story telling as a means of conveying values and giving life to the people, culture and organization. History would be treated as a potential source of positive images for the future, rather than as a singular story of how it was in the good old days.

No particular history or story would be considered more significant than an-other would. Emphasis would be placed on the process of story telling. As people tell the stories of their work lives they place themselves in a relational web of values and meaning. Story telling is a way of giving voice to one's identity and of taking one's place in the organizational world of work. Employees throughout the world are asking to have a say and to be heard. A postmodern organization development would ensure opportunities for public story telling as a process for large-scale change.

The deconstruction and reconstruction of history can be both a healing process and a vehicle for positive change. For example, for women who have heard few if any stories about women in power as business leaders, philosophers, goddesses or military leaders the realm of possibilities for the construction of their identities is limited. Recognizing the potential of history as a source of meaning for the future, feminists have actively engaged in processes to reconstruct history as herstory. To include stories of women in leadership in all of life, including business, government and religion, and to talk about what happened that allowed women to be written out of history liberates the feminine potential for all people.

5. "Post-modernists reject modern views of linear time and predictable space. . . . Without modern time and space, absence and presence become arbitrary, causality an impossibility, and reality an invention."

Organization development in the new millennium will recognize not only the impossibility but also the futility of seeking causality. As a field of practice it will turn toward the discourse of creation as a means of organizing, and away from the discourse of causality. In doing so practitioners will seek processes for helping people to understand work life as a social invention. We will need to become facile at helping people see how we socially construct our worlds, and how we might reconstruct them to better suit our values and the demand of a new age. Reality as an invention suggests that we view organizations, business endeavors and work itself as social inventions. An emerging postmodern metaphor for organizations is as social inventions rather than as machines, or as systems.

6. "The affirmatives' post-modern social science is likely to be influenced by their substantive focus on the margins. . . . Their goal is to speak for those who have never been the subject (active, human), but who are rather so often assumed to be objects (observed, studied). They would include new voices and new forms of local narrative."

In every conversation, culture or organization there are voices on the margins. Generally they hold great promise for innovation and for change in the culture or organization upon whose edges they depend for their definition as marginal. There are, however, some voices missing or marginalized from the powerful discourse that gives design and meaning to our lives as global citizens. The voices of women, children, people of color, the environment, and indigenous people are some of the voices that have not had space or attention in the modem scientific era. A postmodern organization development would discover ways for marginalized voices to become active and equal in the creation of our collective future.

We must learn to delight in and learn from the stories of people which give meaning to their local identities as plumbers, mothers, doctors, union members, managers, Americans, Africans or Mexicans; while at the same time fostering the creation of meta-narratives that give meaning to life as global citizens. There is a need for processes of global cooperation that give meaning to local determination and action within the context of global citizenship.

7.   "New post-modern political movements are on the agenda of at least some affirmatives, as are broader and more authentic forms of participation and democracy."

A postmodern organization development would be radically participatory, not for the purpose of commitment and ownership, but rather for the purpose of co-creation and evolution. Acknowledging our essential relatedness, we would seek to engage everyone who is interested in processes of organization development. To act in ways that knowingly influence us all without involving the multitudes becomes an act of "old paradigmitis".

We must seek to further participatory democracy through all means possible, online and face to face. John Nasbitt's 1982 megatrend is unfolding as we continue to balance high tech-high touch. Large-scale processes, public conversations and global cooperation become essential vehicles for broader participation.

8.   "Others need a post-modern social science that emphasizes emotion, personal fulfillment, even faith, spirituality, and the irrational."

Organization development has emerged as a field of study and practice through which views of human and organizational effectiveness are developed and realized in the workplace. Postmodern discourse about human and organizational effectiveness flows with notions of spirituality, consciousness and evolution. Current best sellers about management and organization counsel us to reinvent work so that life and livelihood flow from the same source of spirit (Fox, 1994), to reawaken spirit at work (Hawley, 1993) and to see leadership as art (DePree, 1989).

Postmodern organization development practices must find ways to surface hope among people, hope that the future of their dreams may indeed be realized. We must draw upon sources of wisdom, vision and inspiration that have for centuries been considered the realism of spirituality and faith. Elsewhere I have written of spirituality as a postmodern organizing principle.

Organizing effort that give attention to the virtues and values we hold in highest regard will lead the way into the 21st century. In keeping with a postmodern social science I leave the above text to the reader for interpretation and application. For each of us these ideas afford different insights, learning and action possibilities. It is in conversation that we might make sense together of these words and in doing so give life to collective possibilities that could not exist separate from our relatedness and interactions.

Lessons from the Past Twenty Years

In the past twenty years working as an organization development consultant I have experienced the emergence of several processes for large scale organizing. I have even been privileged to contribute to the invention of some. It seems to me that these processes have been In the process of emergence, a sort of social coming forth, that has them arriving into prominence just-in-time. What follows is a brief review of three of the most commonly deployed large scale processes— Open Space, Future Search and Real Time Strategic Change. My intent is to highlight what each offers from a post-modern framework.

Open Space Technology is said to have been created by Harrison Owen when he recognized that conference attendees seemed to be more energized and excited by coffee break conversations than by the "formal" conference presentations and discussions. It places value on space as a relational context defined by time, place and listeners willing to witness others telling their stories. Story telling is part of the Open Space vocabulary and process. Each meeting no matter what the specific organizational setting begins with a telling of the story of Open Space—how it came into being, which was involved and how it has served over time.

Open Space works on the energy and commitment of choice. A topic is selected for the meeting by its hosts. Attendance and participation are voluntary. Even the nature of participation is a choice that must be made by participating. Open Space is guided by three rules and one law. The Three Rules of Open Space are:

1. Whoever shows up are the right people.
2. What ever happens is the only thing that could happen.
3. When it is over it is over.

Open Space provides the invitation for people to meet with others based on a shared interest, and to interact with one another in whatever ways are most meaningful to them until they determine to move on.

The Open Space Law of Two Feet tells participants to do what they want to do, and to go where they are interested, contributing and/or learning. As Harrison Owen says, "If you are not where you want to be, use the law of two feet and get up and go somewhere else". The law of two feet sets a community norm of coming and going without worry about disrupting someone else's conversational reality. It also ensures that what interests people is what gets attention. In this way it is a forum for the enactment of what is most meaningful to people involved.

Process is central to organizing using Open Space. Ways of becoming speaker and listener are redefined in terms of self-interest and mastery. There are no formal rules defined by Open Space Technology. Whoever gathers as participants do so with equal opportunity to speak and be heard. The potential for full voice exists in Open Space. Participants do, however, bring relational patterns from other contexts to Open Space. In this way Open Space becomes a microcosm for the larger organization and/or society in which participants reside. Open Space can only be as open and full voiced as the participants, in relation to one another are able to create.

While a forum for public conversation, Open Space places a premium on individual responsibility and self-mastery. Individuals propose sessions and make choices about participation. Diversity and the expression of multiplicity may emerge but are not defined into the process. No voice is purposefully excluded, nor are otherwise marginalized voices purposefully included. To this extent Open Space is a mirror of current organizational values and patterns of expression. It is not, in my experience, a technology for the collective deconstruction and reconstruction of patterns of organizing. Because of its voluntary nature it does not ensure that all stakeholders participate in conversations about their collective future.

As a large-scale process, Open Space has been successfully applied to foster discussion and planning about a wide range of topics, in a wide range of settings. As an organizing device it has been used to organize meetings and conferences ranging in size from 30 to 300. A more detailed description of Open Space and its applications can be found in Harrison Owen's book, *Open Space Technology*. As a form of organizing large-scale public conversations and contributing to global cooperation, Open Space is abundant with postmodern possibilities.

Real Time Strategic Change is defined by Robert Jacobs as, "the simultaneous planning and implementing of individual, group, and organization-wide changes." It is further described as, "an informed, participative process resulting in new ways of doing business that position an entire organization for success, now and in the future." The following description relies upon quotations from Real Time Strategic Change by Robert Jacobs. The process itself draws extensively upon the work of Kathleen Dannemiller, herself a brilliant social innovator.

Real Time Strategic Change (RTSC) involves a critical mass of people, generally from the same organization, in the process of change. Participants are invited based on criteria established to ensure that the "right number and type of people" are involved. This guideline allows for the inclusion of all recognized stakeholders. A premium is placed on real time as a process for "working through the real issues with the real people affected by them, and getting real results." What people and how many of them constitute critical mass are a question to be answered with each RTSC event.

RTSC is indeed a conversational process; participation is invited and occurs as those attending engage in structured dialogues. During RTSC people are identified by their organizational roles and positions. Participants are pre-assigned to max-mix groups of 8–12 people.

Participation in max-mix groups encourages people to listen to multiple and diverse voices during their discussions. Max-mix, by design, brings people from cross functions, cross business units and cross-levels in the organization into contact and communication with one another.

Group discussions are guided by specific questions. Group tasks are clearly defined in terms of questions for discussion. A common set of questions deployed following a presentation includes:

1. What did you hear?
2. What are your reactions?
3. What questions for understanding do you have?
4. For whom?

The overall RTSC process aims to influence: "Who is involved in developing broad views (meta-narratives) of the organization? What perspectives (voices) are included? And, how do these views (stories) become the basis of information used to support people in making change?" I have added postmortem textual terms in parenthesis.

RTSC is an inherently cooperative process aimed at creating common understanding within the organization. individual voices are expressed within each group and merge to become the group voice. Individual voices are channeled toward common ground through a structured process. Max-mix groups invite diverse voices to be expressed and also limited as they merge into one group voice.

Application of small group theory in a large-scale context has contributed to the success of RTSC. It uses the best of what we know about small group process and inter-group effectiveness to address the need for greater participation in discussions of strategic importance to an organization. It leverages the advantages of simultaneity and critical mass to achieve greater participation and greater speed in the process.

Designed upon principles of systems theory, RTSC is information oriented. It operates on the basis that informed are better able to make change. A wide variety of information is shared and discussed during RTSC events including leadership's vision for the organization, the customers' perspective, and the views of competition, government and other stakeholders. Throughout the process emphasis is placed upon understanding rather than upon invention or co-creation. Experts speak and small groups discuss what they heard. Questions for understanding are aimed at adoption, or at best adaptation of ideas rather than co-creation.

One interactive process called "valentines" invites cross functional groups to give each other feedback on performance. Based on small group methods and the assumption that feedback leads to change this process again is information centered rather than meaning centered. Functional groups are expected to receive and act on feedback from other groups in their organization without opportunity for collaborative interpretation and meaning making.

RTSC engages large numbers of people, 50–5000, from the same organization in a large-scale process using principles and practices of small group theory. There is much to be learned from RTSC about how to attend small group process in the course of building an organization-wide context rich with strategic information.

"Future Search" was the phrase first used by Marvin Weisbord in his 1987 book, *Productive Workplaces*. Future Search, the process, has evolved through the work of many organizational scholars and practitioners over the past two decades, including Ronald Lippitt, Eva Schindler-Rainman, Eric Trist, Fred and Merrelyn Emery. Future Search, the practice, is delightfully described and illustrated by Marvin Weisbord and Sandra Janoff in *Future Search: An Action Guide to Finding Common Ground in Organizations and Communities*. The following quotes are theirs. "A Future Search is a large group planning meeting that brings a 'whole system' into the room to work on a task focused agenda." It is based on the notion that common ground binds an organization or community. As a result, the Future Search process is designed to assist the search for and creation of common ground.

There is an explicit emphasis on shared vision as a guide for responsible individual and collective action, as the recommended uses of Future Search highlight:

1. "Future Search processes lead stakeholders to create a shared future vision for their organization or community."
2 "Future Search meetings enable all stakeholders to discover shared intentions and take responsibility for their own plans."
3. "These events can help people implement a shared vision that already exists."

The principle of 'global exploration before local action' serves to guide the design of Future Search meetings. The past is explored through wall charting and story telling about memorable personal, global and local events that occurred during the organization's past 30 years. The public and collective remembering of the past serves to invite voices that may have been silenced during the actual events of the past. It serves as a process for the deconstruction of commonly held relational realities. And it creates an open space for the creation of a shared future.

Future Search seeks to manage two essential and at times opposing forces: the desire for common ground and the expression of multiple and diverse voices. There is a recognition built into the design that validating every person's reality is essential as a foundation for common ground.

"We wish to validate every person's reality. We believe that there is great value in making psychological boundaries easier to cross—especially the boundary between what's inside our heads and what we say in public."

Future Search might be described as a multilingual process in that it allows for people's varying ways of knowing, learning and expressing themselves to occur and to be valued. The process invites thinking, feeling, reflecting, drawing, mind mapping, time lining, remembering and envisioning. It involves "the whole person" in a task oriented, future focused exploration and creation of the organizations past, present and future.

Underlying the design of Future Search is a strong and abiding democratic ideal. The aim is to get the whole system in the room, to engage all stakeholders in a simultaneous, interactive process and to ensure that those who must take action are involved in its determination. While the preferred number of participants is 64, Future Search methods have been used with smaller groups as well as integrated into processes involving hundreds.

Future Search allows for the remembering and re-interpreting of history and for the co-construction of a shared future vision. It fosters discussion in an open forum, allowing for the expression of multiple voices all aimed toward the organizing principle of common ground. It encourages personal responsibility for ideas and actions in alignment with the collective vision. Based on the commitment to validate every person's reality while aiming for common ground, Future Search illustrates emerging postmodern principles in practice.

The Organization Summit: An Appreciative Inquiry Large Scale Conference

> We have reached the end of problem solving as a mode of inquiry capable of inspiring, mobilizing, and sustaining human system change. The future of Organization Development belongs to methods that affirm, compel, and accelerate anticipatory learning involving larger and larger levels of collectivity.
> —David Cooperrider, *Appreciative Inquiry Workshop Manual.*

Appreciative Inquiry has emerged as a process for social, organizational and global change based on postmodern principles. It is a method that views realities as socially constructed with three bold implications. One, it is radically relational, inviting 100s and 1000s of people into circles of face to face inquiry and dialogue. And, within cyberspace, engaging millions of people in the conversations that shape our global village. Inquiry, based on a sincere desire to learn, guides interactions and invites the process of relational meaning making. Inquiry as a process for learning is simultaneously a process for cooperation, co-creation and change.

Two, Appreciative Inquiry is a dramatically creative process, an ongoing inquiry into of the stories that give meaning to life, work and organizing. It is a process for unfolding history—personal, organizational and global; for deconstructing and reconstructing the past in relation to present and future possibilities; and for discovering those narratives which give life in their expression and continual enactment.

Three, Appreciative Inquiry is decidedly affirmative and constructive in the positive interpretation of the word. It is based on the notion that organizations and communities are "affirmative systems" and according to Srivastva and Cooperrider, "they are guided in their actions by anticipatory 'fore-structurers' of positive knowledge." Organizations are heliotropic, they grow in the direction of the light—the most positive image created and conveyed by their discourse.

The Organization Summit is a large scale event in which organization Co-creators—members, stakeholders and meaning makers (people with the formal and/or informal relational capacity to influence the identity, direction and success of the organizational effort at hand. For example: the media, potential funding sources, students of organization, and leaders from other business or service sectors) engage in an Appreciative Inquiry process.

The Organization Summit engages participants in cycles of discovery, dream, design and destiny rather than diagnosis, problem identification, criticism or gap analysis. Initial Appreciative Interviews along with presentations of anticipatory theory and social construction theory create a shared commitment and curiosity among participants for exploring positive possibilities as a means of learning and organizational development.

The Organization Summit is a mix of dyadic, small group and whole group processes. Based on relational notions of meaning making and social construction theory, interaction among people representing diverse voices is essential. Cross-generational processes have proven most effective in generating stories that enliven leadership as well as hope for the organization's future. The Organization Summit utilizes techniques from other large-scale change processes. From Future Search it borrows the process of creating time lines to tell personal, organizational and global histories. From RTSC it takes ways of orchestrating small group conversations in the context of a large group meeting. It deploys Open Space to foster personal choice and public commitment for unfolding actions.

As the word Summit suggests, The Organizational Summit is a process for moving an organization toward its highest potential—the highest ideals imaginable among its co-creators. It is an invitation for participants to discover what gives life—to themselves, their co-creators and their organization. It is an opportunity for participants to dream of what might be possible if their most cherished values are enacted as organizational realities. It is a rigorous process for participants to design an organization with appreciative competencies. And it is a time to engage with one another in meaningful ways so that today's interactions become the seeds of well lived destiny.

Summary

The new millennium brings with it a context of globalization and a demand for organization development processes that engage large numbers of people, on line and in person, simultaneously in the co-creation of our shared future. Modern behavioral science, small group theory, and systems theory have served us well as foundations for organizational development principles and practices to date. A new generation of organization development practices is being evoked as we enter the twenty-first century. This new generation of practice will be grounded in the postmortem social sciences rather than the physical or mechanical sciences. It will be appreciative in nature, rather than problem oriented. It will be radically participatory as it invites a cornucopia of diverse voices to be expressed and heard in the co-creation of common ground for the future of our global village.

References

Beckhard, R. (1969) *Organizational Development: Strategies and Models.* Reading, MA: Addison-Wesley Publishing Co.

Bergquist, W. (1993) *The Postmodern Organization.* San Francisco, CA: Jossey-Bass.

Boje, D.M. and Dennehy, R.F. (1993) *Managing In the Postmodern World, 2nd Ed.* Dubuque, IA: Kendall/Hunt Publishing Co.

Borgmann, A. (1992) *Crossing The Postmodern Divide.* Chicago, IL: The University of Chicago Press.

Cartwright, D. and Zander, A. (Eds.) (1953) *Group Dynamics: Research and Theory.* New York, NY: Harper and Row.

DePree, M. (1989) *Leadership is An Art.* New York, NY: Doubleday

Fox, M (1994) *The Reinvention of Work: A New Vision Of Livelihood For our Time.* San Francisco, CA: Harper Collins Publishers.

French, W.L. and Bell, C.H. Jr. (1973) *Organization Development.* Englewood Cliffs, NJ:Prentice-Hall, Inc.

Gergen, K.J. (1991) *The Saturated Self.* Basic Books.

Gergen, K.J. (1994) *Realities and Relationships.* Cambridge, MA: Harvard University Press.

Hassard, J. and Parker, M. (Eds.) (1993) *Postmodernism and Organizations.* London, U.K.: Sage Publications.

Hawley, J.A. (1993) *Reawakening The Spirit In Work.* San Francisco, CA: Berrett-Koehler Publishers, Inc.

Jacobs, R.W. (1994) *Real Time Strategic Change.* San Francisco, CA: Berrett-Koehler Publishers, Inc.

Jaworski, J. (1996) *Synchronicity The Inner Path Of Leadership.* San Francisco, CA: Berrett-Koehler Publishers Inc.

Katz, D and Kahn, R.L. (1966) *The Social Psychology of Organizations.* New York, NY: John Wiley and Sons, Inc.

Naisbitt, J. (1982) *Megatrends: Ten New Directions Transforming Our Lives.* New York, NY:Warner Books, Inc.

Owen, H. (1992) *Open Space Technology.* Potomac, MD: Abbott Publishing.

Rosenau, P.M. (1992) *Postmodernism and the Social Sciences.* Princeton, NJ: Princeton University Press.

Srivastva S. and Cooperrider, D. (1990) *Appreciative Management and Leadership.* San Francisco, CA: Jossey-Bass.

Varney, G.H. (1977) *Organization Development For Managers.* Reading, MA: Addison-Wesley Publishing Co.

Weisbord, M.R. and Janoff, S. (1995) *Future Search.* San Francisco, CA: Berrett-Koehler Publishers, Inc.

Whitney, D. (1994) *Postmodern Challenges To Organization Development.* HRD Global Changes and Strategies for 2000 AD. pp. 617–629. New Delhi, India: Allied Publishers Limited.

Whitney, D. (1995) *Spirituality As An Organizing Principle.* World Business Academy *Perspectives.* Vol. 9, No. 4, pp. 51–62. Berrett-Koehler Publishers, Inc.

Chapter 17

ORGANIZATIONAL INQUIRY MODEL FOR GLOBAL SOCIAL CHANGE ORGANIZATIONS

Jane Magruder Watkins
Watkins & Kelly
David Cooperrider
Case Western Reserve University

> Change is not what it used to be. The status quo will no longer be the best way forward. . . . We are entering an Age of Unreason, when the future, in so many areas, is there to be shaped, by us and for us; a time when the only prediction that will hold true is that no predictions will hold true; a time, therefore, for bold imaginnings in private life as well as public, for thinking the unlikely and doing the unreasonable.
>
> —Charles Handy, *The Age of Unreason*, p.4.

Organizational leaders faced with managing in these turbulent times, are trained and grounded in formerly useful theories, methods and mechanisms that grew out of Taylorism and the movement called scientific management. A product of modernity, the management sciences have employed linear procedures, count and measure methods and the basic assumption that organizations are both rational in their operation and problems to be solved. (Cooperrider, 1987).

Today, sailing into the future full of theories of chaos (Gleik, 1987), complexity (Waldrop, 1992), social construction (Gergen, 1994), and that illusive paradigm called "post-modernism", the question looms large: Are there models of social architecture in existence or being created that will enable the organizations of the future to survive and to thrive? Where do we look for them? How can we recognize them? Are they replicable or must each organization create them anew?

We suggest that the management models for the future are already in existence or are being created daily, particularly by that network of organizations around the globe that are humanitarian in focus, value based and mission driven. David Cooperrider and Bill Pasmore write in the introduction to their article, "The Organizational Dimension of Global Change," in the Journal Human Relations (Cooperrider and Pasmore, 1991, p. 1037):

OD Journal, Vol. 14, No. 4, Winter 1996.

in an unprecedented attempt to forge a new vision of the world's cooperative capacity. The people-centered GSCO, we submit, is one of the more important social innovations of the past half-century and is one of the greatest unrecognized resources in the world today.

The first part of this paper briefly traces the history and structure of global social change organizations describing their evolution from aid agencies representing dominant "donor" countries that helped poorer countries in times of disaster, to the emerging global partnership model that is, possibly, the model for all organizations in the global village. The second section suggests conceptualizing GSCOs with "network" structures that consider all major stakeholders as integral parts of the organization requiring internal cooperation at every level. Finally we offer a model for organizational study (called organizational diagnosis in the traditional management methods) that uses the Appreciative Inquiry (Cooperrider, 1987) model to create an in-depth understanding of the organization's strengths as a basis for envisioning the future.

International Development Organizations

Origins

Working in multi-cultural environments, International Development organizations[1] focus on issues of poverty and oppression, environmental degradation, human rights and child survival. They have existed in the West since the first missionaries went into the less "developed" (that is, the less industrialized) continents to bring salvation to the heathen and took with them medical knowledge and a passion for education and clean water.

After World War II, secular organizations emerged based on humanitarian principles. The early post-World War organizations were largely "relief" focused, responding to natural disasters of flood, fire and famine, as well as those tragedies of human making such as war. The concept was that a superior and undeniably richer industrialized world should offer aid and assistance to the less developed nations.

During the late 1950s, these generally North American and European based aid organizations working in countries in Asia, Africa and Latin America, began

---

[1]International development organizations are known by several names currently used in the field: In the U. S., Private Voluntary Organizations (PVOs); in international nomenclature, Nongovernmental Organizations (NGOs); in Africa, some are called Community Development Organizations (CDOs); and increasingly in countries newly democratizing, as organizations that build civil society. In this paper they will be called International Development Organizations or Agencies. In the inquiry model we use the term Global Social Change Organizations (GCSO) (Cooperrider and Pasmore, 1991).

to respond to the growing capacity of local people to solve their own problems. The emerging model became known by names such as "technical assistance," and "appropriate technology." During this era the work was being shifted to locally based staffs, but the expatriates were still very much in charge.

It was not until the late 1980s that concepts of equal partnership, shared decision-making, and sustainable development began to replace the donor/donee, helper and helped models for International Development. Today, as governments democratize and civil society grows, thousands of locally controlled organizations have joined the International Development arena.

Emerging Partnerships

In 1984 at Regent's College in London, representatives of Northern and Southern[2] development agencies met to hold a global dialogue that resulted in a special issue of the World Development Journal. The message from the meeting was clear. The South no longer needed Northerners arriving on their shores to "give" them development or even to direct development projects that purported to consult with local people. What the South needed was partnership.

The Northern partners had access to funding and information needed in the South. Help with management practices, particularly as required by large donors, would be useful. And, specifically, the South needed the North to educate their own people and influence their own government's policies on behalf of their Southern partners. The conference participants called for an equal partnership with multiple levels of cooperation. Many Northern agencies took the message to heart and began to expand their own ideas and practices about what cooperation and partnership could mean for their work.

In Dakar, Senegal, January 1990, representatives of international development organization from the United States and Africa met in the second of a series of "North-South" dialogues. For some years the members of InterAction, a consortium of U.S.-based international development agencies, and FAVDO (Federation of African Voluntary Development Organizations), a consortium of African based development field-the challenge of true partnership between Northern and Southern development organizations.

No longer could outsiders arrive on foreign shores with ideas about what was needed to improve the quality of life for the poor and oppressed of some

---

[2]In the search for inoffensive nomenclature to distinguish between the wealthier industrialized countries and the variably less wealthy countries of the world, the term "North" is used for the first and "South" for the latter. Various other designations existed over time: rich/poor, 1st world/3rd world; developed/ undeveloped; developed/ less developed, LDCs; etc. For this paper, the terms used are North and South.

underdeveloped nation. The time had come to acknowledge that for any kind of development, human or material, to be implemented successfully, it would have to be the product of the work of the people themselves who would, thereafter, assure its continuation. The old stereotypes no longer held. The issue of sustainability had become a dominant concern of all parties. And imbedded in the concept of sustainability is the necessity for a truly equal partnership.

The dialogues, planned and implemented by the two consortia, brought together leaders from U.S. and African development organizations representing three areas: CEOs, Program Specialists, and Development Education Specialists. By the middle of the second dialogue in Dakar, emotions were running high.

The rhetoric of victim and victimizer, of haves and have nots was hot and heavy. But these people had, over the years, become friends of a sort, or at least cordial colleagues with very similar values and goals. At the height of the fracas in the Program Specialist group, after speeches about equity and exploitation and "We don't need you anyway, just send money," the calm that often follows such a venting of feelings fell on the group. And someone said, "Aren't we really all after the same thing?"

The conversation switched to an examination of shared values and the friendships that had developed through the common struggle. The dialogue turned: "We must think of ourselves as an association of people of good will, without regard to race, gender or national boundaries, who are deeply concerned about the issues of poverty and oppression around the globe."

It was a stunning moment as the group relished the rising of the human spirit embracing the possibility of cooperation and common cause. What better way to keep the poor poor than to have them, and those who strive to work with them, fighting over limited resources and limited power? Only through the magic of human cooperation is there any hope of changing the world order for haves and have nots, privileged and underprivileged, higher and lower dichotomies that themselves serve to dehumanize one half of the partnership. In that dialogue, the true spirit of the movement called "International Development" was articulated and embraced by a significantly influential partnership of development professionals.

This conversation was later recorded in the report, "Toward Partnership in Africa" (page 96):

> What becomes clear to participants as this series of consultations ends is that in learning how to be partners, the distinctions of "North" and "South", or "African" and "American" become less important and the values and goals we share come to the fore. Through this process (the consultation), we have built a sense of solidarity, not as Northern PVOs and Southern NGOS, but as a unified group of voluntary development organizations working together to empower the poor and build a better world.

Why did this process work? Much of value has been learned in this process by participants and by their organizations: some specific dos and don'ts involved in effective partnership, and much that is intangible, such as greater understanding of one another's working contexts and outlooks, values and problems, a greater sense of empathy for one another and, perhaps most importantly, a greater sense of solidarity with one another as people engaged in work to empower the poor and oppressed and to build a more just and peaceful world.

In February, 1990, shortly after the Dakar meeting, the first International Conference on Popular Participation in the Recovery and Development Process in Africa gathered representatives from sectors as diverse as governments and grass roots organizations at a conference in Arusha, Tanzania. The preamble to the conference documents referred to the conference as a "rare collaborative effort between African peoples' organizations, the African governments, non-governmental organizations and U.N. agencies in search of a collective under-standing of the role of Popular Participation in the development and transforma-tion of the region."

These organizations working across national boundaries in collaboration with people from every social strata in every corner of the globe have discovered the fact that seems absurd in its simplicity: If we want to create a peaceful and genera-tive globe where poverty and oppression are rare and people share in the bounty of the earth, we must do it cooperatively. The more urgent view is that, without such cooperative, our species may simply vanish from an earth rendered uninhabitable by our divisiveness.

Implications for Management

The evolution of relationships between nations and peoples represented by these development agencies is a precursor to the kind of partnerships and relationships that must be practiced by all global organizations. In the 1970s the U.S. Agency for International Development, USAID, commissioned a study carried out by Stark Biddle and thus known as the "Biddle Report," to determine why corporate and philanthropic foundations were reluctant to fund development agencies. The an-swer reported in the document was that unless these agencies learned to manage themselves more professionally, i.e., more like corporations, there would be no funds forthcoming. The irony today is that corporations are beginning to manage themselves more like these development agencies.

The reason becomes obvious. Development agencies have always had to man-age global programs often without adequate communications links, with limited resources and staffs who carry severely heavy workloads, in an unstable and often hazardous environment, operating with multiple cultural norms and behaviors. While their management styles and methods often seemed unorthodox to the busi-ness sector, in fact many of them were very well managed for the environment in which they operated.

Today, many corporations are finding themselves working with those same constraints. And they are discovering what development agencies have long known—that scientific management methodologies that need predictability and stable environments simply do not work in the global arena. What, then, will work in this rapidly emerging global village? What organizational arrangements are required? What methodologies are appropriate?

We suggest that the growing practices of partnership, cooperation, and common cause that is becoming the norm in development agencies holds valuable lessons for all organizations in this time of discontinuous chance. Cooperation is a concept that is increasingly being applied to every level of organizing and in every form of organization. From the agricultural cooperative to good team work in a small organization, to visions of the global cooperation of governments, the term has come to symbolize the creative edge in the field of organization development in the 1990s. In a wider context, the proliferation of peace studies and conflict transformation methodologies: the concept of "new games" with their win-win focus; the wealth of new writing on the feminine qualities of cooperation; the Internet; all are phenomena of an increased interest in cooperation as a generative process for human endeavor.

New Approaches

In the late 1970s, in response to the Biddle Report, USAID funded the New TransCentury Foundation with a grant called "Management Development Services" (MDS) that was designed to provide management training and consulting to development agencies who wanted to meet the management criteria stipulated by the philanthropic donor organizations. For 10 years TransCentury, under MDS grant, worked with several hundred U.S.-based development agencies. In several cases the U.S. agencies requested assistance for their overseas staffs.

While the original purpose of the grant was to provide fairly typical management training and assistance to the U.S. agencies, the longevity of the grant made it possible for a great deal of learning to take place on the part of the organizational development professionals providing the training as well as for the agencies themselves. Clearly, the models and methods needed by these agencies were, in many ways, quite different from those used in the business sector. While traditional management and organization theory might inform the process, in the final analysis, a unique process was called for, one suited to the unique environment in which these agencies work. Hierarchy was often dysfunctional. Projects were not finished on time or did not last past the departure of the Northern agency. Western management practices often made no sense in societies that value relationships above task.

The U.S. agencies began to experiment. A major issue became the ability to "walk the talk" While the dialogue about and rhetoric for sharing, cooperation and partnership moved forward in the larger arena, the U.S.-based agencies were struggling with their own hierarchical structures and the largely homogenous nature of their own staffs. In a field where the majority of CEOs are white males and the majority of workers are Caucasian (see Interaction's Grafton Report series), the rhetoric of valuing diversity and embracing partnership across cultures was creating cognitive dissonance. The rhetoric was right but the practice was not aligned with that rhetoric.

InterAction again took the lead. They began to document the makeup of their member agencies and provided workshops at their annual forums as well as dialogue sessions and written materials aimed at helping agencies diversify staff, often to the point of adding people from the overseas partner agencies to U.S. headquarters' staff. The more each staff worked to value diversity in its own ranks and to gain experience working with people from different cultures in their day to day work, the more credibility they had in the field.

Appreciative Inquiry

In the last half of this decade another obvious—though invisible until now—reality dawned on those working with development agencies. The traditional organization development "problem solving" approach, standing alone, seems to have outlived its effectiveness. As both the speed and nature of change are changing[3] many consultants and organizational leaders, even in traditional organizations, are finding that by the time a group identifies the problem, analyzes the causes, formulates the plan of action to correct it and sets about to carry out those actions, the original problem is no longer the problem! This is particularly true in international development where the speed of change is often lightning fast and unpredictable.

New models have begun to emerge to help organizations cope with rapid change and unstable environments. One of the most widespread practices is that of helping organizations to formulate visions and mission statements as a first step in moving their organizations forward. Many in the field, as well as those trying to lead and manage organizations in these turbulent times (Drucker, 1980) are

---

[3]George Land and Beth Jarman, in their book Breakpoint and Beyond: Mastering the Future Today comment (pp. 4–5) that, "The surprising fact is that change itself has changed. . . . The old rules mandated changes of degree, not of kind. . . . . These great leaps defy traditional wisdom supporting linear and progressive change. . . . This kind of totally unconventional change process has pushed us to the edge, teetering precariously between two eras. We've reached a Breakpoint!

searching for even more creative methods for understanding their organizations, and more innovative, less mechanistic ways to move them forward.

The pioneering work of David Cooperrider, Suresh Srivastva and their colleagues at Case Western Reserve University has created a methodology called Appreciative Inquiry (Cooperrider and Srivastva, 1987), that has been used successfully as a method of inquiring into the well-being cooperation, a government agency and a large number of non-profit international development organizations.

The Appreciative method of studying organizations is particularly appropriate when organizations want to discover more and varied ways to use cooperative processes. Just as diagnosing problems fits neatly into the image of an organization as a machine to be repaired (Marshak), inquiring appreciatively is congruent with a search for cooperative models. It is an ideal approach for understanding how such values drive organizations as international development agencies.

An Experiment

During the past four years, a group of organization development consultants working under another grant from USAID designed and delivered an Institute for PVO-CFO Excellence for the management teams of nearly 30 nonprofit development organizations. These management teams learned how to use an Appreciative Inquiry method for gaining a better understanding of their own organizations and staffs. Outside consultants trained the teams in the use of the approach, but the teams tailored it to their own environments and they, themselves, did the interviewing. The result of this method is a virtual agency-wide conversation about the generative and life-giving aspects of the organization.

Each organization later attended the 5-day Institute with the appreciative stories in hand. The stories and information became the foundation for creating an image of the organization's future. The advantage of the approach is that it combines the best of what is (tradition), with images of the future so that the images and plans are firmly grounded in the best of what is in the organization.

During the Institute, each organization formed the appreciative information into a pattern that gave a picture of their organization's current reality. Traditionally, in the practice of Organization Development, consultants have found it useful to have management teams analyze data using some diagnostic tool that covers all of the relevant aspects of an organization. The Institute consultants experimented with several traditional diagnostic models before it became evident that most such models were created for large profit-making organizations as a way to ferret out problems that needed to be corrected.

Since, as has been noted, most non-profit development agencies are not structured organizationally like large profit-making companies, a different model begins to emerge. The concept of a development agency as a network both internally and externally began to form. What if the internal organization is conceived as a network of major stakeholders, all of whom are decision-makers, resource providers, and, in a very real sense, key players in every aspect of the organization? What might this say about the organization? And what would be the impact of common understanding of the current state of the organization? And what would be the impact of shifting the process from curative (diagnostic) to an ongoing inquiry process that affirms the health of the organization? Could such a model help to create a true "learning organization"? (Senge, 1990).

Furthermore, if these organizations are internal networks, the implications are vast concerning the need for a high level of cooperative behavior inside the organizations as well as with external groups.

This line of thinking led us to create an appreciative approach to understanding (formerly "diagnosing") the organization using the appreciative process for inquiring into the organizations current reality ("collecting data"). While we created this model particularly for the U.S.-based international development agencies participating in the institute, we suggest that it is a model that can be used by that vast array of organizations that make up civic society across the globe.

Organizational Inquiry Model

The Organizational Inquiry Model for Global Social Change Organizations (GSCOs) is a method of inquiring into the health and wellbeing of organizations whose purpose is to improve the quality of life around the globe. Whatever the name, a GSCO is, in general terms, an organization, nonprofit by nature, that has a mission to address such issues as poverty and oppression, human rights, human potential, and environmental concerns of the globe. Because GSCOs are organizations founded on hope and the belief that human beings can work together to improve life on the planet, this Organizational Inquiry Model is designed to inquire into the current reality of an organization and to plan its future by focusing on the successes and the life-giving forces that support the work and the people. Once those forces are located and articulated, the organization can move to affirm, expand and increase those success factors as they imagine the organization's future. This is a departure form the traditional model of organizational diagnosis that searches for the problems and shortcomings of the organization for the purpose of "fixing" it (Marshak, 1993).

This appreciative approach is grounded in the theory of Social Constructionism (Gergen, 1991 and 1994) that holds organizations as social constructions of those who inhabit and "talk" in them. If organizations are imagined and made by human beings, then they can be remade and re-imagined. The constraints of scientific management theory that images organizations as machines are lifted and the possibility of new approaches and configurations emerges. We create what we imagine!

ORGANIZATIONAL INQUIRY MODEL

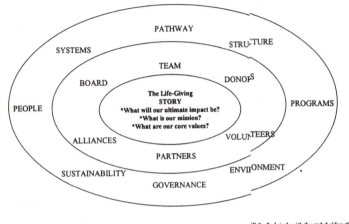

(The terms in rings 2 and 3 of this model are examples only. Each organization needs to fill the 2nd circle with the stakeholders that form the leadership of the organization and the 3rd circle with the tasks and processes that are important to their work.)

Rationale for this Approach

Global Social Change Organizations (GSCOs) are organized around the principles of service and social transformation. They are committed to creating a world constructed for the common good. Because these organizations are founded on hope and the belief that people can organize themselves to make the world a better place, it would follow that any inquiry into these organizations would seek to find the life-giving forces—those things that the organization does well.

A second factor that mitigates an appreciative analysis has to do with the environment in which these organizations work and the nature of change itself. The ambiguity, sudden shifts and discontinuous change that create the environment in which Global Social Change Organizations work, requires maximum flexibility, a core belief that the work makes a difference and a commitment to ride out the storms. There is rarely time to "fix" problems because of the rapidly changing environment. By focusing on what gives life to their work, these organizations are able to have maximum impact, maintain forward motion and assure an environment that is creative and generative.

---

[4]"Breakpoint change abruptly and powerfully breaks the critical links that connect anyone or anything with the past. What we are experiencing today is absolutely unprecedented in all of humanity's recorded history .... At Breakpoint, the rule change is so sharp that continuing to use the old rules not only doesn't work, it erects great, sometimes insurmountable barriers to success."

Assumptions of the
Organizational Inquiry Model

The Organizational Inquiry Model is built on several assumptions:

The first assumption is that the central organizing principles of Global Social Change Organizations are the clarity about the ultimate IMPACT of the work, the work, the CORE VALUES that are shared, and a common MISSION of a group of people who wish to act in the world from a belief that organizations are instruments for the common human good. These are critical ingredients that provide the foundation for the organization. Without clarity and consensus on these ingredients, no amount of organizational excellence related to task and management will ensure survival. Conversely, organizations with clarity on the IMPACT they want to make, shared understanding of their CORE VALUES and agreement on their MISSION, can survive a great deal of imperfection and ambiguity in their organizational forms. Therefore, the premier task of every GSCO is to carry on a continuous dialogue making meaning of their work. The meaning of these terms as used in the paper are as follows:

> **Impact:** The ultimate goal of our work; the conditions that we plan to change; the reason for our existence as an organization.

> **Values:** The core values that we all share and which form the solid foundation for our work together.

> **Mission:** The work we will do in the world to achieve our ultimate impact.

The second assumption is that Global Social Change Organizations are NETWORKS. In this model, what is usually called the 'organization', that is, the staff that works in the headquarters office and in the field offices, is called the TEAM and is seen as the coordinating body for the NETWORK ORGANIZATION. The organization is envisioned as a network of key stakeholders who gather around the desired IMPACT, VALUES, and MISSION to accomplish tasks that lead to social transformation. The NETWORK ORGANIZATION might include the TEAM; a BOARD; DONORS; PARTNERS; ALLIANCES; and, frequently, VOLUNTEERS. Definitions of these terms are described below. However, each organization will have a unique set of actors in this circle. This model describes one possible configuration.

Organizational Inquiry Model Network

Organization Elements

> **Team:** The core staff of headquarters and field offices that work together collaboratively and whose central task is to provide leadership, coordinate and sustain the work and the relationships of the organization;

Board: Whose task is to set policy, provide guidance and ensure that the organization has the resources it needs to sustain itself;

Donors : Those that supply the resources and whose tasks encompass providing financial resources and programmatic guidance;

Partners: Multiple groups of clients' recipients of services who are responsible for collaborating in all planning and implementation of joint programs;

Volunteers: Groups and individuals who contribute time and skills to the organization;

Alliances: Other institutions entities who join in the work of the organization.

The third assumption is that in addition to the core of the organization and the leadership network; there are key areas for inquiry in the ways the organization organizes its work. Inquiry into these areas enables groups to discover the life-giving forces, success stories and generative spirit of their organizations. In this model, examples for inquiry include: PATHWAY; GOVERNACE; SYSTEMS; STRUCTURE; PEOPLE; PROGRAMS; SUSTAINABILITY; ENVIRONMENT. These terms are defined as:

ORGANIZATIONAL INQUIRY MODEL KEY AREAS OF INQUIRY

Pathway: The guiding principles, strategy, plans and tactics for achieving our mission.

Governance: How we organize, govern and manage ourselves, how we make decisions, how we celebrate our achievements, how our governance process aligns with our values and our theory of development.

Systems: The systems and technologies that we use to manage ourselves, to communicate with each other, and to "conference" with the world.

Structure: The way we organize our work and manage our tasks.

People: The well-being, fair treatment and empowerment of our staff team, partners, board members, alliance, and volunteers; the placement of our people in the right positions to make our work flow smoothly; how we value our diversity and celebrate our differences as organizational assets; how we relate to each other; how our rhetoric about valuing people aligns with our organizational behavior.

Programming: Our development paradigm and the theories that underlie our methods of work; the nature of our work and how it aligns with our vision and values; our programming process.

Sustainability: How we guarantee the people and resources to assure the health and survival of all of our organizational entities; how we steadily increase our capacity; how we function as a lifelong learning organization committed to continuous improvement.

Environment: Our understanding of what 's going on in the world that impacts our work, and, overview of the organizational culture and norms that create our work environment.

How to Use the Organizational Inquiry Model

For each of the elements in (1) the core circle; (2) the NETWORK ORGANI-
ZATION circle, and (3) the organization of work circle, you will use the ABCs:

A. Appreciative Understanding of Your Organization;

B. Benchmarked Understanding of Other Organizations;

C. Creation of "Possibility Propositions" To Image Your Organization's Future.

A. Appreciative Understanding Of Your Organization

The process begins with your inquiry into your organization that will provide a
clear picture of your organization's strengths, competencies and life-giving forces.
Using this approach, you look for those moments when your organization is at its
very best. Using an interview process, members of your staff can interview each
other in search of organizational excellence. Questions might include:

Think of a time in your work with this organization when you felt excited,
joyful and at the peak of your form. Tell a story about that time. Describe what
your were doing, what others did and how you felt. Tell the story in a way that
creates an image for the interviewer.

Without being humble, talk about the things that you value about yourself;
what are the things that you value about your job in this organization; and, what is
it that you value about this organization itself, i.e., what, for you, gives life to this
organization?

What do you believe are the core values of this organization? That is, what is
the key thing without which this organization would not exist?

B. Benchmarked Understanding Of Other Organizations

Once you have initiated the process in your own organization, you may want to
seek out and understand the best practices of other organizations. This is best done
as a reciprocal process in which you also share your best practices. Such mutual
sharing gives both organizations a way to inform their own practices and to adapt
and incorporate some ideas that can inspire innovation and improvement.

Often organizations seek out similar groups to "benchmark" but there can be
rich learning and exchange between even the most diverse organizations. Nego-
tiations with potential benchmarking partners should include the parameters of the
exchange and agreement on questions to be asked. Sample questions include:

What is the most exciting and successful time you have had working with
your organization? Please describe for me what made it so exciting. Are there
processes from that event time that you have incorporated into your work here?
Can you tell me about them?

If you had to say the one best thing your organization does when it is at its
most competent, what would that be? Tell me about it. How does it work?

What do you value most about working for this organization?

(These questions are intended to be examples only; you will construct questions appropriate to the study that you want to do.)

C. Creation Of "Possibility Propositions" To Image Your Organization's Future

Once you have gathered information from your own organization and have benchmarked several other organizations, it is time to make sense of that information in search of an image of the current reality that will serve as a spring board to creating an image of your organization's future. This is an exercise that can be carried out at every level of the organization with any mix of staff and stakeholders. The process includes sharing the information and stories gathered from the appreciative inquiry of your own organization and the best practices gathered from other organizations. This sharing is best done as a dialogical process with any written report aimed at capturing the highlights from the stories and sharing the high points of the process itself. A mechanical reporting of facts will not usually lead to exciting "propositions." Once the verbal or written story of the process is finished, the group moves to create the most exciting possible future for the organization that incorporates the best that exists within, plus new and exciting practices discovered from without. Possibility propositions are written as though they are already happening, in the present tense. These become the vision for the organization that guides planning and operations in the future.

This ABC process can be used to study every facet of an organization. This model suggests that a GSCO needs to look, at a minimum, at the two levels described in this model:

The organization itself is conceived of as a network of key stakeholders that make up the decision making and operating body for achieving the mission. The Organizational Inquiry Model suggests in ABC process for each of the 6 elements: Team; Board; Donors; Partners; Volunteer; Alliances (elements should be added or removed according to what is actual in your own organization.)

The second level of inquiry focuses on the various functions and guiding principles of the organization, to include: Impact, Values, Mission, Pathway, Environment, Governance, People, Programming, Systems, Sustainability (Again, you are encouraged to add any other factors that are related to your organization.)

Finally, it is essential that some other interactive process be embedded in the organization as an ongoing dialogue, constantly appreciating, reframeing, and sharing the life of the people and the meaning of the work that make up the GSCO. It is this community meaning-making that creates a flexible, grounded, generative organization. The ABC model can be used as a framework for the ongoing conversations that will create a true learning organization. As the conversation deepens and expands, the framework itself will be changed and embellished as needed to facilitate the learning about the growth and change that are life-giving forces in all organizations.

References

"African charter for popular participation in development and transformation." (1990) New York: U. N. report on International conference on popular participation in the recovery and development process in Africa.

Biddle, S. (1976). Report on the management practices of U.S. private voluntary organizations. Washington, DC: Study from the Office of Private Voluntary Cooperation (PVC),USAID.

Cooperrider, D. and Pasmore, W.A. (1991). The Organization dimension of global change. *Human Relations.*

Cooperrider, D. and Srivastva, S. (1987). Appreciative inquiry in organizational life. In W. Pasmore and R. Woodman (eds), *Research in organizational change and development, Vol. 1.* Greenwich, CT. JAI Press.

Drabek, A. ed. (1994). World Development.

Drucker,P.F. (1980). *Managing in Turbulent Times.* New York: Harper Collins.

Grafton report. Washington, D.C. InterAction.

Gergen, K.J. (1991) *The saturated self: dilemmas of identity in contemporary life.* New York: Basic Books.

Gergen, K.J. (1994). *Toward transformation in social knowledge.* 2nd edition. New York: Sage Publications.

Gleick, J. (1987). *Chaos: making a new science.* NewYork: Penguin Books.

Handy, C. (1989). *The age of unreason.* London: Arrow Books Limited.

Ingersoll, Phyllis and Jerry. Toward review by Africa: An in-depth review by African and U.S. non-profit development agency staff: Consultation report. Washington, D.C. InterAction and FOVAD.

Land, G. and Jarman, B. (1992) *Breakpoint and beyond: mastering the future today.* New York: Harper Collins Publishers.

Marshak, R. J. (Summer 1993) Managing the metaphors of change. *Organizational Dynamics.*

Senge, P.M. (1990). *The Fifth discipline.* New York: Doubleday.

Waldrop, M.M. (1992). *Complexity: the emerging science at the edge of order and chaos.* New York: Simon and Schuster.

Chapter 18

FROM DEFICIT DISCOURSE TO VOCABULARIES OF HOPE: THE POWER OF APPRECIATION

James D. Ludema
Benedictine University

Abstract

This chapter proposes that in today's world of high uncertainty and broad cultural and epistemological variety the purpose of social and organizational inquiry ought to be to create textured vocabularies of hope—stories, theories, evidence, and illustrations—that provide organizations and communities with new guiding images of relational possibility. After showing how the critical methods of contemporary organizational science have contributed to a growing cynicism about the future of human institutions by producing vocabularies of deficit, the dynamics of hopeful vocabularies in human systems are explored. A broad review of the literature suggests that vocabularies of hope serve as powerful catalyst for positive social and organizational transformation. They are ignited when organizational members (1) nurture cooperative relationships, (2) exercise a sense of optimism about their capacity to influence the future, and (3) inquire together into their most deeply held values and highest aspirations. Appreciative inquiry is offered as an alternative to critical and problem-focused inquiry methodologies. Eight core principles of appreciative inquiry that support the creation of textured vocabularies of hope are highlighted. The chapter concludes with an invitation to scholars and practitioners to experiment with new modes of appreciative inquiry that generate vocabularies of hope by posing positive questions about the life-giving, life-enhancing aspects of organizations.

> Think of the tools in a tool-box: there is a hammer, pliers, a screwdriver, a rule, a glue-pot, glue, nails and screws. The functions of words are as diverse as the functions of these objects.   —Wittgenstein.

> We can live three weeks without food, three days without water, and, yes, we can even live three minutes without air, but we cannot live without hope.   —Mumford.

Introduction

It is widely understood that the contemporary world has entered an era in which the complexity and rapidity of social change is virtually unparalleled in human history. The expansion of information technology, the globalization of economic markets, the intermingling of cultures, and the reconfiguration of national and international boundaries are increasing pressures on individuals and organizations to find innovative approaches to addressing their own needs and the needs of society. This shifting global context raises questions of fundamental importance to the social and organizational sciences. Is it possible or even desirable in the current context for social science to play a lead role in building healthy and vibrant social relationships? Can and should social science attempt to remain relevant, or even to become a pioneer of positive possibilities for organizing in the face of such extensive geographical, cultural, and epistemological variety?

Some have grave doubts. Scholars and practitioners from across the social scientific disciplines are becoming increasingly disillusioned with the inability of existing epistemological and methodological alternatives to provide useful insights into human relationships. On the one hand, approaches based in empiricist foundationalism are distrusted for, among other things, resting on shaky theoretical ground and ignoring the impact of context on social phenomena (see e.g., Kuhn, 1970; Feyerabend, 1978; Gergen, 1994a; Denzin and Lincoln, 1995; Argyris, 1973; Bartunek, 1983; Friedlander, 1984). On the other hand, efforts proceeding from the genre of post-empiricist critique are questioned for launching "attacks without alternative" and contributing to a contentious scientific discourse that offers little emancipatory leverage for an increasingly cynical and despairing world (Hazelrigg, 1989, Brown, 1994; Gergen, 1994b; Marcus, 1994).

Thus the questions remain: What should be the role of social and organizational science in the construction of human relationships? How can it recover a central place in making a positive contribution to the enhancement of the human condition? What should be its purposes, commitments, and methods as it attempts to make this contribution in a global context of radical foundationlessness and human plurality?

This paper provides an optimistic response to these questions by proposing that the purpose of social and organizational inquiry ought to be to create textured vocabularies of hope—stories, theories, evidence, and illustrations—that serve as catalysts for positive social and organizational transformation by providing humanity with new guiding images of relational possibility. In much the same way that a hammer, pliers, screwdriver, and rule furnish the tools necessary to build new physical architectures for human inhabitation, textured vocabularies of hope provide the linguistic resources necessary to build new social architectures for transformative human organizing and action.

It is argued that to create powerful vocabularies of hope, two things are needed from organizational scholars and practitioners. First, hopeful research agendas that focus on the life-producing, life-sustaining, life-enhancing aspects of organizations need to be established. Second, constructive methodologies that facilitate the creation of hopeful vocabularies and that themselves become sources of hope by promoting normative dialogue and supporting positive social innovation need to be developed. Appreciative inquiry (Cooperrider and Srivastva, 1987) is highlighted as an approach to social and organizational inquiry that fulfills these purposes. Based on the premises that (1) there is a direct and simultaneous link between our vocabularies of organizing and the ways in which we organize in fact, and that (2) our vocabularies are products of the questions we ask, appreciative inquiry distinguishes itself by posing positive questions that direct our attention to the vital life-giving forces that nourish our best and most valued modes of organizing.

The chapter is divided into four sections. It begins by showing how the critical and problem-focused methods of contemporary social science have contributed to the deconstruction rather than the reconstruction of social relationships by producing vocabularies, not of hope and possibility, but of deficit and deficiency. By so doing, social science has added to a growing cynicism about the future of human institutions and has deepened the despair about its own potential to be a catalyst for positive change. The section ends by suggesting that the time has come to move beyond the limitations of deficit discourse by developing appreciative modes of inquiry that advance vocabularies of human hope.

In section two, the dynamics of hoping in human systems are explored. In order to create methodologies and vocabularies that support human hopefulness, it is essential to understand how hope is generated and sustained in human systems and how it can become a source of social and organizational transformation. A broad review of the literature shows that hope is enkindled in organizations when (1) cooperative relationships are nurtured between organizational members, (2) organizational members have a sense of optimism about their capacity to shape and influence the future, and (3) organizational members inquire together into their deepest values and highest aspirations.

In section three, appreciative inquiry is offered as an alternative to critical and problem-focused inquiry methodologies. It is proposed that the appreciative approach, by intentionally guiding the socially constructive potential of human systems in the direction of their most noble and valued aspirations for the future, generates an ever-expanding selection of textured vocabularies of hope that provide new alternatives for organizing and elevate the human spirit. The process of generating textured vocabularies of hope through appreciative inquiry is illustrated.

The paper concludes with a call to social and organizational science to reaffirm its constructive task by advancing new appreciative epistemologies and methods of inquiry that facilitate the expansion of textured vocabularies of hope. Following Rorty (1980), it is suggested that by advancing vocabularies of hope, social science may, in some small way, reverse the current trends of cultural and organizational cynicism and contribute to a broad and maturing spirit of human hopefulness.

Critical Methods and Vocabularies of Deficit

In the last fifty years, hosts of critical and deconstructive methods for doing social scientific research have emerged (see e.g., Schwandt, 1994; Kincheloe and McLaren, 1994; Olesen, 1994; Stanfield, 1994; and Fiske, 1994). Based on the premise that all claims of truth are arbitrary and should be questioned, these methods provide increasingly sophisticated tools with which to examine, expose, demystify, and debunk existing accounts of reality.

While some scholars celebrate this critical trend because of its emancipatory potential, others see it as a cause for concern. Comparing the methods of post-empiricist critique to those of military combat, Gergen (1994b) writes:

> Critique as a rhetorical move has the effect of demeaning the opposition, generating animosity, atomizing the culture and blocking the way to resolution. . . . [It] carries with it the additional difficulties of favoring the very kinds of totalizing discourses against which it is set, and destroying the grounds of its own rationality (p. 70).

Similarly, for Astley (1985), the arena of management theory has become a "jungle" which is daily becoming "more dense and impenetrable" and is symbolic of "deep fragmentation of the discipline" marked by "intense competing and rival paradigms." For George (1989) the variety of incommensurable perspectives within organizational science has become "a violent babble of competing voices . . . leading nowhere loudly" (p. 269). And for Wollheim (1980) the quicksand of deconstructive reflexivity may lead to complete "immobilization of scholarship."

Of greater concern, however, is the growing awareness that the debilitating effects of critical and deconstructive social science extend well beyond the boundaries of the academic community. Gergen (1994a) argues persuasively that the vocabularies of deficit proffered by much contemporary social science support what he calls broad "cultural enfeeblement" (p. 148). By creating hierarchies of discrimination, eroding naturalized patterns of community, and expanding arenas for self-depreciation, scientific vocabularies of deficit contribute to a pernicious cycle of "progressive [societal] infirmity" (p. 155). To illustrate, the following example (adapted from Gergen, 1994a, pp. 155–161) shows how growth in deficit vocabularies of mental illness have served to compound rather than alleviate individual and societal suffering:

> **First,** based on empiricist presumptions, the disciplines of psychiatry and clinical psychology are formed and begin to create categories of "mental illness."

> **Second,** a collection of mental health professionals emerges and commissions itself with the task and responsibility of diagnosing and curing the multiple forms of mental illness as defined by its members.

Third, mental health professionals translate their clients' problems as presented in everyday language into the alternative language of the profession. Thus, "feeling blue" or "being sad" becomes depression and "getting distracted by everything" or "having a hard time sitting still in school" becomes attention deficit disorder.

Fourth, the mental health profession disseminates its language to the general public through universities, conferences, public policies, books, journals, magazines, newspapers, television, and other electronic media.

Fifth, as vocabularies of mental deficit are disseminated to the culture, they become absorbed into the common language and become encouraged for the construction of everyday reality. In essence, the culture learns how to be mentally ill. Writes Gergen (1994a), "Furnish the population with the hammers of mental deficit, and the world is full of nails" (p. 158).

Sixth, in the final phase of progressive infirmity, vocabularies of deficit are expanded. As people increasingly construct their problems in professional language and seek help, and as professional ranks expand in response to public demands, more resources are available to convert everyday language into a professional language of deficit.

Through this process, deficit vocabularies can come to approximate "small growth industries" (Gergen, 1994a, p. 160) that fuel the progressive enfeeblement of society. See Figure 18.1 for a diagram of this process.

In a similar manner, the vocabularies of human deficit produced by the critical and problem-oriented approaches to social and organizational inquiry diminish the human capacity for positive relational construction by rending and unraveling the intricate social, political, and moral fabrics that make human existence and organizing possible. Writes Gergen (1994b): There is virtually no hypothesis, body of evidence, ideological stance, literary canon, value commitment or logical edifice that cannot be dismantled, demolished or derided with the [arsenal of critical weaponry] at hand" (p. 59). Relying on methodologies that by design are meant to delegitimate and destroy existing organizational understandings, critical and problem-focused methods do little to provide constructive alternative perspectives that point the way to healthier more desired forms of organizing.

In response to the growing body of deficit vocabularies produced by critical and problem-focused methods, a handful of scholars are calling for appreciative approaches to social and organizational science that hold increased potential for revitalizing scholarship and enhancing the human condition. Weick (1982) appeals for an affirmative approach to social science that creates compelling images of human possibility and seeks to discover examples of them in the "real world," even if they are extremely rare. Brown (1994) encourages a "hermeneutic of affirmation" that promotes conversation between scholars and citizens who are committed to "establishing moral authority and inventing positive values as central elements of any polity" (p. 24). Cooperrider and Srivastva (1987), in their original formulation of the now widely applied methodology of appreciative inquiry, call

1. Scientific disciplines are formed
and begin to create categories of illness (vocabularies of deficit).

2. A collection of professionals
emerges to diagnose and cure the
multiple forms of illness.

3. Everyday language of clients is
translated into deficit vocabularies of
the profession.

4. The profession disseminates its
vocabularies of deficit to the general
public.

5. Vocabularies are absorbed into
common language; the culture learns
how to be ill.

6. Vocabularies of deficit are expanded,
becoming "small growth industries"
that fuel the enfeeblement of society.

Figure 18.1. The Link Between Vocabularies of Deficit and the Process of Cultural Enfeeblement.

for modes of inquiry that uncover the "ordinary magic, beauty, and real possibility of organizational life" (p. 165) and help scholars and practitioners to "shape the social world according to their own imaginative and moral purposes" (p. 161). Recognizing the socially constructive power of social theory to determine the direction and quality of organizational life, these appeals, each in its own way, urge scholars and practitioners to reverse the debilitating effects of deficit discourse by developing appreciative modes of inquiry that release the empowering potential of vocabularies of hope. In the final section of this chapter we attempt to show how appreciative modes of inquiry can contribute to this project, but first, to set the stage for that discussion, we explore the role that hoping plays in igniting social and organizational transformation.

Vocabularies of Hope as a Source of Social and Organizational Transformation

In this section it is shown that hoping is often described as a holistic, relational way of knowing that unifies both the tacit and explicit dimensions of experience and puts them to work in transforming the future. When people inquire into the unexplored reaches of their collective norms, beliefs, and assumptions; values, mores, and purposes; plans, desires, and wishes; visions, ideals, and dreams, they engage in the act of hoping by prefiguring a valued and vital future that they hope some day to build, inhabit, and enjoy. These hopeful images of the future, in turn, become powerful catalysts for change and transformation by mobilizing the moral, social, and relational energies needed to translate vision into reality and belief into practice.

This understanding of hope is based on an extensive literature review of the topic from the fields of theology, philosophy, history, political theory, art, music, literature, medicine, psychology, and sociology (see Ludema et al, 1997). While the ways in which hope has been described and understood throughout the ages have varied, many authors suggest that there are four enduring qualities that give hope its power as a source of social and organizational transformation: it is (1)born in relationship, (2) inspired by the conviction that the future is open and can be influenced, (3) sustained by dialogue about high human ideals, and (4) generative of positive affect and action (see Table 18.1 for a summary of these qualities and their relationship to six intellectual traditions of Western thought). The remainder of this section briefly explores each of these qualities.

The Centrality of Relationships

Hope is fundamentally a relational construct. It is engendered in relationship to an "other," whether that other be collective or singular, imagined or real, human or divine. Perhaps the most poignant example of this idea comes from Frankl's (1963) experiences in German concentration camps during World War II. Even in the isolated agony of solitary work duty, Frankl gained hope by imagining himself into a future in which he would be free and reunited with his wife and his most esteemed colleagues at the university. This relational picture of hope stands in marked contrast to much contemporary thought that understands hope as an emotional or cognitive possession of the individual rational agent.

Yet, as Lynch (1965) suggests, hope does not flourish under all relational conditions. It assumes relationships of mutuality in which the value and integrity of all persons is affirmed. Writes Lynch (1965):

I must not be in such a relationship to objects that I vanish out of the picture, I am destroyed. And the reverse is also true: ideally the object in coming to me must find itself. It is the hope for this mutuality that is the secret of all our hopes; it is its absence in substance that makes us hopeless. . . . Hope searches for alternative objects that will not be destructive and that can partake in a relationship of mutuality (pp. 44–45).

Lynch goes on to suggest that this kind of mutuality enlivens hope in the in all relationships, personal or professional: "Hope is the interior sense that there is

TABLE 18.1. Hope's Enduring Qualities as Found in Six Intellectual Traditions of Western Thought.

Intellectual Traditions	Relationality	Future Openness	Ultimacy	Generativity
Greco-Roman		Hope as a source of invention.		Hope spurs creativity and action.
Judeo-Christian	Whether directed at a divine or human other, hope is born when we join with other "efficacious agents."	Hope as a general confidence in God's protection and help.	Love, joy, peace, salvation, redemption, communion with God and others, "the good."	Leads to social involvement.
Enlightenment	Relational hope is a self-fulfilling proposition.	Hope is reasonable when grounded in examples from the past.	Reasonable to hope for the highest good.	Serves as a motive for positive human action.
Phycho-Analytic	Hope is at least partially influenced by past and present others.	Hope is an outgrowth of a pliable vision of wholeness.	Hope as creative urge of Eros.	Hope contributes to social coping, psychosocial development, and individual achievement.
Radical Humanist	Hope as a source of ideological emancipation and authentic consciousness.	Existence is never static; it is always in process of becoming something new, or transcending itself.	Metachronic and transcendent: our most potent hopes offer an image of an ultimate future.	Pursuit of *Ultimum* provides a powerful resource for innovation and action in the present.
Modern (cognitive) Medicine and Psychology	Hope is enlivened in the helping relationship, personal and professional.	Human beings have the capacity to create, evaluate, and alter symbolic constructions.	Hope as a "spiritual" quality; ability to rise above difficult circumstances to renew life.	Hope determines goal-oriented behavior and is a resource for health and vitality.

help on the outside of us . . . when we are especially aware that our purely inward resources are not enough." (p. 40).

In addition to being born in, sustained by, and deepened in relationship, hoping serves as a binding force of community. Kast (1991) shows that hoping allows people to develop a sense of "symbiotic connectedness" with each other. In this symbiosis one feels taken care of, freed from fear of attack, slander and harm, and invested in promoting the health and vitality of others. Similarly, Dauenhauer (1986) suggests that hoping builds community because it encourages exploration of the values and ideals that people share in common. He suggests that when people come together in acts of hoping, they dream and creatively construct the future in ways that reflect their common ideals.

The Importance of Influence-Optimism

Hope springs to life when people understand that the future is fundamentally un-determined and open to human influence. Polak (1973) calls this understanding "influence-optimism." Marcel (1951) describes it as a "fundamental openness," an expectant act of the whole person in which "the soul turns toward a light which it does not yet perceive, a light yet to be born." (p. 31). Moltmann (1991), in a counter-intuitive twist of conventional wisdom, points out that it is only this dy-namically open orientation toward the future that can be considered "realistic." Hope recognizes that no matter what current circumstances might be, "everything is still full of possibilities." Writes Moltmann:

Hope and the kind of thinking that goes with it consequently cannot submit to the reproach of being utopian, for they do not strive after things that have 'no place,' but after things that have 'no place as yet' but can acquire one (p. 25).

This influence-optimism has two important implications for organizations. First, adversity need not be accepted as hope's only starting point. As a response to the fundamental openness of the future, hope can thrive under all conditions. Whether in times of difficulty or in times of well-being, hope draws on people's creative resources and allows them to stretch beyond the status quo in search of even more vital possibilities. Second, hope can be understood as a positive orien-tation toward the future that precedes and anticipates a coherent image of the future. Kast (1991) and Bloch (1986) suggest that, in affirming the "not-yet-seen," hope does not require a clear picture of the future to come alive. On the contrary, hope's positive orientation endures and perseveres even when the future looks bleak or is "still unnamed." As Kast puts it: "By hoping, we walk toward a light that we do not see but sense somewhere in the darkness of the future." (p. 136).

Imagination is portrayed as the engine of hoping: it is the uniquely human func-tion that allows people to participate actively and construct their meaningful realities.

TABLE 18.3. Eight Core Principles of Appreciative Inquiry Support the Four Enduring Qualities of Hope.

	The Centrality of Relationships	The Importance of Influence-Optimism	Conversations of Ultimate Concern	The Generativity of Hope
The Constructionist Principle Social knowledge and organizational destiny are tightly intertwined.				
The Collaborative Principle Collaboration opens the way for the social construction of reality and establishes strong relational connections.				
The Anticipatory Principle The image of the future guides the current behavior of any organism or organization.				
The Provocative Principle The most powerful images of the future are those that stretch, challenge or interrupt the status quo.				
The Poetic Principle Organizations are open books. We can study any topic related to human experience.				
The Positive Principle Organizations move in the direction of what they study. The more positive the topics and questions, the more positive the outcomes.				
The Principle of Simultaneity There is a direct and simultaneous link between inquiry and action. Inquiry *is* intervention.				
The Pragmatic Principle The questions we ask set the stage for what we "find" and how we organize.				

For example, describing it as "the gift that envisions what cannot yet be seen," Lynch (1965) gives imagination a central role in fostering a sense of possibility:

Hope is tied to the life of the imagination—that constantly proposes to itself that the boundaries of the possible are wider than they seem. . . . It is able to wait, to wait for a moment of vision, which is not yet there. . . . It is not overcome by the absoluteness of the present (p. 35).

Hoping, then, involves a continuous inquiry into and affirmation of the best, most positive aspects of people and situations. As Kast (1991) notes, "Hope can be learned first by our being knowingly dissatisfied and rejecting deficiency, and then by our pursuing the daydreams and imaginary worlds that point the way to change" (p. 151).

Conversations of Ultimate Concern

Various authors suggest that not all human vocabularies have an equal capacity to inspire hope. Hope is generated and is sustained when people, facing the mystery of the future, dialogue about their highest human ideals—that which Plato calls the good, the true, and the beautiful; Marcel calls universal values; Bloch calls the absolute, infinite, and unobtainable other; Otto calls the holy; and Fromm calls the transcendent or the spiritual. Tillich's (1957) treatment of "ultimate concern" provides language that illustrates what these authors all seem to be pointing toward. He defines ultimate concerns as those things that sustain and give meaning to life. Tillich writes:

Man, like every living being, is concerned about many things, above all about those which condition his very existence, such as food and shelter. But man, in contrast to other living beings, has spiritual concerns—cognitive, aesthetic, social, political. Some of them are urgent, often extremely urgent, and each of them as well as the vital concerns can claim ultimacy for human life or the life of a social group (p. 1).

Tillich suggests that dialogue about ultimate concerns generates hope by allowing human beings to transcend the relative and transitory experiences of ordinary life and to build for themselves an existence based on a high moral and spiritual ground.

Marcel (1951) talks in similar terms when he claims that there exists a persistent and inescapable transcendent or noble character to the standards by which human beings govern their collective existence, standards which seem to "belong to a different world, founded on kindness, scruples, sacrifice, a world entirely different from this one" (p. 8). For Marcel, the collective pursuit of these ideals, or what he calls universal values, is the essence of human hoping. Likewise for Bloch (1986) hoping is a continuous movement toward the superlative, the sublime, or in his words, "the best as a totality." The best can have many faces—"Happiness, freedom, non-alienation, the golden age, the land flowing with milk and honey, the eternal feminine, the trumpet call in Fidelio, and the Christ pattern of the resurrection day afterwards" (p. 1627)—but it is the condition for hope in any situation.

Frankl (1959) provides a compelling example of how hope grounded in ultimate concern serves as a powerful life-giving force in human communities. While imprisoned in a concentration camp in Germany, he observed that for many prisoners "there was a psychological 'giving up,' a loss of faith and belief in the future resulting in apathy" (p. 64). The hopeless, claimed Frankl, did not long continue to live. However, even the slightest cause for hope enabled people to persevere even under the systemic horrors and daily executions. Hope was defined by those who survived in the language of ultimate concerns as a "spiritual freedom, a freedom which cannot be taken away, a freedom that makes life meaningful and purposeful" (p. 66). Inquiry into ultimate concerns generates a vocabulary of hope and possibility that serves as a potent "life-giving" force for transforming social and organizational relationships. This vocabulary allows people to live beyond current circumstances, transcend the status quo, and transform present reality into one of greater aliveness by placing it in the context of broader and deeper possibilities.

The Generativity of Hope

Hoping in an essential ingredient in social and organizational transformation because it spawns generative action. Tillich (1957), in his treatment of ultimate concerns, claims that all products of human creativity, from works of music, literature, art, and architecture to patterns of social organizing can be seen as symbolic expressions of ultimate concerns. Citing as examples the religious inspiration found in the art and architecture of pre-modern Christianity and the economic inspiration found in the works of modern secular culture, Tillich writes: "[Human] spiritual function, artistic creation, scientific knowledge, ethical formation, and political organization are consciously or unconsciously expressions of an ultimate concern which gives passion and creative Eros to them" (pp. 107–108).

Similarly Bloch (1986), in his three-volume work The Principle of Hope, asserts that hope is the source of all human history and culture. To prove his point, Bloch undertakes a sweeping study of Western culture in which he presents "sketches of hope" from every conceivable area of human activity. He describes "wishful images in the mirror," including culturally defined standards of slimness or beauty, the lure of fairy tales, travel, dance, and comedy, and the wishes for a happy ending that pervade popular culture; he surveys "outlines of a better world," including social, medical, technological, architectural, and geographical utopias, as well as "wishful landscapes" contained in opera, painting, literature, philosophy, and leisure; and finally he sketches "wishful images of the fulfilled moment," including discussions of the contemplative life, music, death, and religion (Aronson, 1991).

Throughout his study, Bloch is careful to point out that hope is at work not only in the magnificent works of art and culture of the "masters," but in the dreams, expectations, intentions, wishes, desires, and longings of every member of society. He claims that hope is rigorously existential and can be seen at every moment in our existence: wanting to lose weight, to travel, to be loved and respected, to be successful, to see our children prosper, in paintings, in gardens, in our dreams of being secure and comfortable in old age. According to Bloch, every human creation (idea, relationship, action), which on the surface seems simply to be a mundane response to the vicissitudes of every day life, is in fact a bold proclamation and announcement of a desired future, a living testimony to the generative power of hope.

Hoping becomes a powerful source of social and organizational transformation because it enlivens the human spirit and guides action. Kast suggests that hope leads to joy which in turn transforms people "into persons who are more alive, who are involved, who have energy to act, who believe in change." (p.108). Similarly, Marcel (1951) draws a connection between hope and what he calls an "ardour for life" (p. 43) that serves as an antidote to despair and stimulates human creativity. Polak (1973) draws the link between hope and action when he claims that human beings exercise influence over the future through the images they project, and in turn these images of desirable future events foster the behavior most likely to bring about their realization. He goes so far as to suggest that the image of the future is the single most important dynamic in the process of cultural evolution:

The rise and fall of images of the future precedes or accompanies the rise and fall of cultures. As long as a society's image is positive and flourishing, the flower of culture is in full bloom. Once the image begins to decay and lose its vitality, however, the culture does not long survive (p. 19).

Polak's conclusion is that for any collectivity its image of the future is not only points the way to the future but also serves as a guiding mechanism that actively promotes certain choices and puts them to work in determining the future (Cooperrider, 1991).

Not all hoping has an equal chance of transforming the future, however. Dauenhauer (1986), Marcel (1951), Moltmann (1991), and Polak (1973) suggest that hoping gains its greatest chances for generativity to the extent that it remains "public property," that is, to the extent that it remains a inclusive act, ever seeking to expand the number of participants and invite open dialogue. Writes Dauenhauer:

Hope promotes the sort of listening or hearing which is not confined merely to having one's own discourse somehow confirmed. It promotes a quest for ever more efficacious and comprehensive discourse . . . [and] works to preserve and expand the number of participants in [this discourse] (p. 99). To this relational formulation Moltmann (1991) adds that hoping, because it is an act of affirming the life and the potential of the other, can never be limited in scope. It must always remain universal in character, committed to inclusiveness and to discovering ultimate concerns that announce "a universal horizon that embraces the whole world" (p. 263).

In sum, the interdisciplinary literature on hope highlights hoping as a primary source of social and organizational transformation. As people come together in relationships of mutuality, affirm a dynamic, open, and evolving future that is "full of possibilities," and collectively dialogue about their highest and most transcendent ideals, they create positive guiding images of the future that provide a compelling logic and source of inspiration for social action (see Table 18.2 for a summary of hope's enduring qualities).

TABLE 18.2. Summary of Hope's Four Enduring Qualities.

Relationship as the Ground of Hope
- Hoping is born and nurtured in a priori relationships of mutual love, care, and support.
- Hoping reaches beyond the self: it prospers when people place themselves in service of the other.
- Hoping is a binding force of community: it provides a sense of symbiotic connectedness with others; promotes feelings of safety and security; and unites people around common values and ideals.

The Contructive Stance of Hope
- Hoping assumes a fundamental openness to the future: it prospers when people recognize the unbounded extent to which relationships and realities are open to creation and reconstruction.
- Hoping precedes and anticipates a coherent image of the future: it comes to life when people assume a posture that is both patient and creative in the face of uncertainty.
- Imagination is the engine of hoping: it allows people to explore the mystery of the future and create promising possibilities for existence.

The moral Dimension of Hope
- Hope is nourished and sustained when people collectively dialogue about their ultimate concerns in a spirit of love and action.
- Hoping is a life-giving act: it renews life by enabling people to place immediate circumstances in the context of broader and deeper possibilities.
- Hoping is a source of Moral Vision: it is a holistic way of knowing that draws on a range of affective, normative, spiritual, and relational resources to spawn moral action.
- Hoping integrates the modes of time: it allows people to draw on the brightest images, ideals, and values of the past to inspire positive possibilities for the future.

The Generativity of Hope
- Hoping is a source of human creativity and culture: everything from works of music, literature, art and architecture to patterns of organizing can be seen as expressions of the hopes of their authors.
- Hoping is a source of positive affect and action: it leads to feelings of joy, well-being, relaxation, and fullness of life and stimulates action by bringing the future into the present as a causal agent.
- Hoping is most generative when it is inclusive; it inspires collective action most powerfully when it remains "public property," invites open dialogue, and seeks to expand its horizon to include all mankind.

Appreciative Inquiry and Vocabularies of Hope

These four qualities of hope—that it is (1) born in relationship, (2) inspired by the conviction that the future is open and can be influenced, (3) sustained by dialogue about high human ideals, and (4) generative of positive affect and action—can be seen at play in the creation of textured vocabularies of hope. In this section we demonstrate how appreciative modes of inquiry, by creating the conditions necessary to nurture these qualities, support the construction of hopeful vocabularies. We begin by demonstrating how textured vocabularies of hope are generated and sustained in society and in organizations. We then explore the ways in which eight core principles of appreciative inquiry support and reinforce the creation of textured vocabularies of hope.

The Structuring of Vocabularies of Hope

As mentioned previously, textured vocabularies of hope can be defined as linguistic constructions that create new images of positive relational possibility, illuminate fresh avenues for moral discourse, and expand the range of practical and theoretical resources available for the construction of healthy social and organizational relationships. In contrast to vocabularies of deficit that erode individual and social well-being, vocabularies of hope serve as linguistic tools that promote the (re)construction of relationships in ways that conform to collective images of the good. The process of social and organizational transformation through vocabularies of hope can be outlined as follows:

First, based on a constructionist epistemology, communities of inquiry and action are formed and begin to explore the most positive, life-giving, life-sustaining aspects of their collective existence. To enrich the range of discourse, communities of inquiry are intentionally designed to include as many relevant voices as possible.

Second, communities of inquiry construct vocabularies of hope by sharing stories, theories, evidence, and illustrations that highlight "best practices" and compelling examples of the forces and factors that give life and sustain their collective existence.

Third, communities of inquiry expand and enrich their vocabularies of hope through processes of normative dialogue and collective visioning.

Fourth, communities of inquiry disseminate their vocabularies of hope through personal relationships, books, journals, magazines, newspapers, universities, conferences, public policies, television, other electronic media.

Fifth, as vocabularies of hope are disseminated to the culture, they become absorbed into the common language and become available for the construction of everyday reality. Best practices and positive examples provide a range of possibilities for societal and organizational innovation. In essence, the culture learns how to be hopeful and inventive.

Sixth, in the final phase of social and organizational transformation, vocabularies of hope are expanded. As people increasingly build their relational vocabularies with "best" examples from the past and "most vital" hopes for the future, more linguistic and normative resources become available to convert dreams into reality and possibilities into practice (see Figure 18.2 for a diagram of this process).

Vocabularies of hope come in all shapes and sizes—theories, ethnographies, case studies, vignettes, empirical data, personal narratives, rhetorical speeches, stories told in the classroom, boardroom, or around the kitchen table. One of the most famous and influential vocabularies of hope in the United States is Martin Luther King Jr.'s speech given at a civil rights march in Washington, August 28, 1963. The speech, and particularly the sentence "I have a dream that my four children will one day live in a nation where they will not be judged by the color of their skin, but by the content of their character," gave voice to the aspirations of an entire nation and has served as a hopeful harbinger of cultural change for more than a generation.

6. Vocabularies of hope are expanded and fuel social and organizational (re)construction.

5. Vocabularies of hope are absorbed into common language; organizations and society learn how to be hopeful and to innovate.

4. Communities of inquiry disseminate vocabularies of hope to the general public through multiple channels.

3. Communities of inquiry consensually validate vocabularies of hope through moral dialogue.

2. Communities of inquiry create vocabularies of hope by searching for positive example and "best practices" in society and organizations.

1. Inclusive communities of inquiry are formed and select positive topics for collective inquiry and action.

Figure 18.2. The Link Between Vocabularies of Hope and Social and Organizational (Re)Construction.

On a more scholarly note, the writings of Tavistock Institute founders which brought the principles of social science to bear on the challenges of post World War II reconstruction; McGregor's (1960) Theory X-Theory Y which offered possibilities for a new human-centered form management; Gilligan's (1982) different voice which for the first time highlighted the unique patterns of women's moral development; Kolb's (1984) experiential learning which revealed and affirmed multiple ways of knowing; and Freire's (1994) pedagogy of hope which championed dialogue and advanced the concept of full voice, are but a few of the vocabularies of hope that have emerged in the social and organizational sciences in recent years. Each of these, in its own way, created new images of positive relational possibility, illuminated fresh avenues for moral discourse, and expanded the range of resources available for the construction of enhanced social and organizational relationships.

The Power of Appreciation

Eight core principles of appreciative inquiry support hope's four enduring qualities and make it ideally suited for generating vocabularies of hope (see Cooperrider and Srivastva, 1987 and Cooperrider, 1990). The first two are the constructionist principle and the collaborative principle. According to the constructionist principle, knowledge is a social artifact rather than a product of empirical observation or of individual cognition. It is created by agreement within communities of people. At the same time, knowledge determines action. What a given community of people knows at any particular moment essentially defines for them the options they have available for organizing. In this sense, social knowledge and organizational destiny are tightly intertwined. Consequently, appreciative inquiry affirms that all inquiry into organizational life should be collaborative. A collaborative relationship between participants is essential on the basis of both epistemological and practical grounds. Epistemologically, collaboration opens the way for a truly social construction of reality in which a broad range of participants contribute to the creation of the future. Practically, it facilitates the establishment of strong relational connections.

These two principles support the first enduring quality of hope, that it is born and sustained in relationship. When people come together to inquire into what gives them life, they create positive affect and a strong social bonding which in Kast's terms leads to a strong sense of "Geborgenheit (safety, security, protectedness) upon which all higher feelings—and the energy for action—nourish themselves" (p. 138). It is also in this collaborative act that organizational members literally create new knowledge—new conversations, vocabularies, ways of understanding things—that open up fresh and previously undiscovered alternatives for organizing. Thus the collaborative dimension of appreciative inquiry ignites hope in two ways: it builds strong, supportive relationships between organizational members, and it creates a context, a "holding environment" if you will, in which organizational members can contribute to the social construction of their common future.

The second set of principles that support vocabularies of hope includes the anticipatory principle and the provocative principle. According to the anticipatory principle, it is the image of the future that guides the current behavior of any organism or organization. Just as a flower grows in the direction of the sunlight, so to organizations evolve in the direction of their most compelling images of the future. The anticipatory principle goes on to suggest that because our images of the future are fashioned through discourse (talking to each other), they are indeed open to human influence. In fact, the most important resource we have for generating constructive organizational change may well be our collective capacity to create and exchange shared vocabularies of meaning.

The provocative principle extends this logic into practice by suggesting that the most powerful images of the future are those that stretch, challenge or interrupt the status quo. Such images are rarely strictly rational. As Polak (1973) suggests, it is precisely the picture of a world that is radically different emotionally, aesthetically, spiritually, and relationally that gives images of the future their gripping appeal. By stimulating normative dialogue about how we can and should organize ourselves, these images present provocative new possibilities for social action. In this sense, appreciative inquiry supports the second enduring quality of hope, that it springs to life through imagination in a context of influence-optimism. By affirming that (1) through systematic inquiry and the creation of new textured vocabularies of hope organizational members can shape the social world according to their own moral and imaginative purposes, and (2) the most powerful vocabularies of transformation are those that offer an intuitive, visionary logic for change, appreciative inquiry opens the way for the creative construction of preferred organizational futures.

Third are the poetic principle and the positive principle. According to the poetic principle, organizations are an open book. They can be endless sources of learning, inspiration, and interpretation (like for example, the endless interpretive possibilities in a good piece of poetry or a Biblical text). Thus we can study virtually any topic related to human experience in organizations. We can study alienation or we can study joy; we can study conflict or we can study cooperation; we can study cynicism or we can study hope. According to the positive principle, human beings and organizations move in the direction of what they study. The more positive the topics of inquiry and the more positive the questions asked, the more positive will be the "theories" we come to discover and the vocabularies we come to create. In addition, because of the positive affect and social connection that occurs, the more we inquire into the life-giving aspects of organizational existence, the more effectively momentum for organization change and development will be catalyzed.

These two principles support the third enduring quality of hope, that hope is sustained through dialogue about ultimate concerns. By expanding the universe of our exploration to include the phenomena that claim ultimacy for our collective existence, appreciative inquiry promotes alternative patterns of discourse and generates new bodies of constructive vocabulary that contribute to human hopefulness. Moreover, as the poetic and positive principles would suggest, since the ontological, epistemological, and methodological commitments upon which we base our inquiry will largely determine what we come to discover, know, and contribute to the world of human organizing, the more we inquire into and promote constructive dialogue about our ultimate concerns, the more hopeful will become our theory, the more promising will become its potential for positive action, and the more we will become a source of hope to each other.

The fourth set of principles includes the simultaneous principle and the pragmatic principle. According to the principle of simultaneity, inquiry and change are not truly separate moments but are simultaneous. Inquiry is intervention. Thus the questions we ask as organizational scholars and practitioners set the stage for what we later "find," and what we find becomes the "data" and the "theories" out of which the future is conceived, conversed about, and constructed. According to the pragmatic principle, to be significant in a human sense, organizational inquiry must lead to the generation of knowledge that can be used, applied, and validated in action. It needs to be relevant to the everyday experience of organizational members.

These two principles support the fourth enduring quality of hope—its generativity. They suggest that there is an isomorphic relationship between our modes of inquiry and the kind of social realities we help to create. If we, as organizational scholars and practitioners, want our methodologies to support hopeful organizations and produce hopeful social theory, then our methods themselves need to be hope-filled. First, they need to support the kind of human interaction that inspire human hope through relational connection, dialogue about our highest ideals, and co-construction of preferred futures. Second, they need to continuously refocus our attention on the most life-giving, life-enhancing dimensions of our collective existence. As both appreciative inquiry and the construct of organizational hope suggest, such methodologies will generate practical social and organizational theory that expands the range of possibilities for societal and organizational innovation and, in essence, allows our cultures to learn to be hopeful and inventive.

Conclusion

The language of hope in human systems has important implications for our continuing task as social and organizational scholars and practitioners. If the premise that hope is a primary source of positive knowledge and action in organizational life is accepted, and the tenets of social constructionism—that knowledge is a social artifact, that language is the means by which knowledge is developed, that there is an inextricable link between language, knowledge, and action—are embraced, then it can be concluded that the creation of textured vocabularies of hope may well be the most powerful tool available to us if our aim is to generate constructive organizational understandings that open new possibilities for human organizing and action.

Yet, the structuring of vocabularies of hope is less a technique than it is a commitment. As Rorty (1980) points out in his comparison of Dewey and Foucault, the methodological approach that we adopt is in no way forced upon us by the "nature of things;" it is simply a matter of choice, tone, or moral outlook. Dewey contributed to the growth of human hope by promoting inquiry into high human ideals—notions of truth, rationality, progress, freedom, and democracy. He affirmed the human will to truth, not as the urge to dominate but as the urge to create, an urge to enhance the human condition. By so doing, Dewey made a simple methodological choice to pursue a constructive option that, according to Rorty, eventually filled his theory with an "unjustifiable hope, and an ungroundable but vital sense of human solidarity" (p. 208).

It is to this kind of commitment that we are invited as social and organizational practitioners by appreciative modes of inquiry. Deep and appreciative exploration into ultimate concerns has the capacity to inspire hope precisely because it compels us to transcend the ego, to put ourselves in service of a cause that is beyond us yet that we make our own, and to move toward "the best as a totality." Much needed is further experimentation with new modes of appreciative inquiry based on a theory of hope with a specific agenda of ultimate concerns. We may find that the more we inquire appreciatively into life's fundamental and ultimate concerns, the more our instrumental, transitory, and provisional issues (which at times seem so focal) will take care of themselves because of the human hope and solidarity that has been enlivened. We will most certainly find, as this chapter would suggest, that the very act of appreciation will itself contribute to transforming our organizations into places of genuine human hopefulness.

References

Argyris, C. Action science and intervention. *The Journal of Applied Behavioral Science*, 1973, 19, 115–140.

Argyris, C., and Schon, D. *Theory in practice: Increasing professional effectiveness*. San Francisco: Jossey-Bass, 1974.

Aronson, R. The principle of hope by Ernst Bloch. *Review Essays*, 1991, 46, 220–232.

Astley, G. Administrative science as socially constructed truth. *Administrative Sciences Quarterly*, 1985, 30, 497–513.

Bartunek, J. How organization development can develop organization theory. *Group and Organization Studies*, 1983, 8, 303–318.

Bloch, E. *The principle of hope* (translated by N. Plaice, S. Plaice and P. Knight from the German Das prinzip hoffnung). Cambridge, MA: MIT Press, 1986.

Brown, H. B. Reconstructing social theory after the postmodern critique. In H. W. Simons and M. Billig (eds.), *After postmodernism: Reconstructing ideology critique*. London: Sage Publications, 1994.

Cooperridder, D. L., and Srivastva, S. Appreciative inquiry in organizational life. In W. A. Pasmore and R. W. Woodman (eds.), *Research in organizational change and development (Vol. I)*. Greenwich, CT: JAI Press, 1987.

Dauenhauer, B. P. *The politics of hope*. New York: Routledge and Kegan Paul, 1986.

Denzin, N. K. and Lincoln, Y. S. *Handbook of qualitative research*. Thousand Oaks: Sage Publications, 1994.

Fals-Borda, O., and Rahman, M. A. (eds.) *Action and knowledge: Breaking the monopoly with participatory action research*. New York: Intermediate Technology/Apex, 1991.

Feyerabend, P. K. *Science in a free society*. London: Thetford Press, 1978.

Fiske, J. Audiencing: cultural practice and cultural studies. In *Handbook of qualitative research*, N. K. Denzin and Y. S. Lincoln (eds.). Thousand Oaks, CA: Sage Publications, 1994.

Frankl, V. E. *From death camp to existentialism*. Boston: Beacon, 1959.

Frankl, V. E. *Man's search for meaning*. New York: Washington Square, 1963.

Freire, P. *Pedagogy of the oppressed*. New York: Continuum, 1984.

Freire, P. *Pedagogy of hope: Reliving pedagogy of the oppressed* (translated by R. R. Barr). New York: Continuum, 1994.

Friedlander, F. Producing useful knowledge for organizations. *Administrative Science Quarterly*, 1984, 29, 646–648.

George, J. International Relations and the Search for Thinking Space, *International Studies Quarterly*, 33, 179–269.

Gergen, K. J. *Toward transformation in social knowledge*. New York: Springer-Verlag, 1982.

Gergen, K. J. *Realities and relationships: Soundings in social construction*. Cambridge: Harvard University Press, 1994.

Gergen, K. J. The limits of pure critique. In H. W. Simons and M. Billig (eds.), *After postmodernism: Reconstructing ideology critique*. London: Sage Publications, 1994.

Gilligan, C. *In a different voice: Psychological theory and women's development*. Cambridge: Harvard University Press, 1982.

Hazelrigg, H. *Claims of knowledge: On the labor of making found worlds*. Talla-hassee: The Florida State University Press, 1989.

Heron, J. *Experience and method: An inquiry into the concept of experiential re-search*. Surrey UK: University of Surrey, Human Potential Research Project, 1971.

Kast, V. *Joy, inspiration and hope* (translated by D. Whitcher). College Station, TX: Texas AandM University Press, 1991.

Kilmann, R., Thomas, K., Slevin, D., Nath, R., and Jerrell, L. (eds.) *Producing useful knowledge for organizations*. New York: Praeger, 1983.

Kincheloe, J. L. and Mclaren, P. L. Rethinking critical theory and qualitative re-search. In *Handbook of qualitative research*, N. K. Denzin and Y. S. Lincoln (eds.). Thousand Oaks, CA: Sage Publications, 1994.

Kolb, D. A. *Experiential learning: Experience as the source of learning and de-velopment*. Englewood Cliffs: Prentice-Hall, 1984.

Kuhn, T. S., *The structure of scientific revolutions, 2nd rev. ed.* Chicago: Univer-sity of Chicago Press, 1970).

Ludema, J. D., Wilmot, T. B., and Srivastva, S. Organizational hope: Reaffirming the constructive task of social and organizational inquiry, *Human Relations*, 50(8), 1997.

Lynch, W. F. *Images of hope*. Notre Dame: Notre Dame Press, 1965.

Marcel, G. *Homo viator* (translated by Emma Craufurd). Chicago: Henry Regnery, 1951.

Marcus, G. E. What comes (just) after "post"? The case of ethnography. In N. K. Denzin and Y. S. Lincoln (eds.), *Handbook of qualitative research*. Thou-sand Oaks: Sage Publications, 1994.

Mcgregor, D. *The human side of enterprise*. New York: McGraw-Hill, 1960.

Moltmann, J. *Theology of hope* (translated by J. W. Leitch from the German Theologie der hoffnung). New York: Harper Collins, 1991.

Morgan, G. *Images of Organizations*. Newbury Park: Sage Publications, 1986.

Morgan, G. *Imaginization*. Newbury Park: Sage Publications, 1993.

Olesen, V. Feminisms and Models of Qualitative Research. In *Handbook of quali-tative research*, N. K. Denzin and Y. S. Lincoln (eds.). Thousand Oaks, CA: Sage Publications, 1994.

Polak, F. *The image of the future* (translated and abridged by E. Boulding from the Dutch Die toekomst is verleden tijd). San Francisco: Jossey-Bass, 1973.

Reason, P. (ed.) *Human inquiry in action*. London: Sage, 1988.

Reason, P., and Heron, J. Research with people: The paradigm of cooperative experiential inquiry. *Person Centered Review*, 1986, 1, 456–475.

Reason, P., and Rowan, J. (eds.) *Human inquiry: a sourcebook of a new paradigm research*. Chichester, UK: Wiley, 1981.

Rorty, R. *Consequences of pragmatism*. Minneapolis: University of Minnesota Press, 1980.

Schon, D. A. *The reflective practitioner: How professionals think in action*. New York: Basic Books, 1983.

Srivastva, S., and Barrett, F. J. The transforming nature of metaphors in group development: A study in group theory. *Human Relations*, 41, 31–63, 1988.

Srivastva, S., Cooperrider, D. L., and Associates. *Appreciative management and leadership: The power of positive thought and action in organizations*. San Francisco: Jossey-Bass Pubs., 1990.

Stanfield, J. H. II. Ethnic modeling in qualitative research. In *Handbook of qualitative research*, N. K. Denzin and Y. S. Lincoln (eds.). Thousand Oaks, CA: Sage Publications, 1994.

Schwandt, T. A. Constructivist, interpretivist approaches to human inquiry. In *Handbook of qualitative research*, N. K. Denzin and Y. S. Lincoln (eds.). Thousand Oaks, CA: Sage Publications, 1994.

Tandon, R. Participatory research and social transformation. *Convergence*, 21, 5–15, 1989.

Taylor, C. Interpretation and the sciences of man. In P. Rabinow and W. M. Sullivan (eds.), *Interpretive social science: A second look*. Berkeley: University of California Press, 1987.

Torbert, W. R. Why educational research has been so uneducational: The case for a new model of social science based on collaborative inquiry. In P. Reason and J. Rowan (eds.), *Human inquiry: A sourcebook of new paradigm research*. Chichester, UK: Wiley, 1981.

Torbert, W. R. Teaching action inquiry. *Collaborative Inquiry*, 5, 1991.

Tillich, P. *Dynamics of faith*. New York: Harper and Row, 1957.

Whyte, W. F. (ed.) *Participatory action research*. Newbury Park, CA: Sage, 1991.

Weick, K. E. Affirmation as inquiry. *Small Group Behavior*, 1982, 13, 441–450.

Wittgenstein, L. *Philosophical investigations* (translated by G. Anscombe). New York: Macmillan, 1963.

Wollheim, R. *Art and its objects* (second edition). Cambridge, MA: Cambridge University Press, 1980.